Vocabulary in a Second Language

Language Learning and Language Teaching

The *LL&LT* monograph series publishes monographs as well as edited volumes on applied and methodological issues in the field of language pedagogy. The focus of the series is on subjects such as classroom discourse and interaction; language diversity in educational settings; bilingual education; language testing and language assessment; teaching methods and teaching performance; learning trajectories in second language acquisition; and written language learning in educational settings.

Series editors

Birgit Harley
Ontario Institute for Studies in Education, University of Toronto

Jan H. Hulstijn
Department of Second Language Acquisition, University of Amsterdam

Volume 10

Vocabulary in a Second Language: Selection, acquisition, and testing
Edited by Paul Bogaards and Batia Laufer

Vocabulary in a Second Language

Selection, acquisition, and testing

Edited by

Paul Bogaards
Leiden University

Batia Laufer
University of Haifa

John Benjamins Publishing Company

Amsterdam / Philadelphia

TM The paper used in this publication meets the minimum requirements
of American National Standard for Information Sciences – Permanence
of Paper for Printed Library Materials, ANSI z39.48-1984.

Library of Congress Cataloging-in-Publication Data

Vocabulary in a second language : selection, acquisition, and testing / edited by
Paul Bogaards, Batia Laufer.
        p. cm. (Language Learning and Language Teaching, ISSN 1569–9471;
v. 10)
Includes bibliographical references and index.
        1. Language and languages--Study and teaching. 2. Vocabulary--
Study and teaching. 3. Second language acquisition. I. Bogaards, Paul. II.
Laufer-Dvorkin, Batia. III. Series.

        P53.9.V634   2004
    418'.0071-dc22   2004053767
    ISBN 90 272 1709 2 (Eur.) / 1 58811 540 2 (US) (Hb; alk. paper)
    ISBN 90 272 1710 6 (Eur.) / 1 58811 541 0 (US) (Pb; alk. paper)

John Benjamins Publishing Co. · P.O. Box 36224 · 1020 ME Amsterdam · The Netherlands
John Benjamins North America · P.O. Box 27519 · Philadelphia PA 19118-0519 · USA

Table of contents

Introduction

Paul Bogaards and Batia Laufer
Leiden University, University of Haifa

Over the last twenty years much has been done in the field of vocabulary in the context of the acquisition of foreign or second languages (L2). Recurrent research themes over the past two decades include: the construct of vocabulary knowledge, e.g. the distinction between receptive and productive knowledge, and between knowledge and use (Henriksen 1999, Read & Chapelle 2001); the relationship between vocabulary knowledge and language proficiency, particularly in respect to reading (Hazenberg & Hulstijn 1996, Hu & Nation 2000); the role of word frequency in vocabulary learning, e.g. the cost benefit of learning frequent, infrequent and specialized words (Coxhead 2000, Nation 2001); task effect on learning, e.g. task induced involvement (Hulstijn & Laufer 2001, Laufer & Hulstijn 2001); the use of dictionaries, paper and electronic, (Bogaards 1991, Chun & Plass 1996, Knight 1994); interactive tasks (Ellis, Tanaka & Yamazaki 1994); explicit versus implicit learning (Ellis 1994); incidental versus intentional learning (Ellis & He 1999, Horst, Cobb & Meara 1998, Kelly 1986, Qian 1996); learning new words versus learning new meanings of already known words (Bogaards 2001); patterns of vocabulary development over time (Laufer 1998, Meara 1997, Palmberg 1987, Schmitt 1998); strategies used by learners to comprehend and learn new words (Cohen & Aphek 1981, Sanaoui 1995, Schmitt 1997); and testing vocabulary knowledge: size and depth, receptive and productive (Bogaards 2000, Laufer & Nation 1995, 1999, Nation 1983, Read 1993, 2000, Wesche & Paribakht 1996). The growth of interest in L2 vocabulary since the days of 'a neglected aspect of language learning' (Meara 1980) has also been reflected in authored and edited books specifically devoted to vocabulary (Arnaud & Béjoint 1992, Bogaards 1994, Coady & Huckin 1997, Hatch & Brown 1995, Nation 1990, 2001, Schmitt & McCarthy 1997, Schmitt 2000, Read 2000).

Most of the contributions that have been selected for this volume are papers that were presented at the Second-Language Vocabulary Acquisition Colloquium, which took place at Leiden University in March 2002, and which was organised under the auspices of the European Second Language Association (EUROSLA) by the editors of this book. This Colloquium was sponsored by the University of Haifa, the Universiteit Leiden Center for Linguistics (ULCL), the Leids Universiteits Fonds (LUF), and the Universiteit van Amsterdam.

1. Overview

The contributions that appear in this volume have been grouped under three themes:
   – Selection
   – Acquisition
   – Testing

We will first provide a brief summary of the three sections and then address the issues of agreement and differences between the contributors that result in an agenda for further research.

The first section is devoted to the selection of words to be taught. Paul Nation presents a comparison of two frequency lists: the General Service List, supplemented more recently by the Academic Word List, and the new, more up-to-date lists of words compiled on the basis of the British National Corpus. Tom Cobb and Marlise Horst raise the question whether a word list similar to the Academic Word List in English can also be found in French. Svenja Adolphs and Norbert Schmitt study the coverage of frequent words in different spoken contexts.

The second section is devoted to questions of L2 vocabulary acquisition. Frank Boers, Murielle Demecheleer and June Eyckmans investigate whether etymological elaboration can be exploited to enhance the learning of figurative idioms. Jan-Arjen Mondria and Boukje Wiersma examine whether the extra effort that is necessary for bi-directional learning from L2 to L1 and from L1 to L2 is more beneficial for the retention of word meaning and form than unidirectional learning. In a controlled experiment, Nan Jiang demonstrates the pervasive influence of L1 semantic structures on L2 semantic development, and shows that semantic transfer continues to mediate L2 word use in proficient L2 speakers. Jean-Marc Dewaele addresses a feature of lexico-pragmatic competence, the use of colloquial vocabulary in L2 speech, and shows that such use is not only related to L2 proficiency but also to personality factors. Though David Qian's paper does not address vocabulary acquisition as such, it is, nevertheless, relevant to the topic since it examines the strategies learners use when encountering unfamiliar words in a text, particularly the strategy of inferring meaning from context. Researchers often claim that inferring a word's meanings is the first step to its acquisition, and that to infer the meaning properly one should use clues from the global meaning of the text. Qian, however, shows that though learners think they use global clues, they most often do not. In fact, they practice a variety of different strategies.

The last section of this book is devoted to testing. Anne Vermeer presents a Measure of Lexical Richness (MLR), which takes into account the difficulty of the words used by the learners. Tine Greidanus, Paul Bogaards, Elisabeth van der Linden, Lydius Nienhuis and Tom de Wolf study the content and concurrent validities of a deep word knowledge test for advanced learners of French. In the last chapter, John Read discusses three distinct lines of development in the application of depth to second language vocabulary acquisition: precision of meaning, comprehensive word knowledge, and network knowledge.

2.   Some items for a research agenda

Although all the papers address one of the three themes of selection, acquisition, or testing, they often diverge on the conceptualization of central issues. We will now examine these points of divergence and suggest that they constitute a starting point of a research agenda in the next decade. We will also offer an additional perspective on some issues discussed by the authors in the hope that this too will inspire future researchers of L2 vocabulary.

The basic unit selected for vocabulary research is different for different researchers. Whereas Nation mainly deals with word families, the study by Adolphs & Schmitt is, for practical reasons, about individual word forms. Mondria & Wiersma present one-word verbs and nouns as learning material, whereas Boers, Demecheleer & Eyckmans examine idiomatic multi-word expressions. In the acquisition section, the words to be learned have, in most cases, one particular sense, or several closely related meanings (Jiang). However, the different formats discussed in the section on testing all have to do with aspects of polysemy. In a comprehensive theory of L2 acquisition, one that explicitly takes the lexical component into account, these different aspects of the lexical material will need to be integrated. Studies in lexical semantics conducted from an L2 perspective may lead to more explicit stands on this subject.

In the domain of selecting vocabulary for language syllabi and tests, several questions arise with regard to using word frequency as the basic criterion for selection. We do not contend that the most frequent meanings appear in most texts that learners read. But in some contexts, these frequent words can be used in a less frequent, possibly non-related sense, or else be a part of an idiomatic expression that has to be understood as a whole. If this additional sense goes unnoticed, lack of comprehension may occur. In productive use, on the other hand, knowledge of the most frequent sense(s) of a lexical item does not necessarily imply that the learner will be able to use it properly. One research avenue can therefore explore how unknown word properties hinder comprehension and production, particularly with respect to advanced learners. A question of inquiry would investigate what aspects of meaning, grammar, phonology, and discourse would still have to be learned to enable correct comprehension and correct use of frequent vocabulary items for which the learner already possesses a single or several central meanings.

A related theoretical question concerns the effect that multiple meanings have on a word's frequency. Words with several meanings, polysemes or homonyms, may appear higher up on frequency lists than monosemous words by virtue of the combined frequencies of their multiple meanings. Hence, the content of these lists cannot be taken to be homogeneous in terms of learner tasks. More learning effort must be invested to acquire words with multiple meanings.

From the learner's point of view, a crucial factor in L2 vocabulary acquisition regardless of word frequency, is word 'learnability'. This is the ease or difficulty with which a particular word can be acquired. Two words may have the same frequency, but one may be more difficult to learn than the other due to factors which have to do with the features of the word, or with other words related to it in the target language, or in the learner's L1 (Laufer 1990, 1997, Swan 1997). For example, a word which is a cognate in a learner's L1 may be infrequent, but it may present no difficulty in learning. On the other hand, a word that is frequent in L2 which has no semantic equivalent, or is lexicalized differently in L1 is hard to understand and acquire (cf. Jiang, this volume).

Because of the aforementioned limitations of frequency lists in terms of text coverage and word learnability, we feel that frequency lists cannot be the sole basis for the selection and gradation of vocabulary for language instruction. Further research should explore other factors that may determine selection, such as word learnability, or the specific needs of particular learners.

As to the acquisition section, it is noteworthy that the different chapters stress different aspects of the learning process and present rather different learning conditions. Whereas Boers, Demecheleer & Eyckmans (with the exception of one of their tests) investigate receptive vocabulary learning, Mondria & Wiersma study receptive as well as productive learning. Jiang measures the speed of response, the degree of confidence in providing an answer, and the learner's perception of task difficulty. Dewaele counts the proportion of colloquial words in a sample of speech. Qian investigates the mismatch between what learners think they do when encountering new words and what they actually do. Furthermore, the subjects in Mondria & Wiersma's experiment learn vocabulary intentionally, whereas Boers, Demecheleer & Eyckmans look into forms of incidental acquisition, defining incidental vocabulary learning as learning words without the intention to learn them, as a by-product of another activity. While most researchers of incidental learning use reading texts as context for new words, Boers, Demecheleer & Eyckmans use a computerized program. Further research could compare the various media (reading, listening, CALL) to see to what extent they would make a difference in acquisition. Following one of Dewaele's ideas, relating proficiency to the use or non use of a certain type of vocabulary, further research could address the phenomenon of lexical avoidance in a developmental perspective.

Vocabulary learning has been measured, not only immediately after the learning session, but also after some delay: two weeks in Mondria & Wiersma's study, and one week in Boer, Demecheleer & Eyckmans's study. The fact that the effectiveness of different learner treatments is no longer exclusively measured immediately after the learning, as was the practice not very long ago, is an important step forward.

The papers differ in their approach to what is traditionally called 'semantisation', i.e. the process of getting acquainted with the meaning of the items to learn. Mondria & Wiersma present their subjects with translations in the other language. Boers, Demecheleer & Eyckmans' subjects had to infer the meaning of the idioms from their membership in a particular category of source domains and they were provided with feedback to their answers. In Qian's study, the task was to infer meaning from text context using all possible clues, but without verification of meaning. Qian's finding that learners don't use contextual clues properly, together with what is known about the perils of guessing without verification of meaning, suggest that semantisation through guessing alone may not be appropriate in vocabulary research, let alone vocabulary instruction.

The importance of instructional intervention is convincingly demonstrated by Jiang. Multiple exposures alone are sometimes not enough to overcome learnability problems and plateaus in semantic development. Further research could seek empirical evidence for the effectiveness of instruction which takes into account interlingual semantic differences.

One of the most important phases in vocabulary learning which has not been researched sufficiently is consolidation of knowledge after initial presentation, with or without a word focused task. Without such consolidation, the number of words learnt is bound to be low. The results of the studies in this book show that this is indeed the case. The overall recall results on the delayed test showed not higher than 50% retention, even in the intentional learning condition. Further research should investigate the efficiency of various consolidation tasks. This is essential to our understanding of vocabulary acquisition, as in real life, new words are rarely remembered after practice in one task, or after one or several exposures in a single text.

The testing section demonstrates the importance of conceptualizing the construct of word knowledge, as stated by Read. Perhaps good correlations between the depth, breadth and lexical richness tests indicate that we are basically testing the same construct of knowledge. A more rigorous definition of vocabulary knowledge in the future will also provide a better insight into the tests used by researchers. The chapters by Greidanus et al. and by Vermeer clearly show that the construction and validation of vocabulary tests is an intricate and time consuming endeavour, but one that will be crucial for all types of vocabulary learning research.

We hope that the papers in this book will provide a useful contribution to the ever growing research on second language vocabulary, and will inspire students and scholars to pursue the various research avenues that the field can offer.

References

Arnaud, P. and Béjoint, H. (eds), 1992. *Vocabulary and Applied Linguistics*. London: Longman.

Bogaards, P. 1991. "Dictionnaires pédagogiques et apprentissage du vocabulaire." *Cahiers de Lexicologie*, 59: 93–107.

Bogaards, P. 1994. *Le vocabulaire dans l'apprentisage des langues étrangères*. Paris : Hatier/ Didier.

Bogaards, P. 2000. "Testing L2 vocabulary knowledge: the case of the Euralex French Tests." *Applied Linguistics*, 21: 490–516.

Bogaards, P. 2001. "Lexical units and the learning of foreign language vocabulary." *Studies in Second Language Acquisition*, 23: 321–343.

Coady, J., and Huckin, T. (eds) 1997. *Second Language Vocabulary Acquisition: a Rationale for Pedagogy*. Cambridge: Cambridge University Press.

Chun, D. M., and Plass, J. L. 1996. "Effects of multimedia annotations on vocabulary acquisition." *The Modern Language Journal*, 80: 183–198.

Cohen,A. D., and Aphek, E. 1981. "Easifying second language learning." *Studies in Second Language Acquisition*, 3: 221–236.

Coxhead, A. 2000. "A new Academic Word List." *TESOL Quarterly*, 34: 213–238.

Ellis, N. C. 1994. "Vocabulary acquisition: the implicit ins and outs of explicit cognitive mediation." In *Implicit and Explicit Learning of Languages*, N. C. Ellis (ed.), 218–282. London: Academic Press.

Ellis, R., Tanaka, Y., and Yamazaki, A. 1994. "Classroom interaction, comprehension and the acquisition of L2 word meaning." *Language Learning*, 44: 449–491.

Ellis, R., and He, X. 1999. "The roles of modified input and output in the incidental acquisition of word meaning." *Studies in Second Language Acquisition*, 21: 285–301.

Hatch, E. V., and Brown, C. 1995. *Vocabulary, semantics, and language education*. Cambridge: Cambridge University Press.

Hazenberg, S., and Hulstijn, J. 1996. "Defining a minimal second language vocabulary for non-native university students: an empirical investigation." *Applied Linguistics*, 17: 145–163.

Henriksen, B. 1999. "Three dimensions of vocabulary development." *Studies in Second Language Acquisition*, 21: 303–317.

Horst, M., Cobb, T., and Meara, P. 1998. "Beyond *A clockwork orange*: acquiring second language vocabulary through reading." *Reading in a Foreign Language*, 11: 207–223.

Hu, M., and Nation, P. 2000. "Vocabulary density and reading comprehension." *Reading in a Foreign Language*, 13: 403–430.

Hulstijn, J., and Laufer, B. 2001. "Some empirical evidence for the Involvement Load Hypothesis in vocabulary acquisition." *Language Learning*, 51: 539–558.

Kelly, P. 1986. "Solving the vocabulary retention problem." *ITL Review of Applied Linguistics*, 74: 1–16.

Knight, S. M. 1994. "Dictionary use while reading: the effects on comprehension and vocabulary acquisition for students of different verbal abilities." *Modern Language Journal*, 78: 285–299.

Laufer, B. 1990. "Words you know: how they affect the words you learn." In *Further Insights into Contrastive Linguistics*, J. Fisiak (ed.), 573–593. Amsterdam: John Benjamins.

Laufer, B. 1997. "What's in a word that makes it hard or easy? Intralexical factors affecting the difficulty of vocabulary acquisition." In *Vocabulary: Description, Acquisition and Pedagogy*, N. Schmitt and M. McCarthy (eds.), 140–155. Cambridge: Cambridge University Press. 140–155.

Laufer, B. 1998. "The development of passive and active vocabulary in a second language: same or different?" *Applied Linguistics,* 19: 255–271.

Laufer, B., and Hulstijn, J. 2001. "Incidental Vocabulary Acquisition in a Second Language: The Construct of Task-Induced Involvement." *Applied Linguistics,* 22: 1–26.

Laufer, B., and Nation. P. 1995. "Vocabulary size and use: lexical richness in L2 written production." *Applied Linguistics,* 16: 307–329.

Laufer, B., and Nation. P. 1999. "A vocabulary size test of controlled productive ability." *Language Testing,* 16: 33–51.

Meara, P. 1980. "Vocabulary acquisition: a neglected aspect of language learning." *Language Teaching and Lingjuistics: Abstracts,* 13: 221–246.

Meara, P. 1997. "Towards a new approach to modelling vocabulary acquisition." In *Vocabulary: Description, Acquisition and Pedagogy,* N. Schmitt and M. McCarthy (eds.), 109–121. Cambridge: Cambridge University Press.

Nation, P. 1983. "Testing and teaching vocabulary." *Guidelines* 5 (RELC supplement): 12–24

Nation.P. 1990. *Teaching and Learning Vocabulary.* New York: Newbury House.

Nation, I. S. P. 2001. *Learning Vocabulary in Another Language.* Cambridge: Cambridge University Press.

Palmberg, R. 1987. "Patterns of vocabulary development in foreign language learners." *Studies in Second Language Acquisition,* 9: 201–220.

Qian, D. D. 1996. "ESL vocabulary acquisition: contextualization and decontextualization." *The Canadian Modern Language Review,* 53: 120–142.

Read, J. 1993. "The development of a new measure of L2 vocabulary knowledge." *Language Testing,* 10: 355–371.

Read, J. 2000 *Assessing Vocabulary.* Cambridge: Cambridge University Press.

Read, J., and Chapelle, C. A. 2001. "A framework for second language vocabulary assessment." *Language Testing,* 18: 1–32.

Sanaoui, R. 1995. "Adult learners' approaches to learning vocabulary in second languages." *Modern Language Journal,* 79: 15–28

Schmitt, N. 1997. "Vocabulary learning strategies." In *Vocabulary: Description, Acquisition and Pedagogy,* N. Schmitt and M. McCarthy (eds), 199–227. Cambridge: Cambridge University Press.

Schmitt, N. 1998. "Tracking the incremental acquisition of second language vocabulary: a longitudinal study." *Language Learning,* 48: 281–317.

Schmitt, N. 2000. *Vocabulary in Language Teaching.* Cambridge: Cambridge University Press.

Schmitt, N., and McCarthy, M. (eds.). 1997. *Vocabulary: Description, Acquisition and Pedagogy.* Cambridge: Cambridge University Press.

Swan, M. 1997. "The influence of the mother tongue on second language vocabulary acquisition and use." In *Vocabulary: Description, Acquisition and Pedagogy,* N. Schmitt and M. McCarthy (eds), 156–180. Cambridge: Cambridge University Press.

Wesche, M., and Paribakht, T. S. 1996. "Assessing second language vocabulary knowledge: depth versus breadth." *The Canadian Modern Language Review,* 53: 13–40.

Selection

Chapter 1

A study of the most frequent word families in the British National Corpus

Paul Nation
Victoria University of Wellington

Abstract

This study compares the General Service List (West 1953) and the Academic Word List (Coxhead 2000) with three 1000 word lists from the British National Corpus. Even though these two sets of lists were developed from quite different corpora and at widely different times, overall they contain much the same vocabulary. This vocabulary however is not distributed in the same way in each set of lists, with the AWL words occurring across the three BNC lists. The BNC lists provided slightly better coverage of a variety of texts and corpora. The BNC lists reflected the adult, British, formal nature of the BNC.

1. Word lists

Making word lists in the field of L2 learning and teaching is usually done for the purpose of designing syllabuses and in particular it is an attempt to find one way of determining necessities (what needs to be learned) as a part of needs analysis. In any needs analysis it is important to decide *whose* needs are being investigated, and then to ensure that the investigation draws on data that is relevant to the people whose needs are being investigated (Nation 2001).

This paper looks at high frequency word lists developed from a very recent analysis of the British National Corpus and shows that it is not appropriate to use these lists unchanged as the basis for syllabus design for learners of English as a second or foreign language in primary or secondary school systems. The reason is that the British National Corpus (BNC) is predominantly a corpus of British, adult, formal, informative language, and most English learners in primary and secondary school systems are not British, are children, and need both formal and informal language for both social and informative purposes. That is, if the BNC lists were used as a basis for school curriculum design, there would be a mismatch between the nature and goals of the learners, and the nature of the corpus that the lists are drawn from.

This paper will estimate the size and nature of the mismatch and then provide evidence for the mismatch. The procedure used to do these two things involves comparing the high frequency word lists from the BNC with the General Service List and the Academic Word List (GSL+AWL). Let us start by looking at how the BNC high frequency lists were made.

The British National Corpus consists of 100,000,000 running words of English with 10% of the total running words drawn from spoken sources and 90% from written sources (see Figure 1). Leech, Rayson and Wilson (2001) rearranged the corpus into 100 one million running word sub-divisions keeping similar texts together in each sub-division. They then created a list of lemmas occurring 1000 times or more in the corpus. A lemma consists of a headword and its inflected forms where the headword and its inflected forms are all the same part of speech. For example, *diminish, diminished, diminishes, diminishing.* For each lemma they provided frequency data (how often the lemma and each of its members occurred in the 100,000,000 word corpus), range data (how many of the 100 subdivisions the lemma and each of its members occurred in), and dispersion data (how evenly the word occurred across the 100 subdivisions, that is, how similar the frequencies are across the subdivisions of the corpus). If the frequencies were very similar in the different subdivisions, the dispersion figure is close to 1, like 0.89. If they are very different, the dispersion figure is much less than 1. This list is available in written form in a book (Leech *et.*) and in electronic form http://www.comp.lancs.ac.uk/ucrel/bncfreq/flists.html. Table 1 presents two sample entries from the electronic list.

Table 1. Two samples of entries from the electronic list.

Headword	Part of Speech	Members	Freq	Range	Dispersion
assault	NoC	%	26	98	0.89
@	@	assault	22	98	0.89
@	@	assaults	4	84	0.87
assemble	Verb	%	17	99	0.94
@	@	assemble	4	96	0.92
@	@	assembled	10	97	0.94
@	@	assembles	0	33	0.83
@	@	assembling	2	83	0.92

The first line of each entry is the headword with the total figures for the lemma. The first column gives the headword, the second the part of speech, and the members of the lemma are in the third column. % indicates that this is the headword of the family. @ indicates family members. Note that the headword occurs twice, once representing the whole lemma and once as a member of the lemma. The second column gives the part of speech of the lemma. The fourth column gives the frequency. Note that for the sake of saving space the frequency is given out of 1,000,000 not 100,000,000, although the count is based on 100,000,000 running words. The fifth column gives the range of occurrence with the highest possible being 100. So *assaults* occurs in 84 of the 100 subdivisions of the corpus. The sixth column gives the dispersion with the highest possible being 100 but in practice 99. *assaults* has a dispersion of .87 which is reasonably high. Dispersion is calculated by a formula involving range and frequency in the one hundred subdivisions of the corpus. If the list is downloaded from the web site and put in a word processing programme, it can be sorted on any of the columns.

2.   Making the BNC high frequency lists

The first 1000 word list of the British National Corpus was made by taking the just over 6500 entries in the rank list of lemmas with a frequency of 10,000 or higher for the whole 100,000,000 running word corpus from the web site and sorting these by range and removing all lemmas with a range of less than 98 out of the 100 one million word sub-corpora. Then the remaining list was sorted by dispersion, and all lemmas with a dispersion of less than 80 were removed. The list was then sorted by frequency. The first 1000 families were made starting with the items at the top of the list. That is, the first 1000 lemmas were expanded into families. A full list of days of the week, months, numbers, and letters of the alphabet were included even though several of these did not meet the frequency, range, or dispersion criteria. The items *goodbye, OK*, and *Oh* were also included even though they did not meet the criteria. The frequency of the items was from 89 per million up (from *ball*).

The second 1000 list was constructed in the same way using what was left of the 6500 lemmas after the first 1000 word families had been made. There were no additions ignoring the criteria. The frequency of the second 1000 was from 27 (*request*) up to 89 (*message*), with a range of 97 up, and a dispersion of 80 up.

The third 1000 list contained words with a frequency of 10 up, a range of 95 up and a dispersion of 80 up. Five word families, which were very frequent in the spoken part of the corpus but which did not meet the range and dispersion criteria, were added to this list. These items were

(1)   hesitation procedure (*er, erm, mm, mhm*)
(2)   interjections (*ooh, aye, eh, aha, ha*)
(3)   *alright*
(4)   *pardon*
(5)   *fuck.*

These were included in the third 1000 rather than the first because they were low frequency and narrow range in the corpus as a whole

A high range minimum was chosen to make sure that the words were of wide range (general service) and to ensure they occurred in both speech and writing. 10 of the 100 sub-sections of the corpus were spoken English, so a range of 95 ensured that at least 5 of those 95 sub-sections were spoken.

The three word lists are of families not lemmas. Word families include both closely related inflected and derived forms even if the part of speech is not the same. Here are some examples.

ADD
     ADDED
     ADDING
     ADDITION
     ADDITIONAL
     ADDITIVE
     ADDITIONS
     ADDS
ADMIT
     ADMISSION
     ADMITTEDLY
     ADMITS
     ADMITTED
     ADMITTING
ADVANTAGE
     ADVANTAGES
     DISADVANTAGE
     DISADVANTAGES
     ADVANTAGING

ADVANTAGED
DISADVANTAGED

In the following discussion, BNC 2000 consists of 2000 word families. The BNC 2nd 1000 consists of the second set of 1000 word families within the BNC 2000. Similarly, BNC 3000 contains 3000 families and the BNC 3rd 1000 contains the third set of 1000 families.

3.   The GSL and the AWL

The General Service List (West 1953) is a list of around 2000 headwords (families) largely but not completely chosen on the basis of frequency. The frequency data used in the GSL came from the Thorndike and Lorge counts carried out in the early twentieth century. Frequency was not the only criterion used in making the GSL, but it was the most important. The original GSL did not list numbers, days of the week and months of the year, but in the study described in this paper they were added to the list. When the definition of a word family using Bauer &Nation (1993) level 6 is used, the GSL contains 1,986 word families — a little less than 2000. The GSL has been used as the basis for the early graded reader schemes.

The Academic Word List (Coxhead 2000) was made by looking at the frequency and range of words across the university divisions of Humanities, Science, Commerce and Law. It contains 570 word families that are not in the GSL and that are frequent and of wide range in a wide variety of academic texts. The AWL contains important vocabulary for learners in senior high school and university.

4.   Does the BNC 3000 provide better coverage than the GSL plus AWL?

Coverage refers to the percentage of tokens in a text which are accounted for (covered by) particular word lists. The corpora used in the comparison are

(1)   a 3,500,000 token written academic corpus with a balance of texts from Science, Arts, Law and Commerce (Coxhead 2000)
(2)   a 300,000 token economics text written by one author — M. Parkin *Macroeconomics* (Addison-Wesley, Mass. 1990).
(3)   the 500,000 token Lund corpus of spoken English (Svartvik & Quirk 1980)

(4)   a 3,500,000 word fiction corpus of texts from Project Guthenburg (Coxhead 2000).

These corpora include written, spoken, academic and fiction texts. In the comparison, it must be remembered that the BNC 3000 contains 444 more word families than the GSL plus AWL, and so should have better coverage because of this.

In Table 2 we can see that the 1st 1000 of the GSL covers 70.9% of the 3,500,000 token academic corpus, the 2nd 1000 words another 4.6% totalling 75.5% with the 1st 1000, and adding the AWL results in a total coverage of 85.5%. In other words 14.5% of the 3,500,000 tokens in the academic corpus are not covered by the GSL plus AWL. The BNC lists provide 1% better coverage.

The BNC provides slightly better coverage of all the corpora. If the coverage by the BNC 3rd 1000 is reduced by 33% to account for the 444 extra words it contains compared to the GSL plus AWL, the BNC extra coverage is less than 1% or in the case of the Academic corpus the advantage goes to the GSL plus AWL. The GSL provides slightly better coverage of the fiction corpus than the BNC 2000.

The BNC 3000 does not provide strikingly better coverage than the GSL plus AWL. The range as shown in the Difference row in Table 2 is from 0.9% to 2.0% with most around 1%.

The BNC 2000 provides much better (7.3% better) coverage of written formal text than the GSL alone. This is probably because the most frequent AWL words are in the BNC 2000 (63% of AWL is in the BNC 2000). Seventy percent of the BNC consists of informative text (see Figure 1) which is the type of text where the AWL is most frequent.

Table 2. Cumulative percentage coverage of a range of corpora by the lists from the BNC and GSL plus AWL.

Corpus	Academic		Parkin		LUND		Fiction	
Levels	GSL+	BNC	GSL+	BNC	GSL+	BNC	GSL+	BNC
1000	70.9	75.5	77.7	80.8	85.6	86.5	81.7	79.8
2000	75.5	83.9	82.5	89.8	89.6	91.1	87.1	86.6
AWL/ BNC 3000	85.5	86.5	91.2	93.2	91.4	92.6	88.5	89.6
Difference		1.0		2.0		1.2		0.9

5.   Do most of the words in the lists occur in a range of texts?

Table 3 is based on the same texts as Table 2 but looks to see if *all* the words in the lists are working. That is, does every word family in the lists occur in the various corpora? There could be words in the lists which seem useful but do not occur. For example, the word *chimney* is in the GSL but did not occur at all in the Academic Corpus. In Table 3 we can see that every word family in the BNC 1st 1000 and 2nd 1000 occurred in the Academic Corpus, and 99.2% of the words in the 3rd 1000 of the BNC occurred in the Academic Corpus. In other words, only 8 words did not occur. The GSL plus AWL consists of 2,556 word families. Only 10 word families (0.4%) did not occur in the Academic Corpus. Table 3 shows that the BNC lists are fractionally better than the GSL+AWL but the difference is very small, half a per cent or less which means that less than fifteen out of 3000 word families are affected in each comparison.

6.   Does the BNC 3000 contain most of the GSL plus AWL?

The GSL is an old list and the AWL is one with a narrow focus. In spite of this, virtually all the GSL 1st 1000 is in the BNC 3000 (except four words: *hurrah, ounce, scarce, shave*). Most (97%) of the GSL 1st 1000 is in the BNC 2000. At the slightly lower frequency levels, 80% of the GSL 2nd 1000 is in the BNC 3000, and 80% of the AWL is in the BNC 3000. However,107 out of 570 word families are not (18.7%). In total, 88% of the GSL plus the AWL is in the BNC 3000. Only 12% (301 word families out of 2556) is not. Thus, though the GSL was compiled long before the BNC, when supplemented by AWL, most of it can be found in the BNC 3000.

Table 3. Percentage of word families in the lists occurring in various corpora

Corpus	Academic		Parkin		LUND		Fiction	
	GSL+	BNC	GSL+	BNC	GSL+	BNC	GSL+	BNC
Lists								
1000	99.9	100	94.9	96.6	99.7	100	100	99.5
2000	98.9	100	62.7	85.3	94.9	98.9	99	99.4
AWL/ 3000	100	99.2	93.2	56.1	94.6	91.7	94.7	95.9
Average	99.6	99.7	83.6	79.3	96.4	96.9	97.9	98.2
Difference		0.1	4.3			0.5		0.3

Table 4. Spread of the 10 sublists of the AWL across the BNC

BNC	1	2	3	4	5	6	7	8	9	10	Total (%)
1st 1000	48	29	13	11	9	2	2	1	4	0	119 (21)
2nd 1000	9	28	36	38	33	31	30	21	9	6	239 (42)
3rd 1000	1	1	4	7	9	10	13	17	26	15	105 (18)
Not in BNC	2	2	7	4	9	17	15	21	21	9	107 (19)

7.   What happens to the AWL?

The AWL is divided into 10 sub lists (9 with 60 word families, sub list 10 with 30 word families). Sub list 1 contains the 60 most frequent, widest range words, sub list 2 the next 60 and so on. Table 4 shows for example that for sub list 1 of the AWL, 48 of the 60 word families are in the 1st 1000 of the BNC, 9 AWL sub list 1 word families are in the 2nd 1000 of the BNC, 1 is in the BNC 3rd 1000 and only 2 word families in AWL sub list 1 are not in the BNC 3000.

Most of the AWL (81.3%) is in the BNC 3000, and 63% is in BNC 2000. This boosts the BNC 2000 coverage of formal text. Note the bold numbers in the sub lists, showing that many of the word families in the higher AWL sub lists tend to be in the BNC 1st 1000 and 2nd 1000, while many of the word families in the lower AWL sub lists tend to be in the BNC 2nd or 3rd 1000 or not in the BNC. In the BNC data the AWL does not stand out as a separate list but is spread across the BNC lists. This is a result of the nature of the BNC. We will look at this as it is reflected in the vocabulary in the corpus and in the composition of the BNC.

8.   The nature and composition of the BNC

The following twenty words are all the words in the BNC 1st 1000 which are not in the GSL or AWL.

> American, announce, appeal, British, budget, campaign, career, client, county, drug, Europe, executive, French, German, okay, Parliament, reference, Scottish, species, television.

Table 5 classifies some of these twenty words and adds example words from the GSL which are not in the BNC 3000. In Table 5 in the row *Young learners vs adults*, *chalk*, *aunt* and *wicked* are considered as words more likely to be useful for younger learners. *Budget, campaign, client* and *executive*, are considered to

Table 5. Possible reasons for non-overlapping words in the GSL and BNC

Factors	In GSL, not in BNC	Not in GSL, in BNC
Old vs modern	shilling	television, drug
US vs British	republic, gallon, quart	county, Parliament
Young learners vs adults	chalk, aunt, wicked	budget, campaign, client, executive
Proper nouns	–	American, British, Europe, French, German, Scottish

be words more likely to be useful for adult learners. It is likely that West included *chalk* in the GSL not because of its frequency but because of its usefulness in the classroom.

Figure 1 tries to show the proportional make-up of the British National Corpus. The conversation (4%) and imaginative (20%) parts are largely informal text. The remainder is largely formal, informative text (spoken 6% plus written 70%). In order to get some idea of the size of the BNC, 100,000,000 running words has been estimated as being equivalent to approximately 10 years quantity of a person's language experience (Aston & Burnard 1998: 28). The BNC consists largely of informative text

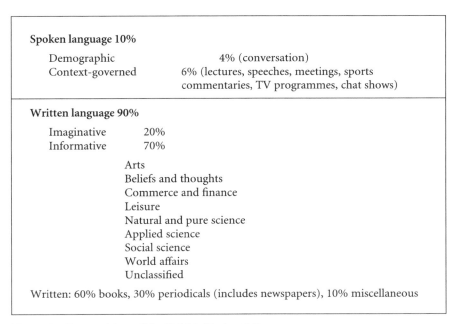

Spoken language 10%

| Demographic | 4% (conversation) |
| Context-governed | 6% (lectures, speeches, meetings, sports commentaries, TV programmes, chat shows) |

Written language 90%

| Imaginative | 20% |
| Informative | 70% |

Arts
Beliefs and thoughts
Commerce and finance
Leisure
Natural and pure science
Applied science
Social science
World affairs
Unclassified

Written: 60% books, 30% periodicals (includes newspapers), 10% miscellaneous

Figure 1. Composition of the British National Corpus

9. Conclusion

The major difference between the BNC 3000 and the GSL+AWL does not lie in the performance of the lists in terms of coverage, but in the way the vocabulary is divided between the three one thousand levels of the BNC, and the two one thousand levels of the GSL and the AWL. The BNC 1st 2000 contains many words from the AWL, whereas in the GSL+AWL, the GSL is largely non-academic and the AWL is wholly academic.

Learners of English as a second language in primary and secondary school systems may be better off using materials based on a replacement for the GSL, with the AWL getting attention at senior high school and university levels. Beginning learners at tertiary level would be better off using materials based on the BNC lists, because of the slightly better BNC coverage.

It is not easy to decide how the GSL could be replaced. As Coxhead (2000) showed, some words could go from the AWL to the GSL, for example *job, sex, percent, area, final.* Some important proper nouns describing countries, people, and languages could be added. A corpus needs to be devised to represent the learning goals of young L2 learners. That is, the corpus would need to contain written and spoken texts that more closely match the uses they would make of their English. At least half of the corpus should be spoken language. Should it be the spoken language of advanced L2 learners or should it be the spoken language of young native speakers? An obvious candidate for the written part of the corpus would be graded readers (also included in the BNC), but many of the graded reading schemes are probably based on the GSL so this could be backward-looking rather than forward-looking. It should probably include school texts as in the Carroll, Davies & Richman count (1971), as this would make the list useful for ESL learners in an English medium school system. Almost one third, 236, out of the top 900 word families in the Carroll et al list do not occur in the BNC 3000. These include *adjective, alphabet, ant, arithmetic, astronaut, aunt, axis,* which are words that may be more immediately useful for school children. It could also include books written for young native speakers. A large number of words (681) in the BNC 3000 are not in the top 5300 types of the New Zealand School Journal corpus. Clearly there is a substantial number of words in texts written for young native speakers which are not in the BNC 3000. Perhaps the language of chat rooms and e-mails should be part of a corpus for making a new GSL.

The main motivation to replace the General Service List is because of its age. There are clearly a few words like *computer, drugs, television,* which are not in it and should be. Perhaps we should respect age rather than see it as an excuse for retirement. However, whatever choices are made, the choices need to represent credible language goals for young learners of English.

References

Aston, L. and Burnard, G. 1998. *The BNC Handbook*. Edinburgh: Edinburgh University Press.

Bauer, L. and Nation, I. S. P. 1993. "Word families". *International Journal of Lexicography* 6: 253–279.

Carroll, J. B., Davies, P. and Richman, B. 1971. *The American Heritage Word Frequency Book*. New York: Houghton Mifflin, Boston American Heritage.

Coxhead, A. 2000. "A new academic word list". *TESOL Quarterly* 34 (2): 213–238.

Leech, G., Rayson, P. and Wilson, A. 2001. *Word Frequencies in Written and Spoken English*. Harlow: Longman. http://www.comp.lancs.ac.uk/ucrel/bncfreq/flists.html.

Nation, I. S. P. 2001. *Learning Vocabulary in Another Language*. Cambridge: Cambridge University Press.

Svartvik, J. and Quirk, R. (eds) (1980) *A Corpus of English Conversation*. C. W. K. Gleerup, Lund.

West, M. 1953. *A General Service List of English Words*. London: Longman, Green & Co.

Chapter 2

Is there room for an academic word list in French?

Tom Cobb and Marlise Horst
Université du Québec à Montréal, Concordia University

Abstract

Extensive analysis of corpora has offered learners of English a solution to the problem of which among the many thousands of English words are most useful to know by identifying lists of high frequency words that make up the core of the language. Of particular interest to university-bound learners is Coxhead's (2000) Academic Word List (AWL). Analyses indicate that knowing the 570 word families on this list along with the 2000 most frequent families consistently offers coverage of about 85% of the words learners will encounter in reading an academic text in English. This finding raises the question of whether such lists can be identified in other languages. The research reported in this chapter provides an initial answer in the case of French. Lists of the 2000 most frequent French word families were built into an online lexical frequency profiling program (*Vocabprofil*) and their coverage powers tested. Analyses of texts using this tool confirmed the usefulness of the lists in identifying distinct and consistent profiles for French texts of three specific genres (newspaper, popular expository, and medical). Comparisons using parallel French and English texts indicated that the 2000 most frequent word families of French offer the reader a surprisingly high level of coverage (roughly 85%), a level that can only be achieved in English with the knowledge of the most frequent 2000 words plus the 570 AWL words. In other words, the French 2000 list seems to serve both everyday and academic purposes more effectively than its English counterpart, such that there appears to be no need for an additional AWL-like list in French to facilitate the comprehension of academic texts. With the coverage powers of the French 2000 list so high, there appears to be little or no space left in the lexis of French for such a list to occupy.

1.   Introduction

Acquiring a second lexicon is a daunting task for language learners, especially if the goal is to achieve literacy in the second language. But the task becomes more manageable if we know which words are more important to learn than others, or which words are most useful to know as a precondition to learning others. In English, computational studies of word frequency and text coverage, in conjunction with empirical studies of learner comprehension of texts with different lexical profiles, have provided valuable information for both course designers and independent learners. It has become clear that words of particular frequencies have predictable degrees of prominence in texts of particular genres. For example, the 1000 most frequent words, along with proper nouns, tend through repetition to make up, or cover, about 90% of the running words in spoken conversations. This type of analysis, known as lexical frequency profiling (or LFP, Laufer & Nation 1995), has been useful in clarifying and resolving specific problems of lexical acquisition in English. Particularly interesting is the Academic Word List (or AWL, Coxhead 2000) component of the LFP framework, which combines frequency, coverage, and genre information to provide learners with a useful solution to a problem in the naturalistic acquisition of the vocabulary needed for reading academic texts.

An interesting question, then, is whether LFP analysis is applicable to languages other than English. While frequency lists have been developed over the years for most European languages, neither the coverage properties nor the genre determination of these lists have been closely examined. This chapter is a preliminary comparison of the vocabulary distributions of English and French using the LFP framework, with emphasis on the question of whether or not there is any lexical zone in French resembling the English AWL that might be useful to learners of French. We begin our investigation with some background on the nature of the problem the AWL resolves for learners of English.

2.   A logical problem in acquiring some second lexicons

Whether the number of words in a modern language is 50,000 or 500,000 or somewhere in between, as variously claimed by different researchers using different counting units and methods, either of these numbers is daunting to an L2 learner. There are at least three factors working against the acquisition of a second lexicon in English. First, many learners are simply unlikely ever to meet a large proportion of the lexicon. The vast majority of English words are found mainly in written texts, while a relatively small handful are encountered in daily conversation and watching television. This means that for the many learners who achieve conversational fluency in an L2 rather than full literacy, the vast majority of words are simply inaccessible for learning through naturalistic acquisition.

Second, even for avid readers, vocabulary acquisition through exposure to texts is slow and uncertain. The classic finding is that there is only .07% likelihood of a first language learner later recognizing the meaning of a new word after encountering it once incidentally in reading (Nagy & Herman 1987). This rate is nonetheless adequate to explain the attainment of an adult-sized English lexicon (defined as about 20,000 word families) based on an average reading program of 1 million words a year. But few L2 learners are likely to read this much; the highest estimate we know of for an extensive L2 reading program is 300,000 words per year, (personal communication from R. Rozell, teaching in Japan 2002).

Third, the probability of word learning from reading is likely to be even lower than .07% for L2 readers. Natural acquisition relies on new words being met in environments where most of the surrounding words are known, as will normally be the case for school-age learners meeting new words in level-appropriate texts in their own language. For L2 readers, however, unknown words are likely to arrive not alone but in clusters. A typical inference exercise in the ESL classroom is to work out the meaning of *date* from lexically dense sentences like, 'Her date eventually motored into view well past the ETA'. The problem of learning from such contexts is real and quantifiable. Research has shown that the minimal ratio of known to unknown words for both reliable comprehension and new acquisition is at least 20 : 1, or in other words when at least 95% of the running words in the environment are known (see Nation 2001 for an overview). These circumstances are unlikely to prevail when L2 learners read unsimplified texts. Thus, the natural acquisition of English as a second lexicon presents a problem: the numbers simply do not add up.

Let us look in detail at a typical learner's progress toward knowing 95% of the running words in an average text. Whether in a classroom or a naturalistic setting, learners tend to acquire L2 vocabulary in rough order of frequency. The 1000 most frequent word families (base words along with their most common derivations and inflections) of English are very frequent in spoken language, and in addition account for around 75% of the running words in most kinds of written language[1] so opportunities for meeting and learning these words are good. Then, learners who read or who join reading-based courses are likely to acquire some or most of the second thousand most frequent words. Words in this category are relatively infrequent in speech but occur often in writing, accounting for another 5% of the running words in many text types. So with just 2000 known word families, the learner already controls about 80% of the running words in an average text. If this rate of return could be sustained (roughly 5% additional coverage per additional 1000 word families learned), then the trajectory from 80 to 95% coverage would be achieved with knowledge of 5000 English word families. But in fact, coverage does not proceed linearly in neat 5% increases with each 1000 words learned. Unfortunately, laying the vocabulary basis for naturalistic acquisition of less frequent items is not so easily accomplished, at least not in the case of English.

It turns out that in natural texts, the chances of meeting less common words drop off rather sharply after the 2000 word zone. Table 1 shows the typical coverage percentages provided by the different frequency bands — percentages for the ten most frequent words (*the, a, of, I*) appear at the bottom of the table, with those for the 100 most frequent words (*house, big, way, girl*) just above, and so on. As mentioned, the 1000 most frequent words are seen to cover about 75% of the words in an average text, and 2000 cover just over 80%.

The coverage curve rises steeply, levels off at around 80%, and thereafter creeps only very gradually towards the 95% mark, as is clearly evident when this information is represented graphically. As Figure 1 shows, the fourth thousand most frequent words account for just an additional 3% of running words, the fifth an additional 1%, and so on — with the 95% mark receding into the distance at 12,000 words. A similar too-much-to-learn problem probably

Table 1. Typical coverage figures for different frequency bands (Carroll, Davies and Richman 1971, cited in Nation 2001).

Number of words	Text coverage
87,000	100%
44,000	99%
12,000	95%
5,000	89%
4,000	88%
3,000	85%
2,000	81%
1,000	74%
100	49%
10	24%

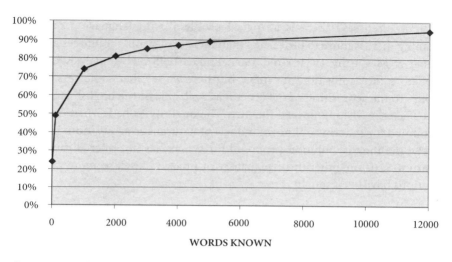

Figure 1. Graphic representation of part of Table 1.

features in any language where a significant proportion of the lexicon is housed mainly on paper. Hazenberg & Hulstijn (1996) reached this conclusion in the case of Dutch, finding that the minimal lexical base for reading demanding texts was knowing 90% of their running words, and that achieving this meant knowing roughly 10,000 word families. For most learners of either language, the 95% or even 90% coverage mark will not be achieved by simple cumulative progression through the frequency levels via courses, contextual inference, dictionary look-ups, or any of the other usual means of natural vocabulary growth. The number of words to learn is simply overwhelming.

To summarize, the deck is stacked against a L2 learner acquiring a functional reading lexicon in English or possibly in any language. It seems the time required for natural acquisition of a second lexicon is approximately all the time available, that is, the time it takes to grow up and be educated in a language. This is time that most L2 learners simply do not have. The natural frequency distribution of words will incline many L2 learners to plateau when they have acquired the resources needed for basic spoken interaction; those who attempt to proceed toward fuller literacy will find the going hard because of the number of words needed for fluent reading and the inhospitable conditions of acquiring them. And yet a large proportion of the world's English learners, if not the majority, are studying English precisely in order to read documents in their academic, professional, or vocational areas.

It is often said there is a 'logical problem' with language acquisition, meaning there is more to be learned than there are learning resources available (Baker & McCarthy 1981; Gold 1967; Pinker 1995). This analysis has been applied to the acquisition of syntax, but here we see that some version of it applies to the acquisition of the lexicon as well, at least the English lexicon for an L2 learner wishing to read fluently. The quantity to be learned cannot be accounted for in terms of known models of naturalistic acquisition. Unfortunately, the innatist solution proposed for syntax has not offered much with regard to lexis on either the explanatory or practical level, so more mundane solutions have been sought.

3.   The AWL as a solution to the problem

A partial solution to the problem of building a second lexicon in English has been found in the form of the AWL (Coxhead 2000). This is a list of 570 words such as *abandonment, abstraction,* and *accessible* that, while not necessarily frequent in the language at large, have been found through extensive corpus analysis to be frequent across the genre of academic texts (Xue & Nation 1984; Coxhead 2000). The AWL, along with the 1000 and 2000 frequency lists, form a combined word list of 2570 families that gives reliable coverage of about 90% of the running words in an academic or quality newspaper text. In other words, the AWL adds another roughly 10% coverage for an additional learning investment of only 570 word families. Learning the meanings of the 570 AWL items presents a challenging but feasible task, and several instructional ideas have been proposed for helping ESL learners get control of its contents (e.g., activities on Coxhead's *Academic Word List* and Cobb's *Lexical Tutor* websites).

The substantial additional coverage that the AWL offers is clear but the reader will recall that the critical point for independent reading and further acquisition is not 90 but 95% coverage. Nation and his colleagues have argued that further coverage shortcuts can be discovered in the relatively definable and manageable lexicons that exist within particular domains, for example in economics (Sutarsyah, Nation & Kennedy 1994). Thus the additional word learning that takes a learner to the 95% criterion will occur more or less naturalistically through content instruction within such domains. The role of the AWL is to provide a reliable bridge between these two relatively accessible zones of lexical acquisition, between the words that are frequent in the language at large and the words that are frequent within a specific domain of study.

The reliability of the AWL's coverage can be demonstrated with the help of a computer program that analyzes texts in terms of their lexical frequency profiles. This analysis is a key component of the LFP framework and is useful both for validating coverage claims and exploiting coverage information instructionally (e.g., for assessing lexical richness in learner productions, and determining the lexical density of reading materials). To analyze a text, the program simply loads the 1000, 2000, and AWL family lists into memory and then classifies each word according to the frequency list it belongs to. Words not on any list are designated off-list. The program keeps tallies of the number of items in each category and calculates the proportion each category represents. A typical output for a newspaper text might show that 70% of the total number of running words are among the 1000 most frequent words, 10% are from the 1001–2000 list, 10% are from the AWL, leaving a rump of 10% off-list items that include a mix of proper nouns and lower frequency items. Various versions of this computer program exist, but for purposes of public replicability the first author's Internet-based version of the program on the *Lexical Tutor* website, *Web Vocabprofile* (henceforth referred to as VP), will be used in the analyses to follow. These analyses will serve two purposes, first to show what the English AWL is and does, and second to provide a specific baseline to measure the success of exporting the LFP framework to a language other than English. The second part of this chapter reports our initial foray into developing and testing the framework for French.

To demonstrate the AWL's reliability and coverage, we submitted a set of seven 2000+ word text segments from the *Learned* section of the Brown corpus (Francis & Kucera 1979) to VP analysis. The results of these analyses are shown in Table 2. While the texts represent a range of disciplines, coverage percentages are remarkably similar. Mean AWL coverage is 11.60%, which as predicted, combines with the coverage provided by the 1000 and 2000 lists to amount to a reasonably reliable 90% figure. Reliability of coverage is evident in standard deviations from means for all four frequency categories: these are small, on the order of 2 to 4%. *Chi*-square comparisons show no significant differences across disciplines, with the exception of medicine-anatomy (possibly owing to the very high proportion of specialist terminology in this field).

A second property of the AWL that can be demonstrated with VP is its genre determination. To make a simple cross-genre comparison, we chose a second genre, that of popular expository writing designed for the general reader. We predicted that texts of this genre would also provide consistent lexical profiles but with smaller contributions from the AWL than was found

Table 2. Lexical frequency profiles across disciplines (coverage percentages).

Brown segment	Discipline	No. of words	1000	2000	1000 + 2000	AWL	1K + 2K + AWL
J32	Linguistics	2031	73.51	8.37	81.88	12.60	94.48
J29	Sociology	2084	74.23	4.75	78.98	13.44	92.42
J26	History	2036	69.3	5.7	75.00	14.49	89.49
J25	Social Psychology	2059	73.63	3.11	76.74	14.38	91.12
J22	Development	2023	76.42	4.55	80.97	12.26	93.23
J12	Medicine (anatomy)	2024	71.05	3.80	74.85	6.72	81.57
J11	Zoology	2026	75.12	6.17	81.29	7.31	88.60
M			73.32	5.21	78.53	11.60	90.13
SD			2.42	1.74	3.01	3.24	4.30

Note 1: In this and subsequent Tables 1K and 2K refer to the first and second thousand word lists respectively
Note 2: Segments from the Brown corpus are described in the Brown University website accessible from the AWL page on the *Lexical Tutor* website.

for the academic texts from the Brown corpus. We profiled 17 randomly selected non-fiction *Reader's Digest* articles of around 200 words each. The results in Table 3 show that coverage percentages are similar across texts on widely differing topics, and that once again standard deviations for category means are low. As expected, the role of AWL items is less prominent (5.56% or about half of what it was in the academic texts). The significant difference found in a *chi*-square comparison for the means of the popular and scientific texts shows that the two genres have distinct lexical profiles.

Other dimensions of the AWL that can be investigated with the help of VP include hypotheses about the list's semantic content. It is arguable that AWL items are not only important because they increase text coverage, but also because of the intellectual work they do in academic texts. These words appear frequently across academic domains for the good reason that they are used to *define, delineate, advance,* and *assess abstract entities* such as *theories, arguments,* and *hypotheses* (the italicized words are AWL items). Researchers in the field of L1 literacy such as Olsen (1992) and Corson (1997) stress the need for English-speaking children to learn to use these Greco-Latin words and to think with the concepts they represent; they argue that a 'lexical bar' faces those who fail to do so (Corson 1985). VP analysis was used in the following way to test the claim that the language of theories and arguments is largely AWL language: the second author performed a *Gedankenexperiment* by typing into the *Vocabprofile* Text

Table 3. Consistent but distinct profiles for non-academic texts (coverage percentages).

TEXT	1000	2000	1000+ 2000	AWL	1K + 2K + AWL
Audubon	71.62	9.46	81.08	4.73	85.81
Computers	76.62	4.98	81.60	10.95	92.55
Drugs	74.46	5.98	80.44	3.26	83.70
Earthquakes	70.89	10.13	81.02	7.59	88.61
Dieting	75.62	6.97	82.59	3.98	86.57
Gas	89.47	0.00	89.47	7.02	96.49
Olympics	72.55	3.92	76.47	5.88	82.35
Origins of Life	69.71	7.43	77.14	4.00	81.14
Plague	75.76	3.03	78.79	5.45	84.24
Salt	81.60	5.66	87.26	3.30	90.56
Stage fright	76.44	9.13	85.57	4.33	89.90
Teenagers	84.03	4.86	88.89	4.17	93.06
Tennis	70.00	7.89	77.89	5.26	83.15
Toledo	69.05	4.76	73.81	6.55	80.36
Vitamins	67.30	9.43	76.73	6.29	83.02
Volcanoes	75.63	7.11	82.74	4.06	86.80
Warm-Up	73.33	6.67	80.00	7.78	87.78
M	74.95	6.32	81.26	5.56	86.83
SD	5.73	2.62	4.47	1.99	4.56

Entry box all the discourse or argument structuring words that came to mind in five minutes and then submitting these for analysis. The items produced by this procedure were as follows:

> concede imply hypothesize infer interpret doubt affirm deny believe reject imagine perceive understand concept promise argue declare assert valid justify confirm prove propose evidence utterance logical status ambiguous observe symbolize acknowledge entail summarize premise contradict paradox consistent theory conclude demonstrate discuss define opinion equivalent generalize specify framework abstract concrete unfounded context analyse communicate implicate

The profile results, shown in Figure 2, show that almost 63% of the spontaneously generated items are from the AWL.

In the remainder of this chapter, the foregoing VP analyses of English will be used as a baseline to investigate the question of whether LFP analysis is applicable to a language other than English, and specifically whether a closely related language (French) can be shown to have a zone of lexis resembling the AWL.

WEB VP OUTPUT FOR FILE: *Gedankenexperiment*

K1 Words (1 to 1000):	10	**18.52%**
K2 Words (1001 to 2000):	3	**5.56%**
AWL Words (academic):	34	**62.96%**
Off-List Words:	7	**12.96%**

0-1000 [TTR 10:10] believe declare doubt generalize observe opinion promise propose prove understand
1001-2000 [3:3] argue discuss imagine
AWL [34:34] abstract acknowledge ambiguous analyze communicate concept conclude confirm consistent context contradict define demonstrate deny equivalent evidence framework hypothesize implicate imply infer interpret justify logical perceive reject specify status summarize symbolize theory unfounded utterance valid

OFF LIST [7:7] affirm assert concede concrete entail paradox premise

Figure 2. Web-VP screen output for thought experiment

Note: In this and subsequent screen outputs, K1 and K2 refer to the first and second thousand word lists, respectively, and TTR refers to type-token ratio.

4.   Are there AWLs in other languages?

As already mentioned, a study by Hazenberg & Hulstijn (1996) indicated that learners of Dutch would need to know the meanings of 10,000 word families in order to be familiar with 90% of the words in an academic text. However, these researchers did not consider the possibility that Dutch might contain a zone of lexis resembling the English AWL that could foreshorten the learning process. It is not obvious that such a lexical zone would necessarily exist in Dutch. For one thing, the Greco-Latin component of academic discourse is visibly less prominent in Dutch than it is in English. Dutch, like German, has 'traditionally turned to its own resources for enriching the vocabulary' (Stockwell & Minkova 2001: 53). In Dutch we find *natuurkunde* instead of *physics, aardrijkskunde* instead of *geography, taalkunde* instead of *linguistics,* and so on. Of course, there is nothing to preclude a home-grown AWL in Dutch, German or any other language, which could presumably be located by contrastive corpus analysis.

On the other hand, the mere existence of Greco-Latin items in a language does not necessarily indicate the presence of an AWL. Many of the Greek and Latin AWL items in the English VP output of Figure 2 have cognate counterparts in many other European languages, but these do not necessarily play the same roles, participate in the same genres, or pose the same learning advantages or difficulties that they do in English. To take a homely example, English speaking children watching a bicycle race in Montreal shout to their heroes 'You can do it!' while their Francophone counterparts shout 'Tu es capable!' The French children are using a word whose equivalent the English children can understand but regard as somewhat formal. In fact, *capable* is an AWL word in English but a high frequency word in French.

The lexical frequency profiles of most languages are not nearly so well known as those of English. One reason is that studies of lexical richness in other languages have often adopted a different methodology, namely type-token analysis, which investigates the amount of lexical repetition in a text rather than the frequency of its lexis with respect to the language at large (e.g., Cossette's 1994 work in French). This methodology has been challenged owing to the way it is influenced by simple text length, which of course is not the case for LFP analysis (see Vermeer, this volume, for an application of LFP analysis to Dutch). Another reason for the limited application of LFP analysis in languages other than English is that the frequency lists that have been developed in these languages have often remained unlemmatized, i.e., do not take the form of word families, so that it is not possible to test their coverage of novel texts (e.g., both Gougenheim, Rivenc, Sauvageot & Michéa's 1967 pre-computational *français fondamental* and Baudot's more recent 1992 computational list). With an unlemmatized list, it is possible for *chat* to be classified as a common word and *chats* as an uncommon word.

In other words, the tools have simply not been available to answer the question: Are there AWLs in other languages? However, in the case of French the situation has recently changed.

5.   Recent lexical developments in French

A disparate group of European scholars have recently laid some groundwork for an LFP approach to the description and pedagogy of French. Verlinde & Selva (2001) at Louvain have produced a substantial frequency list of the French language based on a 50-million word collection of recent newspaper texts (*Le Monde* of France and *Le Soir* from Belgium). Glynn Jones (2001) at the Open University in Great Britain has produced a computer program to automatically lemmatize this list, so that parts of it can be run in an LFP-type computer program and their coverage tested with different types of texts.

Goodfellow, Jones & Lamy (2002) have developed a pilot French version of the LFP for pedagogical purposes, and tested it with British students learning French at the Open University. They broke the larger lemmatized frequency list into the familiar 1000, 2000, and (hypothesized) AWL zones, installed these in another web-based version of VP (available at http://iet.open.ac.uk/cgi-bin/vat/vat.html), and used the program to produce lexical profiles of a set of essays produced by learners of French. They looked for correlations between features of these profiles and grades awarded by human raters and found a moderate correlation between proportions of items in the 1001–2000 frequency band and rater scores.

However, the use of these new French lists in a pedagogical analysis may have been somewhat premature, in that no investigation that we know of has examined their reliability across same-genre texts or their differentiation for different-genre texts. Nor was the hypothesized AWL used in this scheme based on analysis of academic texts per se; it was merely the third thousand most common words of general French. No attempt was reported to determine whether these supposed AWL items were indeed more frequent in academic texts than in other genres. The rest of this chapter outlines our attempt to advance this work by micro-testing the reliability, coverage, and genre characteristics of these potentially useful French lists. But before that a certain amount of preliminary work had to be done on the lists themselves.

The three French frequency lists used in the Goodfellow *et al.* (2002) experiment were generously shared with us by the researchers. We then incorporated these lists into a French web-based version of VP, to be known as *Vocabprofil*, which like its English counterpart allows full inspection of classifications into frequency ranges (see the screen output in Figure 2). A large number and variety of texts were run through the program and output profiles were inspected in detail for anomalies. The output checking was performed by French native-speaker research assistants, but also by general users of the public website who emailed their queries. These users reported both inconsistencies in lemmatization (e.g., *participer* was listed as a first 1000 item while *participant* was listed as second) and simple misclassifications (several French speakers found it odd to see *calme* listed as an off-list or uncommon word). Items flagged as potential misclassifications were checked against a second French frequency list (Baudot 1992), and about 200 items were either reclassified or added to the three lists over a six-month testing period. The size of the lists remained almost identical throughout this process with the number of additions (e.g., *calme*) roughly equaling the number of deletions through reclassification (e.g., *participant* removed as a second thousand entry and reclassified under *participer* in the first 1000).

Our decisions about which words to count as members of the same family were taken in the spirit of the work done in English by Bauer & Nation (1993), where frequency, regularity and transparency of inflection and affixation were the main criteria for family inclusion (e.g., *participant* is an obvious relation of *participer* for anyone likely to be reading a text including these items). It should be noted, however, that the algorithmic lemmatization procedure that had previously been applied by Jones (2001) to these French lists was intended to be exhaustive, such that some low frequency affixes were attached to high frequency base words; hence, some forms that learners might not easily recognize were categorized as frequent. (How readily would a beginning learner of French recognize *échappassiez* as a form of *échapper*?) The word families that emerge from this lemmatization procedure are truly enormous, particularly in the case of verbs with their many suffixes. These French lists, if ever intended for learners, would eventually need to be reworked along the lines of Bauer & Nation's (1993) procedure. An interim solution to their pedagogicalization is suggested in the conclusion.

Once satisfied that the English and French lists were more or less comparable, as signaled by a cessation of anomaly reports from users and research assistants, we shifted our focus from the lists themselves to the comparison of the lexical frequency profiles of English and French that the lists made possible.

6.   Preliminary investigation of French profiles

A large bilingual and multi-generic corpus analysis such as that provided by Coxhead (2000) for English will eventually be required to complete the investigation we are beginning. In this preliminary investigation, we are merely applying our new word lists to French texts in order to test the feasibility of LFP analysis and get a sense of its pedagogical potential. Our methodology is to collect a small bilingual corpus of medium-sized original and translated texts of distinct genres, run these piecemeal through both *Vocabprofile* and *Vocabprofil*, and compare the results. Through this we hope to answer specific questions about the coverage of the lists, and the reliability and genre specificity of the profiles they provide, always with a view to answering the larger question of whether there is anything resembling an AWL in French. We begin with the issue of reliable coverage.

Question 1: Do the new French lists produce reliable coverage profiles within a text genre?
To answer this question, we had our graduate students select and download 100 typical online news texts of between 500 and 1000 words on political topics from different parts of the Francophone world, and submit these one by one to VP analysis using the Internet version of the program running the new frequency lists described above. Proper nouns were not eliminated or otherwise treated, on the assumption that most political news stories would carry similar proportions of these. By analyzing the texts separately, rather than as a single unit, we were able to calculate a measure of variability for frequency categories across the collection. Profiles across these texts proved remarkably consistent, displaying very low degrees of within-level variance. The results of eight of these analyses can be seen in Table 4. The main point of interest is that the standard deviations across the 1000, 2000, and AWL zones are small, even smaller than the figures for English in Tables 2 and 3 above. All adjacent pairs of texts were subject to *chi*-square tests of comparison; none of the profile differences proved to be statistically significant.

Table 4. Consistent profiles within news texts (coverage percentages)

Paper	Topic	1000	2000	AWL	1K + 2K + AWL	Off-list
Le Devoir	CBC coupures	79.65	9.29	1.33	90.27	9.73
La Presse	CBC coupures	82.78	7.50	0.96	91.23	8.77
Le Devoir	Abandon scolaire	78.00	10.85	2.17	91.01	8.99
La Presse	Abandon scolaire	77.15	9.18	2.34	88.67	11.33
Le Devoir	Bush & Irak	75.10	8.54	1.88	85.52	14.48
La Presse	Bush & Irak	77.68	7.40	3.20	88.29	11.71
Le Monde	Bush & Irak	75.99	8.59	1.98	86.56	13.44
Figaro	Bush & Irak	74.75	7.43	1.82	83.99	16.01
M		77.64	8.60	1.96		11.81
SD		2.63	1.19	0.67		2.65

With the new lists apparently able to produce reliable profiles, at least for this type of text, we next turn to the more interesting question of their coverage. Standard deviations will continue to be provided in the analyses to follow, as a continuing reliability check for other types of texts.

Question 2: Do the French lists provide similar text coverage to their English counterparts?

To answer this question, we used French translations of the 18 *Reader's Digest* texts already seen for English above (translated by bilingual research assistants in Montreal[2]). Figure 3 provides a sample translation of one of the texts. The question of interest was whether the French lists as developed to date would produce consistent coverage figures across texts for each of three frequency zones (1000, 2000, AWL), as indicated by small deviations from the mean coverage figures for the 18 texts.

The translated texts were fed through *Vocabprofil* piecemeal. The resulting profile means and standard deviations are shown in Table 5a, and comparison figures for the English profiles of the same texts just below in Table 5b.

The first thing to note in these results is that once again, the experimental French lists provide consistent amounts of coverage across texts on disparate

Traditional methods of teaching are no longer enough in this technological world. Currently there are more than 100,000 computers in schoolrooms in the United States. Students, mediocre and bright alike, from the first grade through high school, not only are not intimidated by computers, but have become enthusiastic users.	Les méthodes traditionnelles d'enseignement ne suffisent plus dans ce monde de technologie. Présentement, on compte plus de 100 000 ordinateurs dans les salles de classe aux États-Unis. Les étudiants, moyens et brillants pareils, de la première année jusqu'à la fin du secondaire, sont non seulement peu intimidés par les ordinateurs mais sont même devenus des utilisateurs enthousiastes.
Children are very good at using computers in their school curriculum. A music student can program musical notes so that the computer will play Beethoven or the Beatles. In a biology class, the computer can produce a picture of the complex actions of the body's organs, thus enabling today's students to understand human biology more deeply. A nuclear reactor is no longer a puzzle to students who can see its workings in minute detail on a computer. In Wisconsin, the Chippewa Indians are studying their ancient and almost forgotten language with the aid of a computer.	Les enfants sont très doués pour ce qui est d'utiliser les ordinateurs dans leur curriculum scolaire. Un étudiant en musique peut programmer des notes pour que l'ordinateur joue Beethoven ou les Beatles. Dans un cours de biologie, l'ordinateur peut produire une image du fonctionnement complexe des organes du corps, permettant ainsi à l'étudiant de comprendre plus en profondeur les principes de la biologie humaine. Un réacteur nucléaire n'a plus de mystères pour les étudiants qui peuvent observer son fonctionnement en détails sur l'ordinateur. Dans le Wisconsin, les indiens Chippewa s'en servent pour étudier leur langue, ancienne et presque oubliée.
The simplest computers aid the handicapped, who learn more rapidly from the computer than from humans. Once a source of irritation, practice and exercises on the computer are now helping children to learn because the machine responds to correct answers with praise and to incorrect answers with sad faces and even an occasional tear. - 198 words	Les ordinateurs les plus simples aident les personnes handicapées qui apprennent plus rapidement d'une machine que d'une autre personne. Jadis une source d'irritation, la pratique et les exercices sur l'ordinateur aident maintenant les enfants à apprendre parce que la machine complimente les bonnes réponses et présente des visages tristes et même parfois une larme pour les mauvaises réponses. - 214 words

Figure 3. Sample translation: Learning with computers/Apprentissage par ordinateur

Table 5a. French VP profiles for popular expository texts (coverage percentages)

TEXT	1000	2000	1000 + 2000	AWL	1K + 2K + AWL	Off-list
Audubon	71.51	8.72	80.23	1.16	81.39	18.60
Computers	78.85	10.13	88.98	3.52	92.50	7.49
Drugs	74.24	6.11	80.35	2.18	82.53	17.47
Earthquakes	73.33	10.26	83.59	4.62	88.21	11.79
Dieting	83.21	6.87	90.08	3.82	93.90	6.11
Gas	74.07	14.07	88.14	5.93	94.07	5.93
Olympics	75.29	6.32	81.61	2.30	83.91	16.09
Origins of Life	70.80	8.41	79.21	3.98	83.19	16.81
Plague	76.29	5.15	81.44	4.12	85.56	14.43
Salt	76.95	5.47	82.42	2.73	85.15	14.85
Stage fright	76.08	7.84	83.92	2.35	86.27	13.73
Teenagers	81.14	8.00	89.14	2.86	92.00	8.00
Tennis	75.95	9.28	85.23	1.69	86.92	13.08
Toledo	71.78	7.92	79.70	2.97	82.67	17.33
Vitamins	70.94	8.37	79.31	3.94	83.25	16.75
Volcanoes	78.74	5.91	84.65	3.54	88.19	11.81
Warm-Up	79.02	8.93	87.95	4.46	92.41	7.59
M	75.78	8.10	83.88	3.30	87.18	12.82
SD	3.61	2.18	3.78	1.20	4.32	4.32

Table 5b. Comparison of French and English profiles (coverage percentages).

	1000		2000		1000 + 2000		AWL		1K + 2K + AWL	
	M	SD	M	SD	M	SD	M	SD	M	SD
English	74.95	5.73	6.32	2.62	81.26	4.47	5.56	1.99	86.83	4.56
French	75.78	3.61	8.10	2.18	83.88	3.78	3.30	1.20	87.18	4.32

topics. Across the 17 texts, the first 1000 most frequent French words account for about three quarters of the lexis of each text, while the second thousand and AWL add approximately 8% and 3%, respectively. Standard deviations from these means are small and consistently lower than their English counterparts, suggesting even greater reliability. The second thing to note is that the overall coverage provided by the English and French lists appears to be similar across the two languages, within a percentage point (86.83% for English and 87.18% for French) for the three lists combined. However, there is a hint of a difference in the components that are providing the coverage in the two languages. The French second thousand list appears to account for more items than its English counterpart, the English AWL for more items than its French counterpart.

This apparent asymmetry will be further explored with texts of a more academic character below.

Question 3: Is there an AWL in French?

To launch an investigation of this question, we first located a set of nine translated medical texts of equivalent size (about 1000 words each) on the website of the *Canadian Medical Association Journal* (CMAJ) and submitted them to piecemeal bilingual VP analysis. Some of these had been translated from English to French, and others from French to English. The results are shown in Table 6a and summarized in Table 6b. It should be noted that medical texts are typically dense in domain-specific terms, which may explain why the off-list component here is high (about 20% of items are not accounted for by the three lists, as opposed to the usual 10 or so). Still, some interesting points of comparison emerge in the more frequent zones (see Table 6b). The first thing to note in the results is that the experimental French AWL does not pull any more weight in these medical texts (only 3.57%) than it did in the

Table 6a. Profiles of medical texts, translated but in no consistent direction (coverage percentages).

Text	English			French		
	1000	2000	AWL	1000	2000	AWL
Dental 1	59.84	7.10	9.56	66.39	11.55	5.57
Dental 2	68.43	9.85	8.37	72.46	7.66	3.79
Breast self exam	65.67	8.50	12.44	73.31	9.37	3.91
Preventive care	63.13	8.94	12.85	72.41	11.35	3.30
Mammography	61.90	9.52	15.00	72.70	10.43	3.13
Lymphedema	57.14	8.12	12.04	69.40	8.62	3.02
Biopsy	54.50	7.63	12.26	67.13	11.95	2.99
Child abuse	60.03	14.46	15.31	76.19	11.19	3.21
Hyperhomocystein-emia	60.84	8.16	10.72	71.04	8.27	3.24
M	61.28	9.14	12.06	71.23	10.04	3.57
SD	4.20	2.17	2.28	3.11	1.60	0.81

Table 6b. Means comparisons for Table 6a (coverage percentages).

	1000		2000		1K + 2K		AWL		1K + 2K + AWL	
	M	SD	M	SD	M	SD	M	SD	M	SD
English	61.28	4.20	9.14	2.17	70.42	5.07	12.06	2.28	82.48	5.54
French	71.23	3.11	10.04	1.60	81.27	3.17	3.57	0.81	84.84	3.02

Readers' Digest texts (3.30%). The second thing is that again the French first and second thousand lists are doing more work (covering 81.27% of running items) than the corresponding English lists (covering 70.42%). It appears that in English, the AWL is needed to achieve the same coverage provided by just the first and second thousand French lists. Our comparison so far suggests that in terms of coverage power, the French first and second thousand lists are stronger than their English counterparts, and that the (hypothesized) French AWL is weak.

We next sought a confirmation of these interesting differences between the French and English lists by working with a different set of texts, this time from a domain with fewer off-list items than the medical texts. We found a set of ten 2000-word translated speeches from the European Parliament which had two characteristics that made them a good test of the French lists. First, they were originally written in French (for the most part) unlike the translations and mixtures of translated and original writing used earlier. Secondly, the fact that the English versions were unusually AWL-rich meant that there was ample scope for any French AWL to emerge. These French and English texts were downloaded from the Internet and run separately through their respective VPs. Summary results are shown in Table 7.

The main thing to note about this second comparison is that, again, English needs its AWL to approach the 90% coverage mark (1000 + 2000 + AWL = 89.43%), while French can get there using its high frequency words alone (1000 + 2000 = 88.32%).

It is tempting to conclude that the French second thousand list is doing some of the work that the AWL does in English. Such a conclusion is consistent with the Goodfellow *et al.* (2002) finding mentioned above that a higher proportion of second thousand-level items tends to predict a higher score on a composition (a role normally played by the AWL in English). This brings us to the central question of our investigation.

Table 7. Mean profiles for 10 EU speeches, translated mainly French to English (coverage percentages).

	1000		2000		1K + 2K		AWL		1K + 2K + AWL	
	M	SD	M	SD	M	SD	M	SD	M	SD
English	79.21	2.17	3.42	0.56	82.63	2.67	6.81	1.74	89.43	1.02
French	78.36	0.92	10.30	1.32	88.32	0.52	2.02	0.59	90.34	0.34

Question 4: Is there room for an AWL in French?

The purpose of identifying the English AWL was to offer university-bound learners of English a shortcut to achieving 90% known word coverage of texts, a target that can otherwise be achieved only when 6000 or more word families have been acquired through naturalistic exposure (see Table 1). From the preliminary data presented here, it appears that learners of French can reach the same level of coverage of an academic text (or any other kind of text) when they have acquired knowledge of the meanings of just the 2000 most common French word families. If we can assume that the remaining 10% of items (or more in some domains such as medicine) comprise proper nouns, domain specific items, and a few other low frequency words in roughly the same proportions as English, then the best guess at this point would have to be that there is no room left in French for an AWL.

The lack of an AWL does not imply that French has fewer resources for academic discourse; rather, it appears to conduct this discourse without the need of a distinct body of words different from those used in everyday life. After all, it is English that is typologically special in having two distinct strands interwoven in its lexicon, the Anglo-Saxon and the Greco-Latin, from whence the phenomenon of the AWL. But in English, or in any language, common words can be used in more or less common ways. Both *To be or not to be* and *Je pense donc je suis* convey complex ideas using common vocabulary, and it is perfectly conceivable that for English this is an option while for French it is the norm. A further test of this idea is presented below.

Question 5: Are the academic words of English the common words of French?

Like all of our questions, this one can receive a definite answer only through large corpus analysis, but in the meantime the methodology of the *Gedanken-experiment* developed in our introduction may provide a hint. In this experiment we determined that the lexis of argument and discourse in English comprised mainly AWL items (*hypothesize, imply, infer,* etc.). If French has an AWL somewhere beyond its first 2000 words, then presumably the French versions of these words would be in it. To investigate the frequency status of these words in French, we translated all plausible French cognates of the 54 original words and checked them with native speakers. The list eventually submitted to analysis included only obvious cognates (e.g., *context* and *contexte*); unclear cases were eliminated (e.g., *summarize*), leaving the following list of 42 words:

impliquer hypothèse inférer interprétation douter affirmer nier rejeter imaginer percevoir concept promesse déclarer assertion valide justifier confirmer prouver proposer évidence logique statu ambigu observer symbolise contradiction paradoxe consistent théorie conclusion démonstration discussion définir opinion équivalent généraliser spécifier abstrait concrète contexte analyser communication

This word-set was run through *Vocabprofil*, and the output is shown in Figure 4. In English, 63% of these words are AWL items; in French almost 56% (39.53 + 16.28) are first 2000 items. A large role for the 2000 list emerged again when all 570 headwords of the English AWL were passed through Altavista's *Babel Fish* translation routine (http://babelfish.altavista.com/) and the French translation equivalents were submitted to *Vocabprofil* analysis. About 58% of these translations proved to be on the 2000 most frequent list, with 26.69% on the first 1000 list and 30.90% on the second. Both the *Gedankenexperiment* and the translation exercise point to the same conclusion: The French second thousand list seems again to be a main repository of academic words (or, as becomes increasingly apparent, of words that are commonly used but can also render academic service). Of course, it is not the only repository of such words; a further 46% of the AWL equivalents and a similar proportion of the *Gedankenexperiment* items are from less frequent zones (e.g., *abstrait, ambigu, concrète; assertion, concept, douter)* but these are unlikely to constitute a coherent lexical zone comparable in size and function to the AWL, given that these words must share a 10% space

WEB VP OUTPUT FOR FILE: *Gedankenexperiment 2*

Mots K1 (1 à 1000):	7	16.28%
Mots K2 (1001 à 2000):	17	39.53%
Mots K3 (2001 à 3000):	11	25.58%
Mots Off-List:	8	18.60%

0-1000 [7 types 7 tokens]: communication discussion déclarer imaginer opinion proposer

1001-2000 [17 types 17 tokens]: affirmer analyser conclusion confirmer consistent contexte définir hypothèse impliquer interprétation justifier logique observer percevoir prouver rejeter évidence

2001-3000 [11 types 11 tokens]: abstrait ambigu concrète contradiction démonstration généraliser nier paradoxe symbolise théorie valide

Off list [8 types 8 tokens]: assertion concept douter inférer promesse spécifier statu équivalent

Figure 4. French Cognates Gedankenexperiment profile

with proper nouns and domain-specific items. (Note that in the screen picture, the name K3, for third thousand, is now used to designate what the originators of these French lists hypothesized might be an AWL.)

Having answered the main questions to the extent allowed by the scale of our present investigation, we return to one trailing matter — the question of profiles and genres.

Question 6: Do French genres have distinct LFPs?

The evidence needed to answer this question has already appeared in the answers to questions above. With the exception of medical texts, the French profiles are not distinct across genres (according to *chi*-square comparisons). For example, first 1000 mean coverage percentages are very close across text types, with newspaper texts at 77.64%, *Readers' Digest* texts at 75.78%, and EU speeches at 78.36% (Tables 4, 5a, 7, respectively). By contrast, English counterpart profiles are quite distinct, largely owing to the different role of the AWL in the different genres.

7.   Conclusion

First, it has been gratifying to work with the French lexical resources recently made available by Selva, Verlinde, Goodfellow and their colleagues. These resources have long been needed in the pedagogical study of French, and we hope that we have made a contribution. The *Vocabprofil* website is receiving a lot of visitors so perhaps we have at least publicized the LFP approach to the analysis of French.

On the general question of the comparative lexical distributions of English and French, the evidence we have gathered suggests that these distributions may be somewhat different. They are similar in that both English and French (and probably any language) use their most frequent 1000 or 2000 words quite heavily, but different in that French seems to use its frequent words even more heavily than English does. On the specific question of whether there is room for an AWL in French, the provisional answer appears to be that there is not. In almost all of the cases we examined, it appears that the goal of achieving 90% text coverage can be met by mastering the common vocabulary of French

Vocabulary has traditionally not been considered the most important thing to emphasize in the teaching of French, and this is an intuition that appears to have some basis. This is not to say that learning the academic vocabulary of French is easy, because the challenge of learning academic uses of common words is probably just as great as learning new academic words. But it is to say that the acquisition process is able to proceed on a naturalistic basis for learners of French as it is not for learners of English.

Any naturalistic learning can nevertheless be made more efficient, possibly by using some of the resources and technologies we have discussed. For example, teachers could use *Vocabprofil* to tailor reading materials to their learners' level of lexical development. Independent learners might wish to peruse the lists themselves and check for any gaps in their knowledge. This idea has proved to be popular with English-learning users of the *Lexical Tutor* website, who can click on 1000, 2000, or AWL words to hear them pronounced and see them contextualized in concordances and dictionaries. The French lists, however,

Figure 5. Pedagogical version of French list.

Note: The word lists are hyper-linked to a 1 million word corpus of *Le Monde* newspaper texts, provided by Thierry Selva in Louvain (upper right frame); French-English Dictionary was developed by Neil Coffey in Oxford (lower right frame).

with full lemmatization are simply too large for pedagogical presentation (the 2000 list is dozens of pages) let alone for Internet delivery. A solution to this problem was to de-lemmatize the verbs and replace them with the infinitive plus a homemade radical that would generate all the contextualized forms of the word in a French corpus. Figure 5 illustrates the case of the verb *accueillir* and the radical *accuei'* used to search for the corpus for forms beginning with this string.

Finally, on a more general note, it is interesting to contemplate the possibility that each language may have its own lexical shape, each entailing different acquisition strategies for learners and different teaching strategies (not to mention different tutorial computer programs). From the best evidence we have right now, it seems that reading academic texts in Dutch, English, and French may require widely different amounts of lexical knowledge and different kinds of lexical skills. There can be no doubt that this idea is interesting enough to warrant further research.

Notes

1. This and many other factual claims made in this chapter can be tested on the first author's *Lexical Tutor* website (Cobb, online).

2. Translations were generously provided by Norman Segalowitz and his research team in the Psychology Department of Concordia University in Montreal.

References

Babel Fish Translation [Online: available at http://babelfish.altavista.com/].

Baker, C. L. and McCarthy, J. (eds). 1981. *The Logical Problem of Language Acquisition.* Cambridge MA: MIT Press.

Baudot, J. 1992. *Fréquence d'utilisation des mots en français écrit contemporain.* Montréal: Les Presses de l'Université de Montréal.

Bauer, L. and Nation, P. 1993. "Word families". *International Journal of Lexicography* 6: 253–279.

Cobb, T. The compleat lexical tutor for data-driven language learning on the web. [Online: available at http://www.lextutor.ca].

Corson, D. 1985. *The Lexical Bar.* Oxford: Pergamon Press.

Corson, D. 1997. "The learning and use of academic English words". *Language Learning* 47: 671–718.

Cossette, A. 1994. *La richesse lexicale et sa mesure.* Paris: H. Champion.

Coxhead, A. 2000. "A new academic word list". *TESOL Quarterly* 34: 213–238.

Coxhead, A. The academic word list [Online: available at http://www.vuw.ac.nz/lals/div1/ awl/].

Francis, W. N. and Kucera, H. 1979. *A Standard Corpus of Present-Day Edited American English, for Use with Digital Computers.* Department of Linguistics, Brown University.

Goodfellow, R., Jones, G. and Lamy, M.-N. 2002. "Assessing learners' writing using Lexical Frequency Profile". *ReCALL* 14: 129–142.

Gold, E. M. 1967. "Language identification in the limit". *Information & Control* 10: 447–474.

Gougenheim, G., Rivenc, P., Sauvageot, A. and Michéa, R. 1967. *L'élaboration du français fondamental (Ier degré).* Paris: Didier.

Hazenberg, S. and Hulstijn, J. 1996. "Defining a minimal receptive second language vocabulary for non-native university students: An empirical investigation". *Applied Linguistics* 17: 145–163.

Jones, G. 2001. "Compiling French word frequency list for the VAT: A feasibility study". [On-line] Working paper. [Online : available at http://www.er.uqam.ca/nobel/r21270/ cgi-bin/F_webfreqs/glynn_jones.html].

Laufer, B. and Nation, P. 1995. "Vocabulary size and use: Lexical richness in L2 written production". *Applied Linguistics* 16: 307–322.

Nagy, W. E. and Herman, P. A. 1987. "Depth and breadth of vocabulary knowledge: Implications for acquisition and instruction". In *The nature of vocabulary acquisition*, M. G. McKeown & M. E. Curtis (eds), 19–35. Hillsdale, NJ: Erlbaum.

Nation, I. S. P. 2001. *Learning Vocabulary in Another Language.* Cambridge: Cambridge University Press.

Olsen, D. 1992. The World on Paper: *The Conceptual and Cognitive Implications of Writing and Reading.* Cambridge: Cambridge University Press.

Pinker, S. 1995. *The Language Instinct.* New York: Harper-Collins.

Stockwell, R. and Minkova, D. 2001. *English Words: History and Structure.* New York: Cambridge University Press.

Sutarsyah, C., Nation, P. and Kennedy, G. 1994. "How useful is EAP vocabulary for ESP? A corpus based study". *RELC Journal* 25: 34–50.

Verlinde, S. and Selva , T. 2001. "Corpus-based vs. intuition-based lexicography: Defining a word list for a French learners' dictionary". In *Proceedings of the Corpus Linguistics 2001 conference,* Lancaster University, 594–598. [Online: available at http://www.kuleuven. ac.be/ilt/grelep/publicat/verlinde.pdf].

Xue, G. and Nation, I. S. P. 1984. "A university word list". *Language Learning & Communication* 3: 215–229.

CHAPTER 3

Vocabulary coverage according to spoken discourse context

Svenja Adolphs and Norbert Schmitt
University of Nottingham

Abstract

In 1956, Schonell *et al.* found that 2,000 word families provided around 99% lexical coverage of spoken discourse. Based on this, it has been generally accepted that approximately 2,000 word families provide the lexical resources to engage in everyday spoken discourse. However, we recently conducted a study of spoken discourse based on more modern corpora which found that 2,000 word families provide less than 95% coverage rather than 99%, suggesting that a wider range of vocabulary is required in speech than previously thought (Adolphs & Schmitt 2003). These results were for unscripted spoken discourse in general, but we know that spoken discourse is not a homogenous phenomenon; rather it varies to some extent according to a number of factors, such as degree of familiarity between interlocutors and purpose of the discourse. This chapter reports on a follow-up study which explored whether the percentage of lexical coverage also varies depending on the context in which the spoken discourse is embedded, or whether it remains constant regardless of the context. Our results show that in order to reach a vocabulary coverage in the mid-90% range, a larger number of word forms is required in contexts where interlocutors have intimate or friendship-based relationships compared to ones in which the interlocutors have a professional or business-based relationship. This indicates that the percentage of coverage is affected by the spoken discourse context.

1.   Introduction

The study of vocabulary is an essential part of language learning and the question of how much vocabulary a learner needs to know to achieve a particular purpose remains an important area of research and discussion. Schonell *et al.*'s (1956) study of the verbal interaction of Australian workers found that 2,000 word families covered nearly 99% of the words used in their speech. This was a landmark study, but limitations of the time inevitably meant that their hand-compiled corpus would be limited in diversity and size. Miniaturization in tape recorder technology now allows spoken data to be gathered unobtrusively in a wide range of naturally-occurring environments. Likewise, modern technology in corpus linguistics allows the use of far larger corpora than in the past. Using a current 5 million word spoken corpus (compared to the Schnell *et al.* 512,000 word corpus), Adolphs & Schmitt (2003) found that 2,000 word families supply lexical coverage for less than 95% of spoken discourse. This indicates that a wider range of vocabulary is necessary to engage in spoken discourse than previously thought.

However, a limitation of the Adolphs & Schmitt study is that it looked at spoken discourse in general, treating all types of speech the same. This clearly oversimplifies the situation, as different spoken contexts have at least somewhat different characteristics. For example, Stenström (1990) compared the frequency and function of a range of discourse markers across different situations of speaking and found considerable differences in the use of these items between the situations. The spoken contexts she compared were a casual conversation between a couple and a narrative delivered to an audience. As the levels of interactivity in the two speaking situations differed, so did the frequency of certain discourse markers. McCarthy (1998) discovered similar variation when he looked at a number of other linguistic features, such as the frequency of deictic items and the use of full lexical words, while Carter & McCarthy (1995) found that different types of spoken discourse had different profiles of grammatical features. Spoken discourse also varies according to the discourse setting, for instance, 'language in action' contexts where interlocutors are doing something together at the moment (such as when mutually assembling a piece of furniture) typically produce spoken discourse with a substantial number of deictic items (*that, there, here, it*) and discourse markers (*I see, okay*) which mark the stages of the process they are trying to complete (Carter & McCarthy 1997).

Because context affects spoken discourse in these ways, one might expect that the diversity of the lexis contained in the discourse would also be affected by different speech contexts. This study explores this issue, by analysing five corpora which differ according to interlocutor relationship and purpose of discourse. It will explore whether any difference in percentage of lexical coverage can be found between the corpora, and if so, what size of vocabulary is necessary to reach viable levels of coverage in each of the context types.

2.   Spoken discourse contexts and the CANCODE corpus

It is now accepted that the context in which discourse takes place has considerable influence over that discourse. Halliday & Hasan (1985) suggested that the *field* (the environment of the discourse), *tenor* (who is taking part in the discourse and their relationship to one another), and *mode* (the role the language plays in the context) all shape the nature of the discourse, and this work has been taken forward by scholars working in areas such as corpus linguistics (e.g. Biber *et al.* 1999) and genre theory (e.g. Martin & Rothery 1986; Hammond & Deriwianka 2001). However, there is a relatively small amount of research which explores how spoken discourse differs according to context, compared with written discourse. One consequence of this is that the aspect of vocabulary coverage in different spoken contexts has received little attention. This may be a result of the lack of spoken corpora or the lack of corpora that are suitably categorised.

The categorisation applied to conversations in the CANCODE corpus can be used to examine vocabulary coverage in different contexts.[1] The careful categorisation and annotation of this corpus makes it a valuable resource for such comparisons despite its relatively small size compared to other modern corpora, such as the British National Corpus and the Bank of English for example. The main phase of data collection took place between 1994 and 1999 with a focus on gathering conversations from a variety of discourse contexts and speech genres. In order to ensure a wide demographic and socio-economic representation, conversations were carefully selected to include adult speakers of different ages, sex, social backgrounds and levels of education.

Traditional divisions between formal and informal have been used as general guidelines for achieving diversity in the corpus. The framework adapted for the CANCODE corpus distinguishes between five different context-types. Our research is based on these carefully established categories the validity of which has been illustrated in previous studies (see McCarthy 1998). Other ways of categorising the CANCODE corpus, such as by topic for example, are possible but would require a complete re-organisation of the text files. However, it is unlikely that such a re-organisation would be sensible if we consider the vast diversity of topics and topic shifts that may occur in any one conversation.

In the current model the context-type axis of categorization reflects the relationship that holds between the participants in the dyadic and multi-party conversations in the corpus. These types of relationships fall into five broad categories which were identified at the outset: *Intimate, Socio-cultural, Professional, Transactional* and *Pedagogic*. These categories were found to be largely exclusive while being comprehensive at the same time. They are described in turn below.

Intimate: In this category, the distance between the speakers is at a minimum and is often related to co-habitation. Only conversations between partners or close family qualify for this category in which participants are linguistically most 'off-guard'. At times the *Intimate* category is difficult to distinguish from the *Socio-cultural* one. Alongside the criteria agreed by the corpus compilers as to what shall qualify for which category, it was decided to let participants judge which category they felt they belonged to. All participants in a conversation have to fall under this category for the conversation to be classified as *Intimate*.

Socio-Cultural: This category implies the voluntary interaction between speakers who seek each other's company for the sake of the interaction itself. Most of the texts that did not fall into any of the other categories turned out to be *Socio-cultural*. The relationship between the speakers is usually marked by friendship and is thus not as close as that between speakers in the *Intimate* category. Typical venues for this type of interaction are social gatherings, birthday parties, sports clubs, and voluntary group meetings.

Professional: This category refers to the relationship that holds between people who are interacting as part of their regular daily work. As such, this category only applies to interactions where all speakers are part of the professional context. Thus a conversation between two shop assistants would be classed as *Professional*, while the interaction between a shop-assistant and a customer would be classed as Transactional. Talk that is not work related but occurs between colleagues in the work-place has still been classified as *Professional*, based on the observation that the participants retain their professional relationship even when the topic of the conversation is not work related.

Transactional: This category embraces interactions in which the speakers do not previously know one another. The 'reason' for transactional conversations is usually related to a need on the part of the hearer or the speaker. As such, the conversations aim to satisfy a particular transactional goal. This category has traditionally been referred to as 'goods-and-services' (Ventola 1987), having the exchange of goods as the main aim of the interaction.

Pedagogic: This fifth category was set up to include any conversation in which the relationship between the speakers was defined by a pedagogic context. A range of tutorials, seminars and lectures were included. As the emphasis was on the speaker relationship rather than the setting, conversations between lecturers as well as academic staff meetings were classified as *Professional* rather than *Pedagogic.* At the same time, training sessions in companies were classified as *Pedagogic* rather than *Professional.* Perhaps a better label for this category would have been *Academic* or *Training* language, since the type of interaction recorded under this category included a large proportion of subject specific lectures and seminars. In addition, the language was entirely authentic L1 academic discourse; there was no simplified ESL pedagogic material included. It is also likely that *Pedagogic* is the category that comes closest to including scripted and technical language.

From the classification above we can see a 'cline' of distance emerging between the speakers in four of the categories (*Intimate, Socio-cultural, Professional, Transactional*) which allows for a corpus-based analysis of linguistic choice in those contexts, with the *Intimate* category being the most private, and the *Transactional* the most public. If percentage of lexical coverage varies according to the distance between speakers, then a comparison between the four corpora should demonstrate this. Although the *Pedagogic* category does not fit into the scale of public versus private, it provides an example of a different type of discourse context, and so will be analysed as well.

3.   Methodology

The procedure of the current study is different to that used by Schonell *et al.* (1956) and Adolphs & Schmitt (2003) in that it considers individual word forms rather than word families in the calculation of vocabulary coverage. While there are good pedagogic reasons to analyse vocabulary in terms of word families, such as the observation that learners seem to mentally handle the members of a word family as a group (Nagy *et al.* 1989), unfortunately it is still impossible to program a computer to identify word families automatically. Current software which counts word families, such as Nation's RANGE program (Internet resource), do so by referring to baseline lists of word family members which have already been compiled. The only way to identify the members of a word family reliably for such baseline lists and other purposes is to do it manually. Both Schonell *et al.* and Adolphs & Schmitt used this time-consuming method. On the other hand, concordancers can quickly and automatically count individual word forms. Because the purpose of the present study (comparing the degree of vocabulary coverage across various spoken genres) can be achieved just as well using individual word forms rather than word families as the unit of measurement, we decided to use the more computer-automated approach in order to avoid possible errors in manual tabulation.

The first step in the research involved creating a frequency list of the words in the categories of CANCODE outlined above. The CANCODE is not lemmatised or coded for word class, therefore the word lists generated were based on individual word forms. Any corpus specific codes or annotation markers were deleted from the list. Backchannel verbalisations which do not normally qualify as words, such as *eh, uh uh, mmm, and Oh!*, were included in the count since these items convey a great deal of meaning and are an important feature of spoken discourse (see Biber *et al.* 1999). Once the lists of words and their frequency of occurrence were set in our spreadsheet, we simply divided various frequency levels by the total number of words in the category to arrive at a percentage of text coverage. For example, to derive the coverage figure for the most frequent 2,000 words in the *Transactional* category, we divided the total number of tokens for each of the 2,000 word forms by the total number of tokens in the transactional sub-corpus. The resulting figure was multiplied by 100 to arrive at a percentage of coverage for each form. These numbers were added up for the first 2,000, 3,000, 4,000 and 5,000 word forms respectively.

Whereas the five different categories in the CANCODE were made up of varying numbers of running words (smallest = *Pedagogic* with 456,177 tokens; largest = *Socio-cultural* with 1,709,598 tokens), it was important to ensure that any differences in lexical coverage were not merely an artefact of the different sizes of the categories.

In order to ascertain whether the differences in overall word count within the various corpus categories would effect the degree of coverage, we carried

Table 1. Differences in lexical coverage of a sub-sample and full version of the transactional sub-corpus

	2,000 word forms % of coverage	4,000 word forms % of coverage	5,000 word forms % of coverage
Transactional sub-sample (434,128 tokens)	94.39	97.45	98.20
Transactional full sub-corpus (1,166,825 tokens)	94.30	97.14	97.82

out an analysis that set out to test the relationship between overall number of words in a corpus and vocabulary coverage provided by the first 2,000, 4,000 and 5,000 word forms. For this analysis we used the transactional category which is one of the larger corpus categories with an overall word count of 1,166,825 words. We extracted a set of files with varying word counts from the transactional corpus to form a sub-sample of 434,128 words, which is similar in size to the smallest category — *Pedagogic.* We then carried out a procedure to determine vocabulary coverage as outlined above for the sub-sample and the full transactional sub-corpus. We found that there were small differences in vocabulary coverage based on the size of the corpus (see Table 1), and this fact will have to be considered in the analysis of the study.

4.   Results and discussion

The results of our analysis summarised in Table 2 show noticeable differences in vocabulary coverage according to spoken discourse context. The differences between the category with the highest coverage (*Transactional*) and the least coverage (*Pedagogic*) ranges from between approximately 1.7 percentage points at the 5,000 word level to almost 4 percentage points at the 2,000 word level. While the percentage differences between categories do not seem large in simple terms, (and are not statistically significant in terms of a Chi-squared analysis: χ^2, p>.05), they become very substantial when translated into the number of word forms involved. Let us take the 2,000 word level where the difference is greatest as an example. The difference is 3.94 percentage points (*Transactional* 94.30% — *Pedagogic* 90.36% = 3.94%). We then counted the number of additional word forms required to raise the coverage figure in the

Pedagogic category from 90.36% to 94.30%. We found that it took 1,608 word forms. Thus, with 2,000 word forms you can achieve 94.30% lexical coverage in the *Transactional* category, but to achieve the same percentage of lexical coverage in the *Pedagogic* category, you would need 3,608 word forms. At the 5,000 level, even though the difference in percentage of coverage is smaller, it actually takes more word forms to make up the difference due to the effects of decreasing frequency. To raise the *Pedagogic* coverage figure from 96.11 to 97.82 (equivalent to the *Transactional* figure at the 5,000 level) would require an additional 2,307 word forms, or a total of 7,307 forms. Overall, the various spoken contexts have noteworthy differences in terms of lexical coverage and number of word forms required.

Using the CANCODE classification system which groups texts according to the relationship that holds between the speakers, the results seem to suggest a 'cline' in the degree of vocabulary coverage which is generally at its lowest in the more private/interactional spheres and increases towards the more public/ transactional spheres. The cline is not completely consistent across the categories however. In fact, the lexical coverage figures for the *Intimate* and *Socio-cultural* categories are quite similar, with the *Socio-cultural* figures being the lowest at all frequency levels. Thus, in terms of the diversity of vocabulary required, there does not seem to be much difference between truly *Intimate* interlocutors and those who are merely friends. A greater difference occurs when the categories move to the more goal-oriented discourse of *Professional* and *Transactional* encounters. In these categories, the lexical coverage figures

Table 2. Percentage of lexical coverage of five speech genre categories

Category (Total tokens in sub-corpus)	2,000 word forms % of coverage	3,000 word forms % of coverage	4,000 word forms % of coverage	5,000 word forms % of coverage
Pedagogic (456,177)	90.36	93.15	94.90	96.11
Intimate (957,192)	92.81	94.70	95.84	96.63
Socio-cultural (1,709,598)	92.43	94.34	95.51	96.31
Professional (480,627)	93.28	95.28	96.51	97.35
Transactional (1,166,825)	94.30	96.10	97.14	97.82

are notably higher, indicating that a narrower range of vocabulary is required to engage in transactional and professional interaction than in more casual conversation. We could speculate that the reason for this result is to be found in the wide range of topics discussed in the more private situations as opposed to the more transactional ones which tend to have more focused topics and follow more predictable patterns of language use.

It is interesting to note in this context that the *Pedagogic* category, which does not fit into the original classification scheme of private versus public discourse, displays the lowest degree of vocabulary coverage. The defining feature of this category is the academic/training nature of the discourse context, and so it should contain a relatively high percentage of a more formal, academic type of discourse. Thus the lower percentage of coverage in this category provides evidence for what teachers have always known: that learners need a wider vocabulary to cope with academic or training discourse than to cope with everyday conversation. The figures also argue for the inclusion of a significant vocabulary component in English for Academic Purposes courses, in order to help learners deal with the more diverse vocabulary found in this type of discourse.

In the Methodology section, we explored whether the size of the sub-corpora would affect the lexical coverage percentages. We compared a sub-sample and the full version of the *Transactional* sub-corpus and found that sub-corpus size made only a small difference in lexical coverage. The magnitude of difference in lexical coverage percentage between the context categories in Table 2 are clearly far greater than that found due to corpus size in Table 1, which suggests that any differences in lexical coverage found in this study should mainly be attributable to contextual differences rather than to the different sizes of the CANCODE categories. An examination of Table 2 also reveals no obvious relationship between corpus size and the magnitude of lexical coverage. This supports the case that corpus size, at least with the size of corpora under discussion, does not affect lexical coverage to any great degree. The trend that does emerge is that the rank order of the context categories is the same at each frequency level (in the order: *Transactional* > *Professional* > *Intimate* > *Socio-cultural* > *Pedagogic*), indicating that the influence of context is consistent across the frequency bands. It is useful to note however, that our analysis between corpora of different sizes was based only on individual word forms, and a similar comparison based on word families remains to be carried out. In sum, although corpus size probably has a small influence, the differences in lexical coverage in the table appear to be a result primarily of context category.

5.   Conclusion

Just as the spoken discourse context affects speech in terms of frequency and function of discourse markers (Stenström, 1990), the frequency of deictic items (McCarthy, 1998), and the propensity towards various grammatical features (Carter & McCarthy, 1995), this study shows that the spoken context also has an effect on the diversity of words typically used. Spoken discourse among intimates or friends typically contains a greater range of vocabulary than spoken discourse which is used for more transactional roles. Taken together with Adolphs & Schmitt (2003), the two CANCODE-based studies indicate that operating in a spoken English environment requires more vocabulary than previously thought, and the amount required depends on the spoken context.

Note

1. CANCODE stands for Cambridge and Nottingham Corpus of Discourse in English and is a joint project between Cambridge University Press and the University of Nottingham. The corpus was funded by Cambridge University Press with whom sole copyright resides. For a comprehensive description of the corpus, see McCarthy 1998.

References

Adolphs, S. and Schmitt, N. 2003. "Lexical coverage of spoken discourse". *Applied Linguistics 24*, 4: 425–438.

Biber, D., Johansson, S., Leech, G., Conrad, S., and Finegan E. 1999. *Longman Grammar of Spoken English*. London: Longman.

Carter, R. A. and McCarthy, M. J. 1995. "Grammar and the spoken language". *Applied Linguistics 16*, 2: 141–158.

Carter, R. and McCarthy, M. 1997. *Exploring Spoken English*. Cambridge University Press.

Halliday, M. A. K. and Hasan, R. 1985. *Language , Context, and Text: Aspects of Language in a Socio-semiotic Perspective*. Oxford: Oxford University Press.

Hammond, J. and Deriwianka, B. 2001. "Genre". In *The Cambridge Guide to Teaching English to Speakers of Other Languages*, R. Carter and D. Nunan (eds), 186–193. Cambridge: Cambridge University Press.

Martin, J. R. and Rothery, J. 1986. "Writing Project Report No. 4". *Working Papers in Linguistics*, Linguistics Department: University of Sydney.

McCarthy, M. 1998. *Spoken Language and Applied Linguistics*. Cambridge: Cambridge University Press.

Nagy, W., Anderson, R. C., Schommer, M., Scott, J. A., and Stallman, A. C. 1989. "Morphological families in the internal lexicon". *Reading Research Quarterly* 24: 262–282.

Nation, P. RANGE vocabulary analysis program. Available free of charge at <http://www.vuw.ac.nz/lals/>.

Schonell, F. J., Meddleton, I.G, and Shaw, B. A. 1956. *A Study of the Oral Vocabulary of Adults.* Brisbane: University of Queensland Press.

Stenström, A.-B. 1990. "Lexical items peculiar to spoken discourse". In *The London-Lund Corpus of Spoken English: Description and Research,* J. Svartvik (ed), 137–175. Sweden: Lund University Press.

Ventola, E. 1987. *The Structure of Social Interaction.* Pinter: London.

ACQUISITION

CHAPTER 4

Etymological elaboration as a strategy for learning idioms

Frank Boers, Murielle Demecheleer and June Eyckmans
University of Antwerp, Université Libre de Bruxelles, Erasmus College of Brussels

Abstract

Various paper-and-pencil experiments have shown that L2 learners can be helped to comprehend and remember figurative idioms by raising their awareness of the literal origins or source domains of these expressions. We have called this technique *Etymological elaboration*. The beneficial effect on comprehension is in accord with cognitive semantic theory, which holds that the meaning of many idiomatic expressions is 'motivated' rather than arbitrary. The beneficial effect on retention is in accord with dual coding theory, which holds that storing verbal information as a mental image provides an extra pathway for recall.

The central aim of the present study is to estimate how far the proposed pedagogical pathway can lead learners into the realm of L2 idioms. We describe two larger-scale on-line experiments, targeting 400 English figurative idioms (including both transparent and opaque idioms). The results reveal that a fair proportion of idioms are etymologically quite transparent to learners, that information about the origin of an idiom often enables learners to figure out their idiomatic meaning independently, and that giving learners explanations about the origin of etymologically opaque idioms can have the same mnemonic effect as applying this technique to transparent idioms.

1. The relevance of figurative idioms in SLA

Figurative idioms (conventional multi-word figurative expressions) have received considerable attention in the SLA literature in recent years (e.g. Cooper

1999, Cornell 1999, Deignan *et al.* 1997, Lazar 1996, Lennon 1998). This interest in idioms since the 1990s contrasts sharply with the earlier days of SLA research when idioms were largely neglected. That past lack of concern for idioms in educational linguistics was probably due to three widely held (but meanwhile outdated) assumptions about the nature of language in general and the relevance of teaching figurative expressions in particular.

Firstly, language was generally conceived as a grammar-lexis dichotomy with grammar 'rules' on the one hand and 'lists' of individual words on the other. Idioms (along with other multi-word expressions) did not fit into this dichotomy. Secondly, figurative expressions were generally considered to serve merely stylistic purposes that were confined to rhetoric and poetry. Consequently, figurative idioms were thought to be merely ornamental — a way of dressing up messages in a colourful way. Thirdly, it was generally assumed that the meaning of idioms was absolutely unpredictable. Because of this alleged arbitrary nature of idioms, it was believed they could not be taught in any systematic or insightful way. The only available option for students to master idioms was to 'blindly' memorise them, an assumption which made idioms rather unappealing to educational linguists.

Meanwhile, however, new insights in the cognitive sciences and in linguistic theory have gradually trickled down to the field of applied linguistics, showing educational linguists the possibilities for more appealing pedagogical approaches to figurative idioms. Firstly, the grammar-lexis dichotomy has been discarded and replaced by a more realistic conception of language as a continuum from simple units to more complex ones (e.g. Langacker 1991: 2). In this conception it becomes easier to view multi-word expressions as occupying a central zone in the linguistic system. SLA research has now acknowledged the importance of learners mastering prefabricated multi-word lexical chunks (fixed and semi-fixed expressions, strong collocations, pragmatic functions, idioms, etc.). Mastery of such ready-made chunks helps learners produce fluent language under real-time conditions (Skehan 1998). This emphasis on holistic and syntagmatic organisation is now strongly advocated in educational linguistics (e.g. Lewis 1993).

Secondly, studies of metaphor have revealed that — far from being an optional ornament — figurative expressions are omnipresent in everyday language (e.g. Lakoff & Johnson 1980). It is very difficult (if not impossible) to describe intangible phenomena or abstract concepts without resorting to metaphor. Cognitive semanticists actually consider metaphor to be a central cognitive process that enables us to reason about abstract phenomena (e.g.

Gibbs 1994, Johnson 1987). Whenever conversations revolve around non-concrete subjects (emotions, psychology, society, vocabulary acquisition, the meaning of life, etc.), we are bound to hear and use figurative expressions. Corpus data have shown that metaphoric expressions do indeed constitute a very rich lexical resource (e.g. Deignan 1995). If metaphor is so pervasive in everyday language, then language learners will inevitably be exposed to a bombardment of figurative expressions throughout their learning process. Furthermore, in order for them to successfully convey messages that go be-yond the realm of concrete objects, learners will need to build a large repertoire of figurative expressions for active usage.

Thirdly, the quest for a pedagogical method to tackle figurative idioms has become much more appealing with the recognition that a large proportion of figurative language is not arbitrary at all. Studies in cognitive semantics (e.g. Kövecses 1990, Lakoff 1987) have revealed that many figurative expressions (including idioms) are in fact 'motivated' rather than arbitrary. While it is true that the figurative meaning of many idioms may not be fully predictable from their constituent parts, it is nonetheless often possible (in retrospect) to explain how and why that figurative meaning has arisen (Lakoff 1987: 153–154, 379). If the meaning of figurative idioms is 'motivated', then it may be possible to teach or learn them in an insightful and systematic way, after all. In this chapter we propose and evaluate such a strategy, which we shall call 'etymological elaboration'. Before doing so, however, we shall first outline relevant aspects of cognitive semantic metaphor theory.

2. A cognitive semantic perspective on figurative idioms

According to cognitive semantics, many figurative expressions can be traced back to a relatively small set of concrete 'source domains' whose structure is mapped onto our conception of abstract 'target domains' via 'conceptual metaphors'. For example, the following conventional figurative expressions can all be traced back to the source domain of travelling via the conceptual metaphor LIFE IS A JOURNEY: *You still have a whole life ahead of you, She needs moral guidance, Without you, I'd be lost, Follow my example, We've reached the point of no-return, She's taken some steps on the road to maturity, The quest for love, I've found my destiny — it's you.*

Metaphoric expressions may be divided into two broad categories. The first category results from mapping so-called 'image-schemas' onto abstract experience (Lakoff 1990). Image-schemas structure our experience of general physical space. Examples are UP-DOWN, NEAR-FAR, IN-OUT and MOTION. These 'bare' schemas are used to lend structure to abstract domains through conceptual metaphors like MORE IS UP (e.g. *An IQ above average*), POWER IS UP (e.g. *He served under Bush*), THE BODY IS A CONTAINER FOR THE EMOTIONS (e.g. *Don't keep all that anger bottled up inside you*), MENTAL INACCESSIBILITY IS DISTANCE (e.g. *Conceptual metaphor theory is still way beyond me*), and MENTAL ACTIVITY IS MOTION ALONG A PATH (e.g. *Is this chapter leading anywhere?*). These image-schema-based metaphors are motivated by correlations in the domain of general physical experience. For example, if you add objects to a pile, the pile will grow (hence MORE IS UP). Since this kind of general physical experience is universal, we would expect to find similar image-schema-based conceptual metaphors in communities around the world. Hence they are not so likely to constitute a major hurdle for language learning at the level of cross-cultural variation.

The second category of metaphoric expressions is probably more interesting from an SLA perspective, because they map our experience of more specific or 'richer' source domains onto our understanding of abstract phenomena . For example, details can be added to the fairly generic LIFE IS A JOURNEY metaphor by drawing from more specific source domains involving vehicles, such as trains (e.g. *It's about time you got back onto the right track, My life seems to have been derailed*), ships (e.g. *She's been drifting without a real purpose in life, My career is on an even keel now*), and cars (e.g. *He's in the fast lane to success, I think I'll take a back seat for a while*). It is this category of 'imageable' expressions that are most commonly referred to as 'figurative idioms', as these tend to arise from (proto)typical scenes in specific source domains (Lakoff 1987: 447). Unlike general physical experience, specific experiential domains are more likely to be culture-dependent and thus to vary from place to place. As a result, a particular domain may not be (equally) available for metaphorical mapping in all cultures. For example, the source domain of boats and sailing appears to be especially productive in English, which is reflected in the wide range of English 'boats and sailing' idioms: *Rock the boat, Steer clear of something, All hands on deck, In the doldrums, On an even keel, Miss the boat, Learn the ropes, Plain sailing, Show your true colours, A steady hand on the tiller, Be left high and dry, Run a tight ship, Take the wind out of your sails, When your ship comes in, Clear the decks*, and many more.

A straightforward example of the type of source domain that is culture-dependent is sports, since cultures differ with respect to the kinds of sports that are especially popular. Baseball, for instance, is evidently more popular in the

United States than in Europe, and consequently American English is likely to produce more baseball-based figurative expressions (e.g. *I had a date with Alice last night, but I couldn't even get to first base with her, Three strikes and you're out*). In British English, the same observation holds for the source domain of cricket (e.g. *Bat on a sticky wicket, Hit someone for six*) and horse racing (e.g. *A dark horse, Hear it from the horse's mouth*).

One of the ways in which cross-cultural variation in metaphor usage can be detected is through comparative corpus-based research, i.e. through counting the frequency of occurrence of a conceptual metaphor and the diversity of its figurative expressions (e.g. Boers & Demecheleer 1997, Deignan 1999). Differences in the relative productivity of shared metaphors may seem trivial at first, but there is some evidence to suggest that they do have an effect on learners' comprehension of L2 figurative idioms. For example, French-speaking learners of English have been shown to find it harder to infer the meaning of English idioms derived from the domain of sailing than of those derived from the domain of eating (Boers & Demecheleer 2001).

To a degree, the high frequency and diversity of a particular metaphor can be taken as a reflection of a country's history (e.g. the comparatively high number of sailing metaphors in British English) or even its national stereotypes (e.g. the relatively high number of gardening metaphors in British English) (Boers 1999). Although the connection between metaphor and culture is an intricate one (Boers 2003, Deignan 2003, Kövecses 1999), variation in metaphor usage could be considered as a reflection of a community's established world views (e.g. Lakoff 1987: 295, Palmer 1996: 222–245). Such a culture-metaphor connection certainly supports arguments to include 'cultural awareness' objectives in the foreign language curriculum (e.g. Byram 1997, Byram *et al.* 2001, Kramsch 1993). In that framework, 'metaphor awareness' could offer the learner a window onto the culture of the community whose language he or she aspires to master. Moreover, the learning experiments reported in this chapter suggest that knowledge of the culture-specific source domains behind particular figurative expressions may help learners comprehend and remember them.

3. Extracting a strategy for learning figurative idioms: 'etymological elaboration'

Apart from serving as a window on culture, an enhanced metaphor awareness has been shown to be useful to learners' in-depth reading comprehension (Boers 2000a) and retention of vocabulary in various semantic fields (Boers

2000b). In this chapter we shall focus specifically on the use of metaphor awareness to facilitate recall of figurative idioms, i.e. conventional 'imageable' expressions that can be traced back to specific source domains. Helping learners appreciate the metaphoric nature of such an idiom can simply be done by reactivating the literal sense of the expression, and by tracing the idiom back to its original use or context. We shall call this mental operation 'etymological elaboration', as it can serve as a particular instance of the more general strategy of 'semantic elaboration', i.e. the learner's active and 'rich' processing of an item with regard to its meaning (Cohen *et al.* 1986).

The effectiveness of etymological elaboration as a mnemonic technique can be predicted on the basis of two complementary theories of learning and memory, namely 'dual coding theory' (e.g. Clark & Paivio 1991, Paivio 1986) and 'levels of processing theory' (e.g. Cermak & Craik 1979, Craik & Lockhart 1972). On the one hand, the activation of the literal or original sense of a figurative idiom is likely to call up a mental image of a concrete scene. Storing verbal information as a mental image is believed to pave an extra pathway for recall because the information is thus encoded in a dual fashion. On the other hand, carrying out the task of identifying the source domains behind figurative idioms involves a certain degree of cognitive effort. This 'identify-the-source' operation probably occurs at a 'deeper' level of processing than 'shallow' rote learning, and deep-level processing is believed to enhance memory storage.

As mentioned above, the beneficial effect of cognitive semantic approaches to SLA has been evidenced by several controlled paper-and-pencil experiments (also see Boers & Demecheleer 1998, Kövecses & Szabó 1996). One of those experiments (reported in full detail in Boers 2001) looked specifically at the effect of the 'identify-the-source' task on learners' retention of figurative idioms. As the outcome of that particular experiment gave the impetus to the larger-scale studies that are reported in this chapter, it is useful to sum it up here. Two parallel groups of Dutch-speaking college students (n = 54) were asked to consult a dictionary with a view to explaining the meaning of ten figurative idioms (*Pass the baton, Champ at the bit, A poisoned chalice, A chink in someone's armour, Haul someone over the coals, Go off at half cock, A steady hand on the tiller, Gird your loins, Run someone ragged* and *A dummy run*). The control group were then given the task to invent contexts in which each of the idioms could be used, while the experimental group were given the task to hypothesise about the origins of each of the idioms. Both tasks required cognitive effort or deep processing, but the 'identify-the-source' task aimed at calling up a mental image and thus at encouraging dual coding. In subsequent tests measuring participants' recall in a gap-fill exercise (after 1 week) and their retention of the meaning of the idioms (after 5 weeks), the experimental group scored significantly better than the control group (p.<001).[1] Overall, the experimental group had clearly benefited from the identify-the-source task.

The encouraging results of this paper-and-pencil experiment encouraged us to start applying the strategy of etymological elaboration on a larger scale. This is how *'Idiomteacher'* was born — a battery of on-line exercises for insightful mastery of figurative idioms. While *Idiomteacher* is used as a straightforward pedagogical tool, it also serves various research purposes. One of these is to find out how far into the world of idioms the proposed strategy can be stretched before it loses its pedagogical effect. After all, it is quite conceivable that the idioms we selected for the pilot experiments were intuitively felt to be suitable candidates for dual coding in the first place, due to their relatively high degree of 'imageability' (which in turn is due to their relative degree of 'etymological transparency').

4.   Idiomteacher as pedagogical tool[2]

With *Idiomteacher* we chose to use computer and internet facilities to implement the pedagogical approach on a larger scale. The programme was set up in a spirit of learner autonomy. Students accessed the on-line exercises from their home computer or from a computer at the college. The self-study battery consisted of 1200 exercises on 400 idioms. These were selected from the *Collins Cobuild Dictionary of Idioms* along the following lines:

(1)   With a view to accommodating learners of varying levels of proficiency, we included roughly equal numbers of expressions from the four frequency bands that are indicated in the dictionary (based on the frequency of occurrence in *The Bank of English*).

(2)   Idioms were chosen that could be related to 'rich' source domains (rather than instances of 'bare' image-schema-based metaphors), such as fighting/warfare, health/fitness, food/cooking, games/sports, agriculture/gardening, handicraft/manufacturing, boats/sailing, entertainment/public performance, religion/superstition, and commerce/accounting.

(3)   Idioms whose source domains were too obvious due to a one-to-one correspondence of keyword and source domain descriptor were not retained as exercise material. For example, the expression *To rock the boat* was filtered out because it would be too evident to the learner that it

was derived from the source domain 'boats/sailing'. Such cases would not present the user with any challenge when the source domain needs to be identified and so they were excluded from our selection.

The programme consists of three types of exercises. The precise implementation of the exercises has varied over time along with research questions, but the following description covers the general design.

One exercise is a multiple-choice task in which learners are invited to hypothesise about the idiom's origin. For example:

What domain of experience do you think the following idiom comes from?
to show someone the ropes
a.   Prison/torture
b.   Boats/sailing
c.   Games/sports

As feedback, a short explanation about the origin or literal use of the expression appears on the screen. In the case of *To show someone the ropes*, the learners would be told that experienced sailors have to teach novice ones which ropes they should handle. Tracing back the idiom to its original source domain is a task that supposedly requires cognitive effort (deep processing). At the same time the exercise stimulates mental visualisation, first via the identify-the-source task and subsequently via the etymological feedback. In our example, the learners are expected to associate the idiom *To show someone the ropes* with sailing imagery and thus to process the verbal information through a visual channel (dual coding). The feedback given in this exercise is brief (usually one or two lines) and it is confined to explanations about the origin of the idioms. No explicit information is given about the idiom's present-day figurative meaning.

Another multiple-choice exercise, on the other hand, consists of a 'conventional' comprehension task , where learners need to identify the correct figurative meaning of the idiom. For example:

What is the figurative meaning of the following idiom?
to show someone the ropes
a.   to disclose the truth to someone
b.   to give someone a severe penalty
c.   to teach someone how to do a task

Both multiple choice tasks are meant to complement one another. By making a connection between the figurative sense of an idiom and its origin, the learner may realise that the idiom is actually 'motivated' (its present figurative meaning 'makes sense', given its etymological origin). This realisation, we hope, will help create a certain metaphor awareness in the learners.

The identify-the-source task and the comprehension task clearly focus on receptive knowledge. More active knowledge is aimed at in the third type of exercise, which is a gap-fill task where the learners read a meaningful paragraph and need to recognise it as an appropriate context to (re)produce (the keyword of) the idiom. For example:

> 'When I started working here as a novice, nobody bothered to teach me how things were done around here. I had to find out all by myself how to do my new work properly. You could say that nobody showed me the _____ .'

When the response is incorrect, the targeted word within its context appears on the screen as feedback.

In the experiments reported below, the gap-fill exercise was used to measure participants' recall of the idioms they had encountered in the multiple choice exercises.

5.   Idiomteacher as research instrument

5.1   Research questions

The acquisition of figurative idioms via etymological elaboration invites a panoply of research questions with regard to two sets of variables:

(1)   variables to do with the idioms themselves (especially whether etymologically transparent idioms are easier to learn than opaque ones), and

(2)   variables to do with learner characteristics (whether the learning process is impacted by proficiency levels, cognitive styles, culture, etc.).

The present report will be confined to the first type of variable. More specifically, the following central question will be addressed: Is the strategy of etymological elaboration equally effective for the retention of etymologically opaque idioms as for the retention of etymologically transparent ones?

Different hypotheses can be put forward in this respect. Etymologically transparent idioms may be most readily 'imageable' and thus especially susceptible to dual coding, which should then result in surplus retention. However, identifying their source domain may be too self-evident to require much cognitive effort. Etymologically more opaque idioms may not call up a mental image as easily and dual coding may only take place when the etymological feedback is given. On the other hand, finding the source domain of opaque idioms may require more cognitive effort and longer semantic elaboration. Retention may also be enhanced by positive affect, for example when the learner finds the etymological explanations that are offered surprising and/or relevant to the learning process. In sum, whether or not a particular idiom is retained well under etymological elaboration may depend on the complex interplay of at least three dimensions:

(1)   degree of cognitive effort,
(2)   likelihood of dual coding, and
(3)   affect (e.g. motivation).

With a view to working towards an answer to the central research question, two computer-aided experiments were set up, the first in 2002 and the second in 2003.

5.2   Experimental design in 2002

In our first experiment, the participants were given access to only one of the two multiple choice exercises before they were asked to do the gap-fill exercise. Under the control condition learners did the comprehension task (i.e., '*What is the figurative meaning of this idiom?*'), whereas under the experimental condition learners did the identify-the-source task (i.e. '*What domain of experience do you think this idiom may come from?*'). In this first version of *Idiomteacher*, there were five options in the identify-the-source multiple-choice task, and learners clicked as many options as necessary for them to find the correct source domain. Only on clicking the right option did learners receive feedback about the origin of the expression. The comprehension task (matching the idiom with the correct definition) offered three options per idiom, and again learners clicked options until they found the correct one. One week after either multiple-choice exercise, all students were asked to do the gap-fill test. This was meant to measure recall of the idioms in a meaningful figurative context.

Participants were students at a Flemish tertiary education college that offers four years of training in modern languages and translation. At the time of our study, there were about 200 students of English (between 19 and 22 years of age), who were all invited to do the exercises. On-line exercises on 400 idioms were distributed over the student population by matching the idioms' frequency bands (as indicated in the *Collins Cobuild Dictionary of Idioms*) with the students' proficiency levels: first-year students were offered exercises on idioms drawn from the highest frequency band, second-year students were offered exercises on idioms drawn from the second highest frequency band, and so on. Teaching experience and pilot experiments with previous generations of students had shown that a distribution along these lines meant that each grade of students were likely to be confronted with a number of idioms that were still unknown to them.[3]

A pre-test was not administered at this stage, because we did not want to encourage the participants to think about the figurative use of the idioms prior to the exercise, as one of the aims of this first experiment was to estimate whether it might be possible for learners (in the experimental group) to infer the figurative meaning of idioms solely on the basis of etymological information. If figuring out the meaning of idioms on the basis of etymological information were not feasible, then the experimental group would experience difficulty matching the idioms with the meaningful contexts presented in the gap-fill exercise. In that case, their gap-fill scores would be lower than those of the control group, who had been asked about and informed of the figurative meaning of the idioms.

Per grade, students were randomly split up into an experimental group and a control group. Per grade, the idioms were divided over four series (each containing between 20 and 30 idioms). Since all students of each grade had taken the same English courses, taught by the same teachers, the likelihood of a series containing known idioms was considered to be the same for the experimental and the control groups.

As mentioned above, the experimental groups were invited to try the multiple choice task aimed at eliciting imagery, while the control groups were invited to try the 'conventional' multiple choice task. One week later, both groups were given the gap-fill exercise, targeting the same series of idioms.

5.3   Results and discussion of the 2002 experiment

The on-line exercises were not part of the students' compulsory study programme. Although we regularly invited the students to take part, only a minority of the student population covered all the exercise sessions that were made available to them. Many students tackled the exercises in a random fashion, which means that they tried the input stage but forgot about the gap-fill test, or vice versa. A considerable number of students did not participate at all.

Table 1. Number of idioms and participants in the 2002 experiment

	Number of idioms	Experimental participants (identify-the-source task + gap-fill test)	Control participants (comprehension task + gap-fill test)
1st grade, series A	28	7	11
1st grade, series B	29	11	13
1st grade, series C	28	8	13
1st grade, series D	30	8	9
3rd grade, series A	30	8	15
3rd grade, series B	30	9	9
TOTAL	175		

An additional problem we encountered was of a purely technical nature. The experiment was run in a period when the school's internet server was very unstable. We found out too late that a number of exercises had stayed inaccessible to students. Due to all these problems, many idioms generated insufficient data for analysis. Of the 400 idioms that were included in *Idiomteacher*, only 175 could be retained for the study. These were idioms for which at least seven students in the experimental condition and at least seven students in the control condition had covered both the input stage and the gap-fill test. Of the idioms that were retained, 115 belonged to the four series aimed at first-year students, and 60 idioms belonged to two series aimed at third-year students. Table one gives an overview.

Despite the small number of participants, we hoped the resulting data could reveal general trends and inspire plausible hypotheses to be examined further in the follow-up experiment.

The first finding pertains only to the experimental condition and shows the relative degree of ease with which students carried out the task of identifying the source domain. For 68% of the idioms, identifying the source domain required on average between one and two clicks (among the five multiple choice options). This is a measure of the ease with which students carried out this problem-solving task. We shall call these 'etymologically transparent idioms'. For 32% of the idioms, however, the average participant needed more than two clicks to identify the source domain. We shall call these 'etymologically opaque idioms'. High numbers of clicks in some cases (4.5 in the worst case, namely for the expression *To follow suit*) were due to some participants' obstinately clicking their first choice repeatedly, as if convinced that the computer programme had not recorded their choice. For other items, students appeared to resort to random guesswork to get past the identify-the-source task. Nevertheless, the finding that the vast majority of figurative idioms could fairly easily be traced back to their origins may be taken as indirect support for the cognitive semantic view that — although their meaning is certainly not fully predictable — most figurative idioms are 'motivated'. If the meaning of idioms were totally unpredictable, finding the source domains would have been pure guesswork, resulting in a more even distribution of the number of clicks. We shall provide more indirect evidence of the motivated nature of idioms when reporting the results of the follow-up experiment below.

Let us now turn to the issue of retention as measured by the gap-fill tests that were administered one week after each input stage. Per item, students could score either nought or one. The average score for the 175 idioms was 0.39 under the experimental condition as compared to 0.28 under the control condition. In other words, on average each idiom was remembered by 39% of the experimental students and 28% of the control students. These relatively low overall scores are probably due to the fact that in either condition the input stage only involved a comprehension task, which does not necessarily lead to retention of form for purposes of language production. Moreover, both types of input stage involved semantic rather than structural elaboration, which may not have contributed to learners' retention of the formal features of the idioms very much (e.g. Barcroft 2002).

Nevertheless, the data suggest that despite the 'handicap' of lacking explicit instruction about the present figurative meaning of the idioms, the experimental students were at least on a par with the control students when it came to (re)producing the expressions in a context which they apparently found compatible with the figurative meaning of the idiom. This lends some strength to the hypothesis that insight into the origins of idioms can help learners interpret the figurative meaning of those expressions.

An additional way of comparing the gap-fill results is to count the number of idioms for which the experimental condition led to a better average score than the control condition, and vice versa. The experimental group's score was better than the control group's in 65% of the cases. A 2-way Sign Test revealed that the likelihood of an idiom being better retained under the experimental condition than the control condition was significant at p < .001. These findings offer general confirmation of the results of pilot experiments that showed a beneficial effect of etymological elaboration on idiom retention.

In a first attempt to answer the question whether the proposed mnemonic strategy is equally suited to etymologically opaque idioms as etymologically transparent ones, we separated the average gap-fill scores under both conditions for etymologically transparent idioms and etymologically opaque ones. The former category contained idioms for which the average participant in the experimental group needed only one or two clicks to identify the source domain. The beneficial effect of etymological elaboration on retention was quite pronounced with regard to the category of transparent idioms: an average score of 0.4 under the experimental condition as compared to 0.32 under the control condition. By contrast, in the category of opaque idioms the effect seemed negligible: average scores of 0.31 and 0.29, respectively.

This trend was confirmed by the additional comparison, where we counted idioms for which either condition resulted in a better average gap-fill score. Idioms that required one or two clicks in the identify-the-source task (i.e. those that were transparent to students), yielded superior retention under the experimental condition in 69% of the cases. For idioms that required more than two clicks, this proportion went down to 55%.

The comparatively weak effect of etymological elaboration when it came to opaque idioms could be grasped by language teachers and course developers as a reason to relegate the proposed strategy to the realm of learner autonomy ('It only works well for idioms whose origins are sufficiently transparent for students to figure out independently'). Teachers and course developers might thus conclude it is not worth 'bothering' students with etymological explanations about idioms whose origins are too opaque for them to retrace themselves. However, we have reason to believe that such a conclusion would be premature. The comparatively weaker effect of etymological elaboration when applied to opaque idioms in our first experiment may in fact have been due to the characteristics of the task design that we used. More specifically, we may not have given sufficient attention to the affective dimension in our task design, including motivation (e.g. Arnold 1999, Crookes & Schmidt 1991).

In a number of our learners, negative affect may have short-circuited the mnemonic device of etymological elaboration when applied to opaque idioms in roughly two ways. Firstly, spending too long on a task (e.g. three clicks on the same item) without any reward may have been frustrating. After a while, the learner may have resorted to random clicking ('Let's get this over and done with'). Secondly, finding out (on reading the feedback) that the origin of the given idiom was maybe too 'far-fetched' to be guessable in the first place may have led to scepticism with regard to the exercise. In such cases, learners may not only have experienced the identify-the-source task as beyond them, but also as a waste of time and energy ('Why not give the explanation straightaway, as I couldn't have guessed it anyhow?'). Either way, the identify-the-source task may have come across to some learners (but not all) as off-putting when it was applied to idioms they perceived to be too opaque.

The reduced success of etymological elaboration when it came to opaque idioms was not absolute, though. Even within the group of idioms whose source domains proved difficult to identify, a small majority yielded better retention under the experimental condition. This invites complementary questions: What may have been the reasons why learners found it hard to identify the source domains of certain idioms? How could these reasons have influenced the likelihood of dual coding taking place?

What follows is an impressionistic typology of four scenarios along which students in the experimental groups may have tackled the idioms whose source domains proved hard to identify. This really is an impressionistic analysis, as it is based on our records of participants' clicking behaviour, our occasional observations of students working on the exercises in the school's computer room, and informal conversations with students when the experiment was over.

(1) Scenario one: The idiom contained a keyword that was likely to be misinterpreted by the learner and consequently associated with the 'wrong' source domain. In other words, the learner was likely to be put on the wrong track by the presence of a word that was supposedly 'known'. This commonly happened when the keyword was homographic. For example, when confronted with the expression *To follow suit* students needed several clicks to get to the right source domain (i.e. card games), because they naturally assumed that the keyword 'suit' referred to clothing. Only when the etymological feedback was given, did they come to understand that 'suit' in this case refers to one of the four types of cards in a set of playing cards. Other examples of idioms whose homographic keywords misled students were *To go against the grain, A track record, To have had one's chips,* and *Above board.* Although negative affect may have set in at first when the student's inferences were repeatedly rejected, recall of these (and similar) idioms in the gap-fill tests was typically better under the experimental condition. Once the misunderstood keyword was disambiguated by the etymological feedback, the idiom became easily 'imageable' and thus susceptible to dual coding. On reading the feedback, students may have realised that they could have guessed the correct response and so the task design was not to be 'blamed' for their failure to do so. A variant

occurred when the learner mistook an unknown word in the idiom for a more familiar one. For example, when confronted with the expression *To give someone free rein*, some of our participants appeared to mistake *rein* for *reign*. Nonetheless, after feedback where the literal meaning of *reins* was explained (i.e. the straps attached to a horse's bridle which are used to control the horse), this idiom was also typically better retained by the experimental group. Once explained, the idiom lent itself well to mental imagery. Similarly, *A bone of contention* was misinterpreted by many students as 'a source of great satisfaction', probably because of the cognate *content* (which means 'happy' in these students' mother tongue). Another instance of this 'false friend' phenomenon occurred when students associated *To work in harness* with the source domain of warfare, because in their mother tongue *harnas* means 'suit of armour'.

(2) Scenario two: The idiom contained a keyword whose literal sense was unknown to the learner. Consequently, the identify-the-source task was reduced to random guesswork. The unknown word may have been an item belonging to a relatively low frequency band. For example, since our learners may not have understood the keywords *mould*, *loggerheads*, and *tether* in the idioms *To break the mould*, *To be at loggerheads*, and *To be at the end of one's tether*, they may have resorted to random guesses as to their source domains. We may assume that this involved neither cognitive effort nor deep processing, and yet these cases still typically resulted in better recall under the experimental condition. Finding out about the literal meaning of the keywords on reading the etymological explanation may actually have been perceived as newsworthy, and may have been sufficient to make this sort of idioms susceptible to dual coding again.

(3) Scenario three: The idiom contained a keyword whose literal usage has become obsolete. To our knowledge, the keywords 'doldrums' and 'shrift' in *To be in the doldrums* and *To get short shrift* are not commonly used outside these idioms anymore. Consequently, our students were highly unlikely to know their literal sense, and so the identify-the-source task was probably a matter of mere guesswork again. Only on reading the feedback did the learners find out that: 'sailors used the word *doldrums* to refer to a region around the equator where there was often no wind to make any progress' (Flavell & Flavell 2000: 72), and 'a *shrift* was a confession made to a priest after which absolution is given' (Flavell & Flavell 2000: 169). The gap-fill scores for this sort of idioms did not show superior retention under the experimental condition anymore. We speculate that learners may not

have felt knowledge of (what were explained to be) obsolete words to be 'useful' enough to them. In addition, they may have felt that the identify-the-source task had been 'unfair' to them, since they could hardly be expected to be familiar with such obsolete lexis

(4) Scenario four: Finding the origin of the idiom required cultural or even 'anecdotal' historical knowledge. Good examples were *To hear something on the grapevine, To be on the wagon* and *To give someone the cold shoulder.* Although each of these idioms contained apparent lexical clues as to their source domains, they were likely to put students on the wrong track, because these words have found their way into the expressions through peculiar metonymic associations that present-day learners (or even native-speakers) may find hard to relate to. The explanations given by Flavell and Flavell (2000) for the above three idioms can briefly be summed up as follows. *To hear something on the grapevine* goes back to the 19th century and refers to hastily erected telegraph lines in the US. They often collapsed and then looked like wild grapevines. During the American Civil War the telegraph was used to send military messages, but often the messages were meant to mislead the enemy (p. 96). *To be on the wagon* goes back to the era when water was delivered to people's homes by wagons. Someone who was trying to give up alcohol was jokingly referred to as being dependent on the water wagon (p. 195). *To give someone the cold shoulder* goes back to medieval times when the welcome guest to the family home would be given a warm welcome and a lavish meal. On the other hand, the less welcome visitor would be served from a cold shoulder of mutton, probably the leftovers from dinner the night before (p. 59). On finding out about these origins, the learners probably realised that they could not have guessed this anyhow. Consequently, the identify-the-source task, which they may have invested effort in (being distracted by the apparent lexical clues), was probably perceived as a waste of time. Because the thread between the origin and the present figurative meaning seems to have become rather thin, the etymological explanation may also have been perceived by the learners as far-fetched. This type of idioms did not show superior recall under the experimental condition.

Whether these impressionistic scenarios correspond fully to psychological reality needs to be confirmed by think-aloud procedures and/or follow-up experiments. If confirmed, then the negative way some of the learners experienced the task with regard to etymologically opaque idioms may have stopped them from processing the information at a 'deep' level. For a problem-solving task to be optimally effective, its design needs to balance out cognitive effort and affect: the task needs to be challenging, but still feasible, it needs to be effortful, but also gratifying (e.g. Robinson 2001). If these principles hold for task design in general, they also hold for our own task design in *Idiomteacher*. If negative affect was to blame for the reduced success of etymological elaboration when applied to opaque idioms in our first experiment, then a more user-friendly task design might well solicit more idioms to qualify for learning along cognitive semantic lines. A straightforward way of reducing the risk of negative affect in our task design is to give learners the etymological explanation of the idioms much sooner, for instance already after one identify-the-source attempt.

In order to find out if under a modified task design etymological elaboration could also embrace opaque idioms, we set up a second experiment with *Idiomteacher* in 2003.

5.4   Experimental design in 2003

Four major changes were made to the way *Idiomteacher* was implemented:

(1)   The students were asked to do the on-line exercises during teaching hours, i.e. under teacher supervision. This meant that more students participated and more data were collected than in 2002 when the exercises were made available as an optional self-study package.

(2)   All students were asked to do the three exercise types: first the comprehension task, followed by the identify-the-source multiple-choice task, and ending with the gap-fill task. The comprehension task now served the purpose of a pre-test (to separate unknown idioms from the ones the students already appeared to understand).

(3)   In both multiple-choice exercises, students were now given only one chance per item to click the right option before proceeding to the next idiom. After each series of comprehension exercises, students were told which items they had answered incorrectly, but the correct answer was not given as feedback. The number of options in the identify-the-source multiple choice task was reduced to three (one correct response and two distracters). When the source domain of an idiom was correctly identified by a student (i.e. in one click), then the idiom was classified as etymologically transparent to that student. After each response, concise feedback on the etymological origin of the idiom (but again without explicit reference to its present-day figurative meaning) was presented on the screen.

(4)   Per series of idioms, all three exercise types were tackled in the same
       teaching period (fifty minutes). This was done to avoid some of the
       problems with data collection we had experienced in 2002. Nonetheless, a
       number of students occasionally progressed through the input stage but
       failed to do the gap-fill exercise.

Because of timetable problems, some series of the exercise package were not
administered during teaching hours and were offered as optional self-study
exercises instead. These were not included in the analysis. Still, the 2003
version of *Idiomteacher* generated data on 274 idioms (a total of 6,006 responses), which was considerably more than its 2002 precursor did. Table 2
gives an overview.

Table 2. Number of idioms and participants in the 2003 experiment

	Number of idioms	Number of participants (comprehension task + identify-the-source task + gap-fill test)
1st grade, series A	28	48
1st grade, series B	29	41
2nd grade, series A	25	11
2nd grade, series B	25	14
2nd grade, series C	24	11
2nd grade, series D	24	21
3rd year, series A	29	22
3rd year, series B	30	20
3rd year, series C	30	11
4th year, series A	30	16
TOTAL	274	

5.5   Results and discussion of the 2003 experiment

Let us first report the findings with respect to the two multiple choice tasks,
which were meant to test students' comprehension of the figurative meaning of
the idioms and students' ability to identify the source domain of the idioms. Out
of the responses to the comprehension task, 70.04% were correct. These may
include a fair number of 'lucky guesses', though, as the multiple choice offered
only three options (one correct and two distracters) per item. Interestingly, a
student's comprehension of an idiom often coincided with that student's ability
to identify its source domain. In 66.08% of the cases where a student clicked the
correct figurative meaning of an idiom, s/he would also opt for the correct
source domain of that idiom in the subsequent exercise. This is significantly

(p < .001) more than would be predicted by chance, and it suggests yet again that the meaning of many idioms is 'motivated', not only for native speakers but also for language learners processing L2 idioms.

Learners appear highly likely to recognise the source domain of idioms whose figurative meaning they understand. This does by no means exclude the possibility of acquiring the figurative meaning of an idiom without awareness of its origin, of course. Neither does recognition of the source domain of an idiom guarantee full comprehension of its figurative meaning. 'Motivated' is not synonymous with 'fully predictable'. For example, *Being in the saddle* can quite easily be traced back to horse riding, but this does not guarantee as precise an interpretation as 'being in control or having power'. A (key)word may sometimes help students recognise the source domain of an idiom without enabling them to infer its precise figurative meaning. For example, idioms containing the word 'play' (e.g., *Playing with a stacked deck*) can easily be related to the source domain of GAMES/SPORTS, without necessitating full comprehension of their figurative meaning. A learner coming across the expression *The gloves are off* may realise that this refers to boxing gloves and may thus identify the right source domain. However, when fighters take off their gloves, this may signify different things — stopping the fight as well as inflicting more damage by using bare fists. In order to figure out the precise meaning of the idiom, the learner would definitely need more (contextual) clues.

Nonetheless, the strikingly frequent correspondence between comprehension of idioms and recognition of their source domains that is evidenced by our data points again to the potential merits of etymological elaboration not only as a mnemonic technique, but also as a realistic pathway for idiom interpretation.[4] Students could be encouraged to try and infer the meaning of an idiom via its etymology, and then verify (or falsify) the interpretation. Such a problem-solving task probably involves 'deeper' processing than rote learning, and may thus be beneficial to retention as well.

Let us now turn to the scores on the gap-fill tests, which were meant to measure retention after the comprehension task and the identify-the-source task. Altogether, there were four possible routes along which a participant could proceed through those tasks, depending on their success or failure at each stage. Table three shows the recall rate in the gap-fill tests for each of the four routes.

Table 3. Recall rates in gap-fill test after both multiple choice tasks

Comprehension	Source domain	Recall
+	+	80.14%
+	−	74.63%
−	+	68.68%
−	−	67.96%

As might be expected, the recall rate of idioms whose meaning had successfully been interpreted in the comprehension test was highest.[5] Interestingly, however, gap-fill scores for these idioms were lower when students had failed to identify the source domain. At first sight, this seems to confirm the general finding in the 2002 experiment that etymologically opaque idioms (i.e. idioms whose origins students find hard to retrace) are less well retained after etymological elaboration than etymologically transparent ones. However, the recall rates of idioms that were misinterpreted in the comprehension task reveal a different pattern. Here, the gap-fill scores with regard to idioms that were experienced as etymologically opaque (i.e. when the participant failed to identify the source domain, which occurred 854 times) were as high as the scores for the transparent ones (i.e. when the participant successfully identified the source domain, which occurred 945 times). With regard to previously unknown idioms, it seems that reading a brief etymological explanation is equally beneficial to retention (through dual coding) as correctly identifying the source domain followed by reading the etymological explanation. This finding is not in accord with the 2002 data which suggested that the proposed mnemonic technique was less suitable for etymologically opaque idioms. The new data suggest that giving etymological explanations may be an effective dual coding strategy across the idiom board after all.

The question then arises why presenting an etymological explanation did not result in stable recall rates for opaque idioms whose meaning had been interpreted correctly in the comprehension test. We cannot rule out the possibility that the number of 'known' idioms may have been overestimated (lucky guesses), but we also suspect that affective elements were at play again. It is possible that students who had already correctly interpreted the meaning of a given idiom were less interested in finding out about its origin than students who had been confronted with a gap in their knowledge. To students who already understood the meaning of the idiom, learning about its origin may have seemed a bit redundant. As a result, they may not have felt sufficiently motivated to carefully read the etymological explanation. By contrast, students who had failed the comprehension task may have given more attention to the etymological explanation, as it was a tool at hand to help solve their diagnosed comprehension problem.

To estimate the plausibility of this account, we took a closer look at a small number of idioms whose source domains had proved opaque to the majority of the students, and whose etymology required unusually long explanations (four or five lines instead of the usual one or two lines).[6]

If the etymological explanations were perceived as a bit redundant to participants who (thought they) already understood the idioms, then comparatively lengthy explanations on the screen would have been especially off-putting and thus more likely than short ones to have been (partially) skipped. Ignoring the etymological information would then have reduced the chances of dual coding taking place. Indeed, for this particular set of idioms, the average gap-fill scores by students who had passed the comprehension task dropped by 10.27%, while they actually rose by 6.79% for students who had misinterpreted them.

This finding is compatible with the speculation that motivation may have influenced students' appreciation of the etymological information, and thus the probability of dual coding taking place. Accidentally, it was this category of opaque idioms with comparatively complicated origins that appeared least suited to the strategy of etymological elaboration in the 2002 experiment (when participants got access to the explanation only after — finally — clicking the correct source domain). Unless negative affect puts a damper on learning, such opaque idioms turn out to be susceptible to dual coding after all.

6.   Conclusion and perspectives

The overall findings reported in this chapter confirm earlier studies in which a cognitive semantic approach to teaching figurative language proved beneficial to second or foreign language learners. In our experiments we have tried to evaluate the effect of one particular learning strategy, i.e. etymological elaboration, on learners' retention of idioms. The results reveal that the proposed strategy can successfully be applied to a wide range of idioms, comprising both etymologically transparent and opaque ones. In a context of learner autonomy, where learners are encouraged to try and figure out the origins of idioms independently, the strategy is obviously applicable only to comparatively transparent idioms. In a context of explicit instruction (e.g. the language classroom or on-line learning tools), similar retention rates can be obtained for opaque idioms, simply by giving learners concise explanations about the origins of the expressions.

The beneficial mnemonic effect of etymological elaboration can be explained with reference to dual coding theory, since associating an idiom with its origin is likely to call up mental images. The experimental data also show evidence, however, that this mnemonic effect can be dampened by negative affect, which may set in when the identify-the-source task proves frustratingly difficult or when the etymological explanation is perceived as unhelpful or irrelevant. Decisions about task design can have profound effects on pedagogical outcomes. For example, it might be worth measuring the effectiveness of giving etymological explanations after telling learners explicitly that this will definitely help them remember.

Apart from the encouraging findings with regard to etymological elaboration as a mnemonic technique, the experiments provide further evidence in support of the cognitive semantic view that the meaning of idioms is motivated rather than arbitrary, and that this also holds for learners processing L2 idioms. It appears that learners' comprehension of L2 idioms frequently coincides with their recognition of the source domains, and that knowledge of the origins of idioms can help learners figure out their meaning. This is an invitation to further investigate the merits of etymological elaboration, not just as a mnemonic technique, but also as a channel for in-depth comprehension.

Acknowledgements

We would like to express our gratitude to the Research Fund of the Erasmus College of Brussels, to the school's webmaster Arnout Horemans, to several generations of students at the Erasmus College for their eager participation, and to the book and series editors for their insightful comments on earlier drafts of this chapter.

Notes

1. The average scores in the gap-fill test were 30.86% under the experimental condition and 9.09% under the control condition. The average scores in the comprehension test were 68.89% and 34.94%, respectively.

2. At the time of writing this chapter, we had piloted *Idiomteacher* with students at the college for two years, with a view to making the exercises available to outsiders afterwards. For an update on that project and for access to the on-line exercises, please contact the authors.

3. Overall 63 % of the control groups' first responses to the comprehension tasks were correct. A fair number of these direct hits may have been lucky guesses, though, since the multiple choice consisted of only three options.

4. Boers and Demecheleer (2001) offer more experimental evidence of learners' ability to interpret unfamiliar idioms independently and without any contextual clues.

5. The fact that gap-fill scores were under 100% for idioms that were interpreted correctly in the comprehension test is not surprising given the difference between receptive and productive knowledge. Furthermore, some of the correct interpretations in the first multiple- choice task may actually have been 'lucky guesses', and so pre-knowledge may have been overestimated.

6. These were *Have a chip on one's shoulder, Keep something at bay, Hear something on the grapevine, Kick the bucket, Hit someone for six, Run the gauntlet, No room to swing a cat,* and *A flash in the pan.*

References

Arnold, J. (ed). 1999. *Affect in language learning.* Cambridge: Cambridge University Press.
Barcroft, J. 2002. "Semantic and structural elaboration in L2 lexical acquisition". *Language Learning* 52: 323- 363.
Boers, F. 1999. "When a bodily source domain becomes prominent: the joy of counting metaphor in the socio-economic domain". In *Metaphor in Cognitive Linguistics,* R. W. Gibbs and G. J. Steen (eds), 47–56. Amsterdam and Philadelphia: John Benjamins.
Boers, F. 2000a. "Enhancing metaphoric awareness in specialised reading". *English for Specific Purposes* 19: 137–147.
Boers, F. 2000b. "Metaphor awareness and vocabulary retention". *Applied Linguistics* 21: 553–571.
Boers, F. 2001. "Remembering figurative idioms by hypothesising about their origins". *Prospect* 16: 35–43.
Boers, F. 2003. "Applied linguistics perspectives on cross-cultural variation in conceptual metaphor". *Metaphor and Symbol* 18: 231–238.
Boers, F. and Demecheleer, M. 1997. "A few metaphorical models in (western) economic Discourse". In *Discourse and Perspective in Cognitive Linguistics,* W. A. Liebert, G. Redeker and L. Waugh (eds), 115–129. Amsterdam and Philadelphia: John Benjamins.
Boers, F. and Demecheleer, M. 1998. "A cognitive semantic approach to teaching prepositions". *E L T Journal* 53: 197–204.
Boers, F. and Demecheleer, M. 2001. "Measuring the impact of cross-cultural differences on learners' comprehension of imageable idioms". *ELT Journal* 55: 255- 262.
Byram, M. 1997. *Teaching and Assessing Intercultural Communicative Competence.* Clevedon: Multilingual Matters.
Byram, M., Nichols, A. and Stevens, D. (eds). 2001. *Developing Intercultural Competence in Practice.* Clevedon: Multilingual Matters.
Cermak, L. and Craik, F. 1979. *Levels of Processing in Human Memory.* Hillsdale: Erlbaum.

Clark, J. M. and Paivio, A. 1991. "Dual coding theory and education". *Educational Psychology Review* 3: 233–262.

Cohen, G., Eysenck, M. W. and LeVoi, M. E. 1986. *Memory: a cognitive approach.* Milton Keynes: Open University Press.

Cooper, T. 1999. "Processing of idioms by L2 learners of English". *TESOL Quarterly* 33: 233–62.

Cornell, A. 1999. "Idioms: an approach to identifying major pitfalls for learners". *IRAL* 37: 1–21.

Craik, F. I. M. and Lockhart, R. S. 1972. "Levels of processing: a framework for memory research". *Journal of Verbal Learning and Verbal Behavior* 11: 671–684.

Crookes, G. and Schmidt, R. W. 1991. "Motivation: reopening the research agenda". *Language Learning* 41: 469–512.

Deignan, A. 1995. *Collins Cobuild English Guides 7: Metaphor.* London: HarperCollins.

Deignan, A. 1999. "Corpus-based approaches to metaphor". In *Researching and Applying Metaphor*, L. Cameron and G. Low (eds), 177–199. Cambridge: Cambridge University Press.

Deignan, A. 2003. "Metaphorical expressions and culture: an indirect link". *Metaphor and Symbol* 18: 255–272.

Deignan, A., Gabrys, D. and Solska, A. 1997. "Teaching English metaphors using cross-linguistic awareness-raising activities". *ELT Journal* 51: 352–360.

Flavell, L. and Flavell, R. 2000. *Dictionary of idioms and their origins.* London: Kyle Cathie.

Gibbs, R. W. 1994. *The Poetics of Mind: Figurative Thought, Language, and Understanding.* Cambridge: Cambridge University Press.

Johnson, M. 1987. *The Body in the Mind: The Bodily Basis of Meaning, Imagination and Reason.* Chicago and London: University of Chicago Press.

Kövecses, Z. 1990. *Emotion concepts.* New York: Springer.

Kövecses, Z. 1999. "Metaphor: does it constitute or reflect cultural models?" In *Metaphor in Cognitive Linguistics*, R. W. Gibbs and G. J. Steen (eds), 167–188. Amsterdam and Philadelphia: John Benjamins.

Kövecses, Z. and Szabó, P. 1996. "Idioms: a view from Cognitive Semantics". *Applied Linguistics* 17: 326–55.

Kramsch, C. 1993. *Context and Culture in Language Teaching.* Oxford: Oxford University Press.

Lakoff, G. 1987. *Women, Fire and Dangerous Things: What Categories Reveal about the Mind.* Chicago and London: University of Chicago Press.

Lakoff, G. 1990. "The invariance hypothesis: is abstract reasoning based on image-schemas?" *Cognitive Linguistics* 1: 39–74.

Lakoff, G. and Johnson, M. 1980. *Metaphors We Live By.* Chicago and London: University of Chicago Press.

Langacker, R. W. 1991. *Foundations of Cognitive Grammar. Vol. 2: Descriptive Applications.* Stanford : Stanford University Press.

Lazar, G. 1996. "Using figurative language to expand students' vocabulary". *ELT Journal* 50: 43–51.

Lennon, P. 1998. "Approaches to the teaching of idiomatic language". *IRAL* 36: 12–30.

Lewis, M. 1993. *The Lexical Approach.* Hove: LTP.
Paivio, A. 1986. *Mental Representations.* Oxford and New York: Oxford University Press
Palmer, G. B. 1996. *Toward a theory of Cultural Linguistics.* Austin: University of Texas Press.
Robinson, P. 2001. "Task complexity, task difficulty, and task production: exploring interactions in a componential framework". *Applied Linguistics* 22: 27–57.
Skehan, P. 1998. *A Cognitive Approach to Language Learning.* Oxford and New York: Oxford University Press.

CHAPTER 5

Receptive, productive, and receptive + productive L2 vocabulary learning: What difference does it make?

Jan-Arjen Mondria and Boukje Wiersma*
University of Groningen

Abstract

This experimental study investigated the popular belief of many foreign language teachers that words that are learned both receptively and productively are better retained receptively than words that are learned just receptively. The results of the experiment showed, contrary to expectation, that learning words both receptively and productively leads to a similar level of receptive retention as learning words just receptively. Similarly, learning words both productively and receptively leads to a comparable level of productive retention as learning words just productively. In addition, the experiment showed that productive learning leads to a considerable amount of receptive retention, that receptive learning leads to a certain amount of productive retention, and that productive learning is substantially more difficult than receptive learning.

1. Introduction

A few years ago, an experienced foreign language teacher told us that he always asks pupils to learn words both receptively and productively (i.e. from L2 to L1, and from L1 to L2), even in those cases — mainly at higher levels — where the

---

* An important part of this investigation was carried out by the second author in the framework of her Master's thesis, supervised by the first author in collaboration with Siebrich de Vries. The authors would like to thank her for her help.

focus is on the extension of receptive vocabulary knowledge. The reason for him to do so was that he was convinced that the combination of receptive and productive learning would lead to a higher or more stable level of vocabulary knowledge and that this would reduce the chance of forgetting the words. Furthermore, it was his conviction that when the knowledge of a word learned both receptively and productively decreases as a result of the natural forgetting process, productive knowledge — which is assumed to be more complex — would decrease first and that receptive knowledge would remain.

In order to investigate whether the idea that the combination of receptive and productive learning leads to better receptive knowledge than receptive learning alone is the idea of only one particular teacher or whether it is shared by many teachers, we conducted a small scale written survey on receptive and productive word learning among 90 Dutch foreign language teachers. The results showed that 83% of them agreed with this idea. This raises the question: is there evidence available that supports what we will call 'the combination hypothesis', that is the idea that the combination of receptive and productive learning ('the combination method') leads to a higher or more stable level of receptive retention than receptive learning alone. In other words: is there evidence for the idea that the extra effort put into productive learning results in better receptive retention?

2.   Literature review

In spite of the fact that the distinction between receptive and productive L2 vocabulary knowledge is beyond question (Melka 1997), there are, to the best of our knowledge, only five experimental studies comparing receptive and productive L2 word learning, namely Schuyten (1906), Stoddard (1929), Griffin & Harley (1996), Waring (1997), and Schneider, Healy & Bourne (2002). We focus on studies comparing the effects of receptive and productive *learning* and we will not discuss studies that just compare receptive and productive *knowledge*, as these studies do not provide us with relevant extra information. One peculiar thing we noticed is that earlier studies have been rarely quoted by later studies. The only experiment that was quoted by one or more of the others is Stoddard (1929), respectively by Griffin & Harley (1996) and Schneider *et al.* (2002).

2.1   Schuyten (1906)

Schuyten carried out three classroom experiments with Dutch speaking Belgian pupils learning French, German and English words, respectively. The experimental design in each of the three cases consisted of two parts and each part made use of a different set of target words. For the first set of words the sequence was: productive learning, receptive test and productive test. For the second set the sequence was: receptive learning, productive test and receptive test. The main results were the following.

(1)   In each of the three experiments receptive retention was substantially higher than productive retention, suggesting — the results were not tested for significance — that receptive learning is easier than productive learning.
(2)   Receptive learning led to a substantial amount of productive knowledge, and productive learning led to a substantial amount of receptive knowledge.

However, the conclusions are qualified by the fact that pupils were tested on each set of words both receptively and productively as a result of which performance on the second test might have been boosted by the first test, and the fact that the order of testing is coupled to sets of words, so that effects of testing order and sets of words are mixed up. Furthermore, it should be pointed out that the results are based on an immediate test, and not on a (more informative) delayed test.

2.2   Stoddard (1929)

Stoddard required American high school students without any knowledge of French to learn French words. Half of them learned the words from French to English; the other half learned the words from English to French. The (immediate) retention test was identical for both groups and tested receptive knowledge of half of the words, and productive knowledge of the other half. The experiment showed the following.

(1)   The results on the receptive part of the test were significantly higher — about twice as high — than the results on the productive part of the test.
(2)   The best results on the receptive part of the test were obtained when the words were learned receptively, and the best results on the productive part of the test were obtained when the words were learned productively.
(3)   Productive learning led to a considerable amount of receptive knowledge and receptive learning led to a considerable amount of productive knowledge.

Unfortunately, the conclusions of this elegant experiment are qualified by the fact that the (American) students in question had no experience at all with the foreign language in question (French), which might have had a more negative effect on productive learning and testing — cf. familiarity with the L2 orthography — than on receptive learning and testing. Furthermore, the results are qualified by the fact that they are based on an immediate test, and not on a delayed test.

2.3 Griffin & Harley (1996)

Griffin & Harley required comprehensive (high) school students, in their first year of learning French, to learn French words. Half of them learned the words English-French, and the other half learned the words French-English. Half of the students of each group were tested receptively, the other half productively. Testing took place immediately after learning and on the third, seventh and twenty-eighth day. The most important conclusions were the following.

(1) Receptive learning yielded a substantial amount of productive knowledge, and productive learning yielded a substantial amount of receptive knowledge.

(2) Equivalence of type of learning and type of test (i.e. receptive learning followed by receptive testing, and productive learning followed by productive testing) yielded better results than non-equivalence of learning and testing (i.e. receptive learning followed by productive testing, and productive learning followed by receptive testing).

(3) The overall results on the receptive tests were significantly higher than those on the productive tests.

(4) The total retention — receptive and productive knowledge taken together — as a result of receptive learning did not differ significantly from that as a result of productive learning.

(5) The total retention as a result of receptive learning decayed at a comparable rate as the total retention as a result of productive learning.

A practical conclusion drawn by Griffin & Harley is that productive learning is the better all-purpose direction. This is because the productive association is more effective than the receptive association for the more difficult production task, while the weaker receptive association is needed only for the less difficult comprehension task.

With regard to the interpretation of the results, it is regrettable that the way of presentation of the data does not allow us to compare individual conditions, that is combinations of one type of learning with one type of test. Another point of concern is that repeated testing may have boosted the retention, and it is not clear whether this effect is comparable for receptive and productive retention. Furthermore, the way of scoring the productive data has been rather lenient — 'identifiable approximations to the target items' — which might have had a positive effect on the level of productive retention. Finally, we consider the conclusions with regard to the 'total retention' — receptive and productive knowledge taken together — as invalid, as it is not correct to add up scores on quite different tests.

2.4 Waring (1997)

Waring carried out an experiment rather similar to that of Stoddard. Students learned one set of words receptively and another set productively. The order of types of learning was balanced across students and each set of words was combined with each type of learning. The knowledge of both sets of words was tested productively and receptively ten minutes after learning, the following day, one week later, and three months later. In addition, for homework after the learning session, students were required to write a short essay about their learning during the experiment. The results showed the following.

(1) Productive learning took more time than receptive learning.
(2) Receptive tests yielded higher test scores than productive tests.
(3) Receptive learning led to a certain amount of productive knowledge and productive learning led to a certain amount of receptive knowledge.
(4) The best results on a receptive test were obtained when the words were learned receptively, and the best results on a productive test were obtained when the words were learned productively.
(5) Productive knowledge — whether acquired by productive learning or by receptive learning — decayed faster than receptive knowledge.

However, the results have to be interpreted with caution. First, the productive tests always preceded the receptive tests, which might have had a positive effect on the receptive retention scores. Second, the experiment was carried out using Japanese as a first language and English as a foreign language. It is not clear whether the differences in script have had a comparable effect on receptive and productive learning. Third, the fact that retention tests were administered at four different times might have had a positive effect on the retention, and it is not clear whether this effect is the same for receptive and productive retention.

Fourth, a comparable comment can be made with regard to the essay that the students had to write about their learning. Finally, it is not clear whether the conclusions (4) and (5) are based on significant differences.

2.5   Schneider *et al.* (2002)

Schneider *et al.* carried out two experiments in which they required American college students to learn a set of French words. In each experiment half of the students learned the words receptively and took an immediate receptive retention test. The other half of the students learned the words productively and took an immediate productive retention test. One week later, a delayed retention test was administered. Half of the students of each group were tested receptively, after which they had to relearn the words receptively. The other half of each group were tested productively and had to relearn the words productively. The most relevant results were the following.

(1)   The receptive learning trials showed a higher proportion of correct responses than the productive learning trials. At the *re*learning trials too, receptive learning was more successful than productive learning.

(2)   The receptive retention tests (both immediate and delayed) yielded higher scores than the productive retention tests.

(3)   Receptive learning led to a certain amount of productive knowledge (delayed retention test). Productive learning, however, led to a considerable amount of receptive knowledge (delayed retention test), an amount that was even comparable to that as a result of receptive learning.

(4)   The retention loss between the immediate and the delayed test was greater for words that were learned receptively than for words that were learned productively, suggesting that words that are learned in the more difficult productive way are less susceptible to forgetting.

With regard to the interpretation of the results, it should be borne in mind that the students had no experience with the foreign language in question (French). This might have had a more negative effect on productive learning and testing — cf. orthography — than on receptive learning and testing. In addition, the ecological validity of the experiment suffers from the fact that the words to be learned were presented on a computer screen, at a fixed rate, and without any information about the pronunciation of the words in question. Finally, we do not agree with Schneider *et al.*'s conclusion about the retention loss, because in half of the cases the format of the delayed retention test (receptive or productive) did not correspond to that of the immediate retention test (receptive or productive). In fact, a closer look at the data shows that the productive knowledge of words learned productively decayed faster than the receptive knowledge of words learned receptively.

2.6 Summary

Unfortunately, none of the five experimental studies discussed above investigates our central research question, namely: does the combination of receptive and productive learning lead to a better receptive retention than receptive learning alone? That is, the experiments make comparisons between receptive and productive learning, and between receptive and productive testing, but in none of the experiments subjects learn a set of words both receptively and productively, followed by a retention test. Nevertheless, the experiments do provide us with useful information on three aspects of receptive and productive word learning that are relevant to our research question and that we will discuss below, namely

(1)   the overlap between receptive learning and productive learning,
(2)   the degree of difficulty of receptive learning vs. productive learning, and
(3)   the decay of receptive knowledge vs. productive knowledge.

2.6.1   *Overlap between receptive learning and productive learning*
All the experiments discussed show that productive learning leads to a certain amount of receptive knowledge, as well as the reverse, namely that receptive learning leads to a certain amount of productive knowledge. However, the receptive retention as a result of productive learning in general lags behind the receptive retention as a result of receptive learning, with the exception of Schneider *et al.* (2002). Likewise, the productive retention as a result of receptive learning in general lags behind the productive retention as a result of productive learning, with the exception of Schuyten (1906).

This information supports the combination hypothesis in the following way. On the one hand, productive learning partially overlaps with receptive learning, as a result of which additional productive learning might lead to an extra amount of receptive knowledge. On the other hand, productive learning partially differs from receptive learning, so that adding a productive learning stage might lead to more extended processing (learners spend more time on learning) and more varied processing (two different ways of learning), which in turn might result in better retention.

2.6.2   *Degree of difficulty of receptive learning vs. productive learning*
Productive learning is more difficult than receptive learning. This is evidenced by the fact that in all the experiments the mean scores on the productive retention tests were lower than those on the receptive retention tests. Additional evidence comes from the fact that productive learning took more time than receptive learning (Waring 1997) and the fact that receptive learning trials were more successful than productive learning trials (Schneider *et al.* 2002). The fact that productive learning is more difficult, is an extra argument in favour of the combination hypothesis, as more elaborate processing is generally expected to lead to better retention (Anderson 1990).

2.6.3   *Decay of receptive knowledge vs. productive knowledge*
With regard to the decay of knowledge, Waring (1997) found that productive knowledge — whether acquired by productive or receptive learning — decayed faster than receptive knowledge. Schneider *et al.*'s (2002) data shows that the productive knowledge of words learned productively decayed faster than the receptive knowledge of words learned receptively. Both findings are in line with the earlier mentioned teacher's idea that productive word knowledge is more susceptible to decay than receptive word knowledge.

3.   Experimental research

3.1   Definitions

In order to test the combination hypothesis empirically, we carried out the experiment described below. However, due to the absence of generally accepted definitions of the terms receptive and productive vocabulary learning, knowledge, and testing (see Melka 1997, Read 2000 and Schmitt 2000), it is necessary to first define these terms here. For convenience's sake, we will talk about 'words', where we actually mean 'lexical units', that is 'union[s] of a lexical form and a single sense' (Cruse 1986: 77; cf. Bogaards 2001).

Receptive vocabulary learning: learning the meaning of an L2 word. Prototypically: learning a word from L2 to L1.
Productive vocabulary learning: learning to express a concept by means of an L2 word. Prototypically: learning a word from L1 to L2.
Receptive vocabulary knowledge: knowledge of the meaning of an L2 word. Prototypically: being able to translate a word from L2 to L1.

Productive vocabulary knowledge: being able to express a concept by means of an L2 word. Prototypically: being able to translate a word from L1 to L2.

Receptive vocabulary testing: testing a person's knowledge of the meaning of an L2 word. Prototypically: requiring a person to translate a word from L2 to L1.

Productive vocabulary testing: testing a person's ability to express a concept by means of an L2 word. Prototypically: requiring a person to translate a word from L1 to L2.

3.2   Research questions

The research questions were the following.

(1)   Does learning words both receptively and productively — the combination method — result in better receptive retention, as compared to learning words just receptively?

(2)   Does learning words both receptively and productively result in better productive retention, as compared to learning words just productively?

(3)   What is the overlap between receptive word learning and productive word learning? That is, to what degree does receptive learning lead to productive knowledge, and to what degree does productive learning lead to receptive knowledge?

(4)   What is the degree of difficulty of receptive learning vs. productive learning, as shown by respectively the receptive and the productive retention?

The first question is the central research question, based on the combination hypothesis, suggesting that the extra effort put into productive learning (in combination with receptive learning) results in a higher or more stable level of receptive retention. The second question is the productive counterpart of the first question. It is also based on the combination hypothesis, but now in the productive version. The question was included in order to provide a more complete picture of the combination hypothesis and the relationship between receptive and productive learning. The third and the fourth questions are not new, but were included as they can provide us with useful information for the interpretation of the results of the first two questions. Conversely, research on the combination method (questions 1 and 2) offers new possibilities for answering question four, namely by comparing the receptive and the productive retention as a result of the combination method.

3.3   Method

3.3.1 *Design*

Three types of learning (receptive; productive; receptive + productive) were combined with two types of testing (receptive or productive) in a 3 × 2 between-subjects design (see Table 1). Retention tests were administered immediately after learning — just to give pupils the idea that the experiment had finished — and after two weeks. The innovative element in this design, as compared to the 2 × 2 designs described above, is the inclusion of the third type of learning: the combination of receptive and productive learning.

Table 1. Design of the experiment

Cond.	Learning	Immediate test	Delayed test
1	Receptive	Receptive	Receptive
2	Receptive	Productive	Productive
3	Productive	Receptive	Receptive
4	Productive	Productive	Productive
5	Receptive + Productive	Receptive	Receptive
6	Receptive + Productive	Productive	Productive

3.3.2 *Subjects*

Subjects were 198 Dutch pupils from eight third grades from four schools offering general secondary education at pre-university level. The age of the pupils was 14–16 years, and all of them had been receiving French lessons during three hours every week for at least two and a half years.

3.3.3 *Materials*

Target words. Sixteen French target words (8 nouns and 8 verbs) were chosen that did not occur in the coursebooks used in the schools concerned and whose meanings could not be inferred on the basis of words, stems and affixes already known by the pupils. Furthermore, the selection did not contain synonymous word pairs or word pairs whose meanings could be inferred from each other. The complete set of target words is in the Appendix.

Learning materials. For each of the three types of learning a different learning sheet was made, in all cases containing the same words but differing with regard to their presentation.[1] The words were presented in two columns without context: from French to Dutch for receptive learning, and from Dutch to French for productive learning. In both cases nouns and verbs alternated in the same order. For the combination of receptive and productive learning the front of the sheet presented the words from Dutch to French in the same order as before, and the back side presented the words from French to Dutch, but now in a different order, as the same order might give pupils the undeserved impression that they knew the words already as a result of which they would spend less time to the second type of learning.

The instruction was printed at the top of each learning sheet and mentioned the direction of learning (French to Dutch, Dutch to French, or both), the available time (15 minutes), and the fact that a retention test would be administered immediately afterwards.

Tests. Two tests were made: a receptive and a productive retention test. As a criterion for receptive word knowledge we adopted: recall of the meaning (L1 translation) of the L2 word without a context. The criterion for productive word knowledge was: recall of the L2 word (translation of the L1 word) without a context. To that end, both the receptive and the productive test contained the 16 target words, in French and in Dutch respectively. The instructions were: 'Translate the following French words into Dutch' and 'Translate the following Dutch words into French'. The order of the items differed from that of learning, in order not to overestimate the retention. In addition, the order of the items in the receptive test differed from that in the productive test in order to prevent pupils from cheating. In both tests nouns and verbs alternated (as before).

3.3.4 *Procedures*
The experiment consisted of a learning session followed by an immediate retention test and, two weeks later, an unannounced delayed retention test. The procedures for each of the eight participating classes were identical. Within each class, without their knowledge, the pupils were randomly assigned to one of the six conditions, so that in each class all combinations of learning and testing were present. The experiment took place during the regular French lessons that the pupils attended and was led by the second author.

Learning session. The experimental materials were distributed at the beginning of the learning session and were collected at the end of it. Writing was not allowed. The available time for learning was 15 minutes, that is 56 seconds per word. This amount of time is greater than in the other experiments discussed, as the pupils in the combination conditions had to have sufficient time to carry out their double learning task. (Cf. Stoddard 1929 and Griffin & Harley 1996 allotted 24 seconds per word, receptively or productively. Waring's 1997 subjects used

38 seconds per word receptively and 48 seconds productively. Schneider *et al.* 2002 presented each word pair — receptively or productively — at each of the three learning trials during two seconds, each time followed by testing.)

Immediate retention test. Immediately after the learning session the immediate retention test (receptive or productive) was administered. Pupils were fore-warned that in some cases the test format might be different from the format that they had expected, but that this was done on purpose. Furthermore, pupils were asked to give only one answer per item. The time available for the test was 5 minutes. After the test the pupils were thanked for their participation in the experiment in order to give them the impression that the experiment had finished. They were not told that a delayed retention test would be adminis-tered later on. This was intended to avoid encouraging relearning, which might lead to treatment confusion.

Delayed retention test. Two weeks later (12–14 days) and unexpected by the pupils, the delayed retention test was administered following the same proce-dures as for the immediate retention test. (The fact that for organisational reasons the interval between the immediate and the delayed test varied from 12 to 14 days is not a problem, as the conditions were balanced across and within classes.)

3.3.5 *Scoring*
Scoring was done by the first author and an experienced teacher of French. Independently of each other they judged the correctness (correct/incorrect) of the pupils' answers on the basis of the meanings given in bilingual and mono-lingual dictionaries. Minor spelling errors (e.g. diacritics) were accepted as long as the overall word picture and pronunciation were not affected, and provided there was no confusion with another word. Wrong or missing articles were ignored. The mean agreement between judges was .99 ($r_\varnothing$). Differences between judges were resolved by discussion. Correct answers were assigned 1 point, incorrect answers 0 points.

3.3.6 *Data analysis*
The main unit of analysis was a pupil's test score on the set of 16 items. Thus, for each pupil there was an immediate retention score and a delayed retention score. The techniques of analysis were planned pairwise comparisons.[2] Unless indicated otherwise, the analyses are based on the delayed retention scores, as the immediate retention test, showing a ceiling effect, was mainly intended to

give pupils the idea that the experiment had finished. However, in those cases where analyses of the immediate test data provide useful additional information or information that does not correspond with the analysis of the delayed test, this will be reported. In all cases alpha was set at 5%.

3.4   Results

The mean retention scores on the immediate and the delayed tests are given in Table 2. In addition, the mean retention scores are represented graphically in Figure 1.

Table 2. Mean retention scores (and standard deviations) per condition

Learning	Immediate Test		Delayed Test	
	Receptive	Productive	Receptive	Productive
Receptive	15.7	8.4	7.7	1.9
	(0.9)	(4.1)	(2.9)	(2.2)
	n=33	n=32	n=33	n=32
Productive	13.5	15.5	6.6	4.1
	(2.1)	(0.8)	(2.6)	(3.2)
	n=33	n=32	n=33	n=32
Receptive +	15.4	14.1	7.9	3.8
Productive	(1.4)	(2.5)	(2.7)	(3.0)
	n=34	n=34	n=34	n=34
Total	14.9	12.7	7.4	3.3
	(1.8)	(4.1)	(2.8)	(3.0)
	n=100	n=98	n=100	n=98

Note. Maximum score = 16.

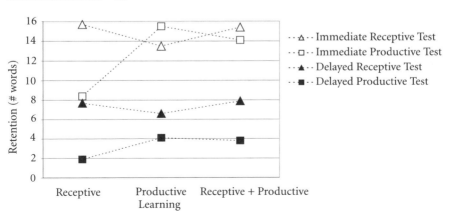

Figure 1. Mean retention scores per condition

Research question 1: The combination method and receptive retention
With regard to the receptive retention, there was no significant difference between receptive + productive learning on the one hand and receptive learning on the other hand (7.9 vs. 7.7 [R+P/R vs. R/R][3]; $t[65] = 0.36$, $p = .36$ [one-tailed]). In order to check whether the pupils in the receptive + productive learning condition had indeed paid attention to productive learning too, the productive retention as a result of this receptive + productive learning was compared to that as a result of receptive learning. The difference was significant (3.8 vs. 1.9 [R+P/P vs. R/P]; $t[64] = 3.03$, $p < .01$ [one-tailed]), showing that the pupils in the combination condition had indeed paid attention to productive learning too.

Research question 2: The combination method and productive retention
As for the productive retention, there was no significant difference between productive + receptive learning and productive learning (3.8 vs. 4.1 [P+R/P vs. P/P]; $t[64] = -0.32$, $p = .75$ [two-tailed]). The fact that no difference was found can not be ascribed to a lack of attention for receptive learning in the combination method, as there was a significant difference in receptive retention between productive + receptive learning and productive learning (7.9 vs. 6.6 [P+R/R vs. P/R]; $t[65] = 1.98$, $p = .03$ [one-tailed]).

As for the *immediate* productive test, there was a significant difference between productive + receptive learning and productive learning (14.1 vs. 15.5 [P+R/P vs. P/P]; $t[39.9] = -3.15$, $p < .01$ [two-tailed]), but in a direction that was contrary to expectations.

Research question 3: Overlap between receptive learning and productive learning
The receptive retention as a result of receptive learning did not differ significantly from that as a result of productive learning, although receptive learning yielded a 16% higher retention (7.7 vs. 6.6 [R/R vs. P/R]; $t[64] = 1.52$, $p = .07$ [one-tailed]). The just mentioned receptive retention as a result of productive learning was substantial and differed significantly from zero (6.6 [P/R]; $t[32] = 14.82$, $p < .001$ [one-tailed]).

The *immediate* test showed a comparable difference between the receptive retention as a result of receptive learning and that as a result of productive learning — receptive learning yielded a 16% higher retention — but here the difference was significant (15.7 vs. 13.5 [R/R vs. P/R]; $t[44.5] = 5.53$, $p < .01$ [one-tailed]).

As for the productive retention, productive learning and receptive learning led to significantly different results (4.1 vs. 1.9 [P/P vs. R/P]; $t[62]=3.19$, $p < .01$ [one-tailed]), receptive learning clearly lagging behind. Nevertheless, receptive learning led to a significant amount of productive knowledge (1.9 [R/P]; $t[31]=4.83$, $p < .001$ [one-tailed]).

Research question 4: Degree of difficulty of receptive learning vs. productive learning
The degree of difficulty of receptive learning vs. productive learning was investigated in two different ways. The first, innovative way compares the receptive and the productive retention as a result of the combination method. The receptive retention turned out to be significantly higher than the productive retention (7.9 vs. 3.8 [R+P/R vs. R+P/P]; $t[66]=5.97$, $p < .001$ [one-tailed]), showing that productive learning is more difficult.

The second way of investigating the degree of difficulty of receptive learning vs. productive learning is by comparing the receptive retention as a result of receptive learning to the productive retention as a result of productive learning. This comparison is based on the idea that the best results on a test are obtained when the way of learning corresponds to the way of testing. Receptive learning followed by receptive testing led to a significantly higher retention than productive learning followed by productive testing (7.7 vs. 4.1 [R/R vs. P/P]; $t[63]=4.75$, $p < .001$ [one-tailed]), confirming that productive learning is more difficult. On the *immediate* test, however, there was no significant difference (15.7 vs. 15.5 [R/R vs. P/P]; $t[63]=0.90$, $p = .19$ [one-tailed]), but this can easily be explained by the ceiling effect in both conditions.

Now that we know that the type of test has a significant effect on the retention, the question rises what the size of this effect is as compared to the effect of correspondence between type of learning and type of test. This question can be answered by comparing the receptive and the productive retention, both as a result of productive learning. On the basis of the type of test, the retention is expected to be higher on the (easier) receptive test, but on the basis of the correspondence between type of learning and type of test, one would expect better results on the productive test. However, retention turned out to be significantly higher on the receptive test (6.6 vs. 4.1 [P/R vs. P/P]; $t[63]= 3.59$, $p < .01$ [two-tailed]), showing that the effect of type of test on the retention is greater than that of correspondence between type of learning and type of test. The *immediate* test, on the other hand, showed the opposite: for productive learning the productive retention was significantly higher than the receptive retention (15.5 vs. 13.5 [P/P vs. P/R]; $t[41.5]=5.16$, $p < .001$ [two-tailed]), showing that the effect of correspondence between type of learning and type of test on the retention is greater than the effect of type of test.

4.   Discussion and conclusions

4.1   The combination method

Learning words both receptively and productively leads to a similar level of receptive retention as learning words just receptively (in the experiment 49% vs. 48% [7.9 vs. 7.7] [R+P/R vs. R/R]). This does not conform to expectations. That is, it had been expected that the combination method would lead to superior receptive retention on the basis of the fact that the extra type of learning (productive learning) in itself leads to a certain amount of receptive retention (as shown by this experiment and the other experiments discussed), in combination with the expectation that learning in two different ways (receptive and productive) would result in more extended, varied and elaborate processing, factors that are supposed to have a positive effect on retention.

This unexpected result can not be accounted for by the way the combination method has been operationalised. That is, the pupils were given ample time — clearly more than in the other experiments discussed — so that they would be able to learn the words both receptively and productively. This is testified by the retention data in two different ways. First, the significant differences on the delayed productive test between receptive learning and receptive + productive learning [R/P vs. R+P/P], and on the receptive test between productive learning and productive + receptive learning [P/R vs. P+R/R] show that pupils in the combination conditions had indeed learned in both directions. Second, the ceiling effect on the immediate test provides evidence that pupils had had enough time.

In view of the above, the explanation for the fact that the combination method does not lead to superior receptive retention must be sought in the combination method itself. In particular, it must be explained why receptive + productive learning, in spite of the extra, productive learning stage, which in itself leads to receptive retention, does not lead to improved retention as compared to receptive learning. The following two explanations are possible.

As a first explanation we may submit that the receptive retention as a result of receptive learning was at the time of learning already so high that additional productive learning was not able to add to that. Evidence for this is the ceiling effect on the immediate test (a mean retention score of 15.7, where the maximum was 16).

As a second explanation we may submit that the fact that productive learning leads to a certain amount of receptive knowledge does not necessarily imply that adding productive learning to receptive learning leads to a higher or more stable receptive retention.

Both explanations account for the fact that the added value of productive learning manifests itself only on the productive test and not on the receptive test.

With regard to the combination method and *productive* retention — the logical counterpart of the main research question just discussed — our conclusions are similar. The experiment shows that learning words both productively and receptively leads to a comparable level of productive retention as learning words just productively (24% vs. 25% [3.8 vs. 4.1] [P+R/P vs. P/P]). This too does not conform to the expectations, as it had been expected that the combination method would lead to superior productive retention on the basis of the fact that the extra type of learning (receptive learning) in itself leads to a certain amount of productive retention (as shown by this experiment and the other experiments discussed), in combination with the expected more extended and more varied processing. The unexpected result can be accounted for along the same lines as just discussed for the combination method and receptive retention, although the productive retention as a result of receptive learning was much lower — both absolutely and relatively — than the receptive retention as a result of productive learning.

On the *immediate* test, however, we found that the productive retention as a result of productive + receptive learning was significantly lower than that as a result of productive learning (88% vs. 97% [14.1 vs. 15.5] [P+R/P vs. P/P]). This is contrary to the combination hypothesis, which had predicted the opposite. A possible explanation is that in the combination method the time spent on receptive learning has been at the expense of the time that would have been spent otherwise on (more difficult and more time-consuming) productive learning. And as we have already seen, productive learning is essential for productive retention. As an explanation for the contrast with the delayed test, where the difference has practically disappeared, we may submit that the initial advantage of concentrating on productive learning is compensated later on by the beneficial effect of the varied processing of the combination method.

Summarising, the combination hypothesis was not confirmed, neither with regard to receptive retention, nor with regard to productive retention.

4.2   Overlap between receptive learning and productive learning

Productive learning leads to a considerable amount of receptive retention, a finding that confirms earlier research. In fact, there was no significant difference between the receptive retention as a result of productive learning and that as a result of receptive learning, although the latter was higher (42% vs. 48% [6.6 vs. 7.7] [P/R vs. R/R]).

Conversely, receptive learning leads to a significant amount of productive retention, a finding that is also in line with earlier research. However, the amount of retention was only half of that as a result of productive learning (12% vs. 25% [1.9 vs. 4.1] [R/P vs. P/P]), a significant difference. Thus, productive learning leads to a substantially better productive retention than receptive learning.

Interestingly, productive knowledge does not in all cases include receptive knowledge, as is often assumed. At the immediate test following productive learning, the receptive retention was lower than the productive retention (85% vs. 97% [13.5 vs. 15.5] [P/R vs. P/P]). This finding is in line with the overall means found by Griffin & Harley (1996), but it contrasts with the (immediate test) findings of Stoddard (1929), who found the opposite. However, this contrast can be accounted for by the fact that Stoddard's students were not familiar with the foreign language in question, which might have hampered productive retention more than receptive retention. Furthermore, our finding differs from Waring (1997), who found no significant difference on the immediate test. A comparison with the results found by Schuyten (1906) does not make sense, because in his experiments the productive retention might have been boosted by the preceding receptive test. Finally, a comparison with Schneider *et al.* (2002) is not possible because they did not administer an immediate receptive test to the students who learned productively. The results on their delayed tests, however, are in line with our results on the delayed tests.

4.3   Degree of difficulty of receptive learning vs. productive learning

Productive learning is significantly and substantially more difficult than receptive learning. This has been demonstrated by the experiment in two different ways. First, by means of a comparison of the receptive and the productive retention of the combination method (the innovative feature of this experiment) (49% vs. 24% [7.9 vs. 3.8] [R+P/R vs. R+P/P]). Second, by means of a comparison of the receptive retention as a result of receptive learning and the productive retention as a result of productive learning (48% vs. 25% [7.7 vs. 4.1] [R/R vs. P/P]). The higher degree of difficulty of productive learning is in line with the experiments discussed earlier and can be explained in two ways (cf. Ellis & Beaton 1993). The first explanation is that productive use requires more precise knowledge of the word form (cf. new output patterns), although this will partly depend upon the degree to which less than perfect responses are scored as correct. This is 'the amount of knowledge explanation', as it is called by Nation (2001: 28). The second explanation has to do with the structure of the lexical system. Ellis & Beaton suggest that a new L2 word for a beginner has no links to other L2 words, but only a (receptive) link to the L1 equivalent. In contrast, the L1 equivalent has many associations within the L1 lexicon, which constitute competing paths to choose from, competing paths that may be stronger than the (productive) link to the new L2 word. This is 'the access explanation' (Nation 2001: 29).

The effect of type of test is greater than the effect of correspondence between type of learning and type of test. This is shown by the fact that productive learning followed by receptive testing led to a substantially higher retention than productive learning followed by the corresponding productive test (42% vs. 25% [6.6 vs. 4.1] [P/R vs. P/P]). Strangely enough, however, this effect was the opposite on the immediate test, where productive learning resulted in a receptive retention that was lower than the productive retention (85% vs. 97% [13.5 vs. 15.5] [P/R vs. P/P]).

How is this interaction to be accounted for? The fact that productive knowledge decreases at a faster rate than receptive knowledge can be explained by the more stringent criterion set in a productive test: while a decreased receptive knowledge may still be sufficient for success on a receptive test, a decreased productive knowledge may be insufficient for success on a productive test. However, the fact that on the immediate test following productive learning, the productive retention was higher than the receptive retention is inconsistent with our conclusion that the effect of type of test is greater than the effect of correspondence between type of learning and type of test. As yet, we did not find a plausible explanation for this finding.

A comparison of our findings with the other experiments discussed, shows that the interaction found is in line with Waring's (1997) results for productive learning: on the immediate test productive and receptive retention were similar, but after a three months delay productive retention was substantially lower than receptive retention. Our results, however, are at variance with Stoddard

(1929), who found — on an immediate test — that for productive learning receptive retention was higher than productive retention, possibly as a result of the unfamiliarity of the students with the foreign language in question. A comparison with the findings of Schuyten (1906), Griffin & Harley (1996) and Schneider *et al.* (2002) is not possible. That is, Schuyten's productive test was always preceded by a receptive test, which might have benefited the productive retention, and Griffin & Harley, unfortunately, do not mention mean results per condition and day of recall. Schneider *et al.*, finally, did not administer an immediate receptive test to the students who learned productively.

4.4 Implications for foreign-language teaching

Receptive learning is still the best way to acquire receptive word knowledge. Contrary to expectations, adding productive learning does not lead to better receptive retention. Productive learning alone, although it leads to a substantial amount of receptive knowledge, is not recommended as an alternative, because it takes extra time, which can be better spent on learning more words receptively.

When productive knowledge is the aim of vocabulary learning, it is advised to learn the words productively. Adding receptive learning is not useful, as it does not lead to improved productive knowledge. Receptive learning alone is not an option, as it only leads to a limited amount of productive knowledge.

When the learning aim is both receptive and productive word knowledge, it is recommended to learn the words both receptively and productively (the combination method). Here again, receptive learning alone is not an option, because of the limited amount of productive retention. Neither is productive learning alone recommended, as the resulting receptive retention lags behind that as a result of the combination method.

If for practical reasons (e.g. materials preparation or simplicity of instruction) a choice has to be made for either receptive learning or productive learning — the learning aim still being receptive and productive knowledge — productive learning is the best candidate because receptive learning does not result in a substantial amount of productive knowledge.

However, it should be pointed out that in all cases the productive retention will be clearly lower than the receptive retention, due to the fact that productive learning is more difficult. Therefore, for a higher productive retention additional learning and/or exercises are necessary.

Notes

1. Originally we intended to use word cards because of its advantages over the fixed list format (cf. Mondria & Mondria-de Vries 1994). But as the learners in the schools concerned were not familiar with this way of learning, and as we did not want to complicate the experiment by introducing a new learning method to the pupils, we had to give up this idea.

2. As the pairwise comparisons were planned a priori, we did not carry out ANOVAs (cf. Hays 1988: 385). Moreover, the most obvious ANOVAs here, namely 3 × 2 (Type of learning × Type of testing) ANOVAs, would not be valid as they assume that it makes sense to add up receptive and productive retention scores in order to calculate a mean retention score per type of learning, which is not the case.

3. P = productive. R = receptive. Characters before the slash refer to learning. Characters after the slash refer to testing. The slash itself can be read as 'followed by'.

References

Anderson, J. R. 1990. *Cognitive Psychology and its Implications* (3rd ed.). New York: Freeman.

Bogaards, P. 2001. "Lexical units and the learning of foreign language vocabulary". *Studies in Second Language Acquisition* 23: 321–343.

Cruse, D. A. 1986. *Lexical Semantics*. Cambridge: Cambridge University Press.

Ellis, N. and Beaton, A. 1993. "Factors affecting the learning of foreign language vocabulary: Imagery keyword mediators and phonological short-term memory". *Quarterly Journal of Experimental Psychology* 46A: 533–558.

Griffin, G. and Harley, T. A. 1996. "List learning of second language vocabulary". *Applied Psycholinguistics* 17: 443–460.

Hays, W. L. 1988. *Statistics* (4th ed.). New York: Holt, Rinehart & Winston.

Melka, F. 1997. "Receptive vs. productive aspects of vocabulary". In *Vocabulary: Description, Acquisition and Pedagogy*, N. Schmitt and M. McCarthy (eds), 84–102. Cambridge: Cambridge University Press.

Mondria, J.-A. and Mondria-de Vries, S. 1994. "Efficiently memorizing words with the help of word cards and 'hand computer': Theory and applications". *System* 22: 47–57.

Nation, I. S. P. 2001. *Learning Vocabulary in Another Language*. Cambridge: Cambridge University Press.

Read, J. 2000. *Assessing Vocabulary*. Cambridge: Cambridge University Press.

Schmitt, N. 2000. *Vocabulary in Language Teaching*. Cambridge: Cambridge University Press.

Schneider, V. I., Healy, A. F. and Bourne, L. E., Jr. 2002. "What is learned under difficult conditions is hard to forget: Contextual interference effects in foreign vocabulary acquisition, retention and transfer". *Journal of Memory and Language* 46: 419–440.

Schuyten, M. C. 1906. "Experimentelles zum Studium der gebräuchlichsten Methoden im fremdsprachlichen Unterricht". *Experimentelle Pädagogik* 3: 199–210.

Stoddard, G. D. 1929. "An experiment in verbal learning". *Journal of Educational Psychology* 20: 452–457.

Waring, R. 1997. "A study of receptive and productive vocabulary learning from word cards". *Studies in Foreign Languages and Literature* (Notre Dame Seishin University) 21 (1): 94–114.

Appendix

Target words and translations

French target word	Dutch translation	English translation
une hotte	een afzuigkap	a cooker hood
entasser	opstapelen	pile up
un tamis	een zeef	a sieve
sautiller	huppelen	skip
un nain	een dwerg	a dwarf
dévorer	verslinden	devour
un fémur	een dijbeen	a thighbone
rôder	zwerven	roam
une bagarre	een vechtpartij	a fight
gaspiller	verspillen	waste
un phoque	een zeehond	a seal
mâcher	kauwen	chew
un cascadeur	een stuntman	a stunt man
luger	sleeën	sledge
une avalanche	een lawine	an avalanche
verser	gieten	pour

CHAPTER 6

Semantic transfer and development in adult L2 vocabulary acquisition

Nan Jiang

Georgia State University

Abstract

A unique aspect of adult L2 vocabulary acquisition is the separation of lexical and semantic development. Unlike first language acquisition, lexical development in L2 is not necessarily accompanied by substantial semantic development. Instead, adult L2 learners often rely on the pre-existing semantic system. Due to the differences in lexical form-meaning mapping between the learner's L1 and L2, semantic restructuring is often necessary in order for them to use L2 words correctly. Disagreement exists among second language researchers regarding how successful such semantic restructuring can be. Existing research evidence suggests that semantic development is a slow, and often incomplete process in adult L2 learning and that even advanced adult L2 learners continue to rely on their L1 semantic system in L2 use. This study examined semantic transfer and development in a sentence completion test, in which Chinese ESL speakers had to complete sentences with pairs of English words provided. An effort was made to separate positive transfer and semantic development by using English word pairs that are not distinguished in the participants' first language, such as *criterion* and *standard*. The ESL participants showed high error rates in the test, which offers further evidence for incomplete semantic development in adult L2 learning.

1.   Introduction

Learning new words in an L2 is a complicated process involving a variety of sub-processes and tasks. Before a word becomes a part of one's automatic linguistic competence, it has to be recognized as a word, its morphosyntactic and semantic properties have to be learned, and it has to be integrated into one's mental lexicon so that it can be retrieved automatically when needed. One can view L2 vocabulary acquisition as encompassing two dimensions, thus classifying these different tasks and processes into two general categories. The first dimension is primarily concerned with the status of a lexical entry in the mental lexicon, i.e., the retention, consolidation, and automatization of words in the lexicon. Examples of the processes included in this dimension are the initial registration of a word in one's memory, the consolidation or loss of a word as a function of the learning strategies used and frequency of use and practice, the conversion of passive knowledge to productive skills, and the integration of lexical knowledge into one's automatic competence. This dimension is related to the aspects of vocabulary acquisition often referred to as size or breadth (Goulden, Nation, & Read 1990, Laufer, & Nation 1995, Qian 1999, Wesche & Paribakht 1996, Vermeer 2001) and automaticity (Kempe & MacWhinney 1996, Segalowitz 1995, Segalowitz, Segalowitz, & Wood 1998, Segalowitz, Watson, & Segalowitz 1995).

The other dimension is primarily concerned with the content of a lexical entry, i.e., the enrichment, expansion, and refinement of lexical information represented in a lexical entry. It involves processes whereby a learner becomes more knowledgeable about a word, such as the increased knowledge about a word's form properties, as reflected in better pronunciation, or the expansion of a learner's knowledge of a word's morphosyntactic properties, as shown in the correct use of a word in a wider variety of syntactic environment. Semantically, it can mean a more precise understanding of a word's meaning, better knowledge of the semantic differences between an L2 word and its L1 translation or of the relationship between an L2 word and other L2 words, and the expansion from knowing the core meaning to knowing peripheral, figurative, and connotational meanings. This dimension covers much of what has been referred to as depth or richness (Bogaards 2000, Haastrup, & Henriksen 2000, Henriksen 1999, Nation 1990, Qian 1999, Read 1993, Richards 1976, Vermeer 2001, Wesche & Paribakht 1996, Wolter 2001), and organization (Meara 1996, Schmitt & Meara 1997). The latter is included in this dimension because how the L2 lexicon is organized, or how L2 words are related to each other is determined to a great extent by what is represented in the lexical entry.

Among these tasks faced by a learner, knowing the meaning of new words is among the most important because it directly affects whether or not one is able to use a word successfully for communication. At the same time, the understanding of a word's semantic properties, including its core, peripheral,

figurative, connotational meanings, its semantic differences from its L1 translation and other semantically related L2 words, is probably the most challenging
task that many adult L2 learners face. Thus, semantic development deserves
primary attention in L2 vocabulary acquisition research. Unfortunately, even
though the importance of form-meaning mapping and semantic development
has been widely recognized (e.g. Ellis 1997, Paribakht & Wesche 1999, Henriksen 1999), semantic development in L2 has been much neglected in empirical
research. Most L2 vocabulary acquisition studies have focused on the retention
dimension, i.e., on how new word retention is affected by various factors (e.g.
Brown & Perry 1991, Chun & Plass 1996, Fischer 1994, Fraser 1999, Grace 1998,
Hogben & Lawson 1994, Hulstijn 1992, Hulstijn, Hollander, & Greidanus 1996,
Laufer & Hadar 1997, Moore & Surber 1992, Prince 1996, Rott 1999 Sanaoui
1995). In this paper, I will report the findings of an empirical study on semantic
transfer and development and discuss the implications of these findings for
understanding adult L2 vocabulary acquisition and vocabulary teaching.

2.   Stages of L2 semantic development

Getting to know the meaning of new words is no doubt a developmental
process. It can be divided into two stages for most L2 words. One is the initial
understanding of a word's meaning, or the initial mapping of new word forms
to existing meanings or concepts in the learner's mind. This initial form-
meaning mapping is a critical part of word retention and production because a
word without meaning is not likely to be retained for long-term use. The other
is the gradual elaboration and modification of the meanings. This can be a long
and continuous developmental process. We can refer to them as the comprehension stage and the development stage.

2.1   The comprehension stage

This is the initial mapping of lexical form and meaning. It allows a new L2 form
to be linked to higher level semantic or conceptual representations so that it
can be stored and used as a meaningful unit in one's lexicon. A central research
issue at this stage is whether an L2 lexical form is linked to a new meaning
created in the L2 learning process or a meaning or concept that is part of the
learner's pre-existing mental representations. This issue arises of course from
the unique learning condition adult L2 learners face, i.e., they already possess
well established conceptual and lexical systems.

There is some consensus among second language acquisition (SLA) researchers regarding this issue. Many suggest that new L2 words are initially mapped to pre-existing concepts or L1 translations. Ellis (1997) for example pointed out that 'in the first instance at least, the acquisition of L2 words usually involves a mapping of the new word form onto pre-existing conceptual meanings or onto L1 translation equivalents as approximations' (pp. 133–134). Similar views have been expressed by Blum & Levenston (1978), Strick (1980), Ringbom (1983), Giacobbe (1992), and Hall (2002).

I'd like to make two further points about this mapping process. First, the mapping onto the pre-existing L1 translation or meaning, or semantic transfer, is likely to occur as far as there is an existing word or concept that is similar in meaning to the target word, no matter what strategies are used by the teacher to convey the meaning of the new word. In this sense, using L1 translations, pictures, objects, definitions, or context does not make a difference. When the meaning of a new L2 word is understood, it is likely to be understood within the existing semantic or conceptual system. A new concept may emerge only if no such concept is present and the context is powerful enough to help create a new concept. Second, because of the strong links between concepts and L1 words, a link will be formed between an L2 word and its L1 translation once the meaning of the L2 word is understood. This L2-L1 link is established regardless of whether L1 is or is not used in the semanticization process.

It is reasonable to assume that most L2 words do have similar concepts or words in the learner's L1 and thus are initially comprehended within the pre-existing L1 semantic system. For this reason, 'comprehension' is a term more appropriate than 'acquisition', a term sometimes used by some researchers (e.g. Ellis 1995), to refer to the semantic processes involved at this stage.

2.2 The development stage

As pointed out by many researchers (e.g. Hudson 1989, Sonaiya 1991), translation equivalents from two different languages may not always share identical semantic properties and boundaries. Subtle to substantial semantic differences may exist between two translation equivalents. Initial mapping onto an L1 concept or translation equivalent allows an L2 word to be used correctly to some extent. But accurate and idiomatic use of L2 words requires the development of semantic structures that are specific to L2 words. This often involves the restructuring of the semantic content originally transferred from L1.

An important research question in this context is, to what extent is an adult L2 learner able to sustain such semantic restructuring or development so that an L2 word contains semantic content that is comparable to that of native speakers (NSs)? Two opposing views can be found in the literature. Some researchers indicated explicitly or implicitly that with continued exposure to contextualized L2 input, the learner should be able to form new concepts or reorganize semantic elements to form new meanings for L2 words (Blum & Levenston 1978, Giacobbe 1992, Ringbom 1983, Strick 1980). Such restructuring is also allowed in de Groot's distributed model of bilingual conceptual representations, where an L2 word may be connected to a different set of meaning elements from its L1 translation (de Groot 1992, 1993).

An alternative scenario is that this restructuring process may be slow, and in many cases, incomplete. Incomplete restructuring can be a result of limited contextualized exposure to the target language, or learners' sometimes successful use of L2 words based on L1 meanings. As a result, an L2 word remains mapped to a largely L1-based concept. Such possibilities are discussed by Weinreich (1953) who talked about 'habitualized and established' transfer. These possibilities are also explored in Selinker and Lakshmanan's (1992) discussion of the relationship between language transfer and fossilization. In bilingual language processing research, it is also widely assumed that a bilingual's two languages share the same conceptual system (e.g. Dufour & Kroll 1995).

I have made an explicit proposition regarding incomplete semantic development and its causes (Jiang 2000, in press). My argument is that if an L2 word is mapped onto an L1 meaning or concept, the latter will become the mediator of this L2 word in communication. Under many circumstances, the core meaning of an L2 word and its L1 translation are identical and a learner can use an L2 word both receptively and productively without making an error based on the transferred core meaning. Even when the transferred meaning leads to an error, such errors are not always noticed by or pointed out to the learner. Thus, contrary to the belief that increased exposure will help extract and create new meanings, it will strengthen the connections between the L2 word and transferred L1 meaning because of repeated co-activation of the two. Restructuring will successfully take place only when the conflict between the transferred semantic understanding and the understanding obliged by the context is powerful enough to override the transferred meaning, sometimes accompanied by a communication breakdown. However, such contexts may be available for some words, but not others.

These two stages are likely to overlap in some way. For example, comprehension can be considered as part of development. However, the two stages can be distinguished on the basis of the primary tasks faced by the learner at these stages and their outcomes. The primary task at the comprehension stage is to understand the core meaning of a new word within the pre-existing semantic system or map a new word form onto a pre-existing concept so that a word-meaning linkage can be formed. As a result, the word is now linked to one's existing lexical and semantic representations and can be registered in the learner's long-term memory or mental lexicon. At the development stage, the learner faces the continuous task of checking the original semantic content of a word against meanings of the word as shown in different contexts for match and mismatch. The outcome of this process may be the consolidation of the original form-meaning links, or the emergence of an L2 word with modified and fine-tuned semantic content. This is also the stage when L2 learners are more likely to adopt strategies and processes of semantic development similar to those involved in L1 semantic development.

3.   Some research evidence and potential limitations

How far semantic development can go in adult L2 vocabulary acquisition is ultimately an empirical issue. A small number of studies have specifically focused their investigation on semantic development by either examining lexical performance by advanced learners or following changes of semantic knowledge over a period of time. Some of these studies (Ijaz 1986, Schmitt 1998, Strick 1980) employed tasks such as sentence completion, semantic judgment, and one-on-one interview. Others (Jiang 2002, in press) adopted an online semantic judgment task in which participants' reaction times were measured.

3.1   Earlier studies

In one of the earlier studies, Ijaz (1986) adopted two tests, semantic relatedness judgment and sentence completion. Five groups of advanced speakers of English as a second language (ESL) with various L1 backgrounds and ESL learning experiences and a group of NSs of English were tested. Six English words and phrases with meaning overlaps, *on, upon, onto, on top of, over,* and *above,* were the focus of the study. In the semantic relatedness test, participants were given two words and asked to indicate how similar one word was to the other.

In the sentence completion task, participants were given sentences with one word missing and asked to decide which one of the words provided fits in the context. Both tests were semantic in nature as one's performance was directly determined by how the participants understood the meaning of the target words. The rationale of the study was to compare the performance of non-native speakers (NNSs) and that of NSs in order to know if NNSs possessed semantic structures of these words similar to those of NS.

The results were mixed. There were both similarities and differences between the performance of NNSs and NSs. In the semantic relatedness test, 49.3% of the ratings from NNSs were significantly different from those of NSs. In the sentence completion test, 15 out of 28 insertions were significantly different between NSs and NNSs as a whole. An analysis of NNSs' deviant responses in both tests showed a clear influence of their first languages. Ijaz concluded that 'native language conceptual patterns appear to be powerful determinants of the meaning ascribed to L2 words and they seem to be very rigid and difficult to permeate' (p. 447). In another study in which a similar semantic relatedness test was employed, Strick (1980) found a similar L1 transfer effect on address terms among Iranian ESL speakers.

In one of the few longitudinal studies of L2 vocabulary acquisition, Schmitt (1998) tested four ESL graduate students from different background languages in three sessions in a 18-month period. Part of the test was to find out, in one-on-one interviews, how many meaning senses of 11 target words they knew productively and receptively. These 11 words had a total of 61 meaning senses. During the interview, the participants were first asked to provide the meanings for each target word. The correct responses were considered as an indication of their productive knowledge of the lexical meanings of the target words. The participants were then given prompts for triggering additional meanings after they had produced all the meanings they could. These prompted responses were considered as an indication of their receptive knowledge. The meaning senses not provided with a prompt were considered unknown senses. The rationale of the study was to track semantic development by comparing the number of senses in the three different categories that were provided by the participants across the three sessions. The results showed that 'the vast majority of meaning senses stayed at the same state of knowledge' (p. 300) over the period of testing. If the participants did not know a particular sense of an English word at the beginning of the study, in most cases (72%), they had no knowledge of that sense after a year of living and studying in a graduate program at a British university. The results led Schmitt to conclude that 'knowledge of meaning senses has a certain amount of inertia and does not change easily. This is probably to be expected, as acquiring a large number of meaning senses quickly and easily might be too auspicious to hope for, at least in L2 learning' (p. 300).

A potential limitation in these studies is a lack of an adequate means to separate authentic semantic development from L1 influence or other factors. In Strick (1980) and Ijaz (1986), errors and discrepancies between NNSs and NSs performance were often attributed to the influence of L1. Native-like performance by NNSs was explicitly or implicitly considered as an indication of semantic development. However, the latter can also be a result of positive semantic transfer. Similarly, it is difficult to tell whether the increase in the number of meanings recalled by Schmitt's (1998) participants was a result of semantic development or variable success in providing meanings across different sessions. It was not impossible for the participants to report meaning senses based on their L1. As the participants might not be able to recall all meanings of a word in one session, the procedure left room for the increase in recalled meanings in later sessions. A further problem was related to the fact that the participants were given unknown meanings at earlier sessions. Under these circumstances, the increase in recalled meanings may have reflected either an improved success in L1-based meaning recall in a later session as a result of repeated tests, or the explicit explanation of unknown meanings in earlier sessions, rather than authentic L2 semantic development in natural settings.

3.2   Two recent reaction-time studies

To examine authentic semantic development, it is crucially important to control the effect of positive semantic transfer. If possible, one also wants to minimize the effect of explicit semantic knowledge obtained through formal instruction because such knowledge should not be equated with semantic knowledge that is developed in the process of communication and can be automatically retrieved in spontaneous communication.

In an effort to control the influence of L1 and explicit knowledge, I adopted an online semantic judgment task coupled with the use of L2 words that shared or did not share the same L1 translations. In this online semantic judgment task, participants were presented with two L2 words simultaneously on a computer monitor. Their task was to decide whether the two words were related in meaning. They responded by pressing one of two buttons, one for *Yes*, and the other for *No*. They were required to respond as quickly and accurately as possible. Their responses and response times were recorded by a computer.

Several mental processes are involved in performing such a task. One is to recognize the two L2 words. Then the meaning for each word must be retrieved and compared. If shared semantic elements are found, or some overlap of semantic space is identified, a positive response is reached and executed. Otherwise, a negative response is given.

It is reasonable to assume that participants' response time is determined in part by the semantic relationship between the two words. Specifically, one can predict that a *Yes* response should be given faster than a *No* response. This is because a positive response can be given as soon as a shared element is found, but a *No* response can be given only after all semantic meanings are retrieved and compared. One can further predict that the degree of semantic relatedness is negatively correlated with response time. More related word pairs will lead to shorter response times, because it is easier to identify a shared meaning element when two words are more closely related than when they are not.

Let us imagine that we have two sets of English word pairs that are equally related. They are also similar in frequency and length, two variables that we know affect reaction times. We give these two sets of items to NSs of English and ask them to complete an online semantic judgment task. Based on the second prediction above, they should show comparable response times on the two sets.

Now imagine that the English word pairs in one set share the same Chinese translation, and the items in the other set do not. We present these items in a random order to a group of Chinese ESL speakers and ask them to complete the same online semantic judgment task. What would be the prediction regarding their response times on the two sets?

The prediction one makes depends on one's view on whether substantial semantic development has occurred in these Chinese ESL speakers. If one believes that substantial semantic development has occurred and successful restructuring of semantic content of these L2 words has taken place as a result, then one should predict similar performance by these Chinese ESL speakers as compared to native English speakers. That is, they will show no difference in reaction time on the two sets of items.

However, if one believes that these English words are still mapped to the L1 concepts or meanings, a very different prediction has to be made. Following this view, the word pairs that share the same Chinese translation, such as *problem* and *question* (both translated into *wenti* in Chinese), or same-translation pairs, are mapped to the same concept or semantic structure. Thus, their semantic content is in principle identical. The word pairs in the other set, such as *interrupt* and *interfere* (translated into *daduan* and *ganrao* respectively), are mapped to two different concepts or semantic structures. Thus, there is less semantic overlap. Based on our discussion of the relationship between degree of semantic relatedness and response time, one would predict that Chinese ESL speakers will take less time to respond to the same-translation pairs than the different-translation pairs.

Thus, L2 speakers' reaction times on the same-translation and different-translation pairs can be used as an indication of whether L2 words have gone through substantial semantic development or are still mapped to the L1 meaning. The predictions discussed above are summarized below:

Prediction 1: Both NSs and NNSs will respond to related items faster than unrelated items.

Prediction 2: NSs will show no difference in response time on two sets of English word pairs that are matched in length, frequency, and semantic relatedness.

Prediction 3: If L2 processing is mediated by L1 semantic structures, NNSs will respond to English word pairs that share the same L1 translation faster than different-translation pairs, even if the two sets of items are matched in length, frequency, and semantic relatedness.

In two separate studies (Jiang 2002, in press), advanced Chinese and Korean ESL speakers were tested in the online semantic judgment task. In both studies, the test materials included a set of related English words pairs and a set of unrelated English word pairs of the same frequency range. Among the related pairs, half of them shared the same translation in the participants' first language, and the other half did not. The materials were constructed separately for the two groups of ESL speakers. A same-translation pair for Chinese ESL speakers shared the same Chinese translation. A same-translation pair for Korean ESL speakers shared the same Korean translation (see Jiang 2002 for more detailed information about material construction). Participants were tested individually on a randomized list of 128 English word pairs presented on a computer monitor. Their response latencies were recorded by a computer. The results of these experiments are summarized in Table 1.

As is clear from the table, for both NNSs and NSs, unrelated items typically took more than 100 milliseconds (ms) longer to respond to than related items. Thus, the first predication was supported. But more importantly, a clear and

Table 1. Non-native and native speakers' reaction times (in milliseconds) and error rates (in percentages, in parentheses) on same-translation, different-translation, and unrelated L2 word pairs.

| | The Chinese Study | | | | The Korean Study | | | |
| | NNs | | NSs | | NNs | | NSs | |
	related	unrelated	related	unrelated	related	unrelated	related	unrelated
Same-translation	1075 (7.8)		886 (11.3)		1549 (7.7)		1058 (8.7)	
Different-translation	1174 (14.5)	1318 (12.6)	895 (7.0)	1133 (10.9)	1662 (13.3)	1797 (8.7)	1074 (8.1)	1152 (11.4)
Differences	99* (6.7)		9 (4.3)		113* (5.6)		16 (0.6)	

* significant at .01 level.

consistent pattern of results emerged for the related items. NSs of English in both studies showed no difference in reaction time on the same-translation and different-translation pairs. Their performance confirms that the two sets of test items were matched in semantic relatedness, i.e., the same-translation pairs and the different-translation pairs were equally related. It also supported the second prediction.

The NNS participants, however, produced a consistent same-translation effect in reaction time. Both Chinese and Korean ESL speakers responded to the English word pairs that shared the same L1 translation approximately 100 ms faster than English pairs that did not, which supported the third prediction. This finding is noteworthy particularly when we consider the fact that the same-translation and different-translation pairs were equally related, as determined by native English speakers in the pre-test and by native English speakers' reaction times in the studies. The same-translation effect observed in L2 speakers in the absence of such effect in L1 speakers suggests that L2 words are still mapped to L1 semantic structures for these proficient L2 speakers. When two L2 words share the same L1 translation, they also share the same semantic content, which leads to faster response time. These findings are consistent with those of Strick (1980) and Ijaz (1986). They all suggest L1 semantic structures continue to mediate L2 word use in proficient L2 speakers.

Furthermore, these findings offer more compelling evidence for the continued role of semantic transfer because of the two advantages of the research method adopted in these studies. The first advantage is the use of semantically related same-translation and different-translation pairs. The identification and use of these two types of word pairs offer us a unique opportunity to isolate L2 words' relationship with L1 as the only variable for examination. By observing how these two types of L2 word pairs behave in a controlled environment, one is able to reveal and pin down the role of L1 or L1 semantic structures in L2 processing with a high level of certainty and objectivity.

Second, because of the online nature of the task and the emphasis on speed, participants are less likely to pause and consider a test item in detail before they make a judgment. This means that they rely more on their intuition about the target words than explicit lexical knowledge. If one looks at their response times, which were within the range of 1000 to 1700 ms for related pairs, it is reasonable to conclude that their performance was not affected by deliberate thinking and conscious application of explicit knowledge. Not contaminated by explicit knowledge, such reaction time data may better reflect how semantic information is represented in the mind of L2 speakers.

4.   The revised sentence completion task and findings

The online semantic judgment task offers a unique approach to the study of L2 semantic representation and development. The use of participants' reaction times as data allows one to uncover subtle differences in learners' observable behaviour for understanding invisible mental representation and processes. Such lab-based research also has the advantage of better controlled intervening variables and its findings are as a result more consistent and replicatable. However, the interpretation of the findings from such research does depend on a number of assumptions. For example, we have to assume that participants' response time in such a task is determined largely by the degree of semantic overlap between two words, not by something else. This in turn assumes that semantic content is retrieved and compared in performing the task. While these are reasonable assumptions and virtually all research on mental representations and human cognition relies to some extent on assumptions and inferences, further converging evidence from a more 'direct' task will no doubt help enhance the validity of the interpretation of such online findings.

In this section, I report the results of a study that used a revised version of the sentence completion task used by Ijaz (1986). The purpose of the study was to explore adult L2 learners' semantic representation and development by directly observing how they use words in context.

In Ijaz (1986), a sentence completion task was used in which participants had to choose one of the six semantically related words to complete a sentence. Through the analysis of deviant and incorrect use of the words, Ijaz found that the participants' performance was influenced by their L1. Correct responses were often implicitly considered as reflecting semantic development. However, correct responses could be a result of positive transfer too. There was little built in the design to differentiate authentic semantic development and positive semantic transfer. Furthermore, participants were free to use explicit lexical knowledge.

To overcome these problems, I constructed testing materials that make the use of explicit knowledge or positive L1 transfer less likely. I chose pairs of English words that shared the same Chinese translation and whose differences are subtle and often hard to verbally describe, such as *criterion* and *standard*, *accurate* and *precise*. If a Chinese speaker relies on L1 semantic structures in using these words, he or she is likely to use them interchangeably, thus subjecting them to errors, because no such distinctions are made in Chinese. For the same reason, we can also rule out the possibility of positive semantic transfer if a Chinese ESL speaker does use these words correctly. Furthermore, based on my many years of experience learning and teaching English in China, the differences between these words are seldom explained in instruction simply because they are difficult to describe. This difficulty can be easily confirmed if one brings a pair of such words to a native English speaker for explanation of differences. For this reason, an L2 learner is not likely to be explicitly taught about the differences between such words. Thus, one is able to use instances of incorrect use of these words as evidence of lack of semantic development, as Ijaz did. More importantly, consistent correct use of such words offers more compelling evidence for semantic development because it cannot benefit from either positive L1 transfer or formal instruction.

4.1   Method

4.1.1   *Materials*

For the present project, six pairs of English words were selected. They were *criterion-standard, complicated-complex, accurate-precise, safe-secure, insist-persist, doubt-suspect*. The two members of each pair can be translated into the same Chinese translation. An important step in developing test materials for the present purpose is to identify a set of sentences for which native English speakers agree which word is appropriate. This turned out to be much more difficult than anticipated. As a first step, 10 sentences containing each of the 12 words were selected from the Bank of English corpus. Consideration was given to sentence length, word familiarity, and content familiarity while selecting these sentences so that they offered an adequate context for word choice and were understandable to the participants to be tested. The 12 target words were then taken out of the 120 sentences, which were given to 10 native speaking college students, along with the missing words, for example *insist* and *persist*. They were asked to decide whether one (and which one), or both of the given words fitted in the sentence context. There was much disagreement among the 10 informants. Eventually, 20 sentences were identified for which at least 9 out of 10 NSs agreed as to which word was appropriate, 4 for *insist-persist*, 4 for *doubt-suspect*, 3 for *safe-secure*, 4 for *accurate-precise*, 3 for *criterion-standard*, and 2 for *complicated-complex*. These sentences became the test materials for the present study (see the appendix).

4.1.2 *Participants*

Ten advanced Chinese ESL speakers and ten native English speakers took the test. All participants were studying at Georgia State University at the time of testing. All NNSs were graduate students from mainland China. Some English learning background information obtained from a questionnaire administered to the NNSs participants before the test is summarized in Table 2.

4.1.3 *Procedures*

The participants were tested individually. They signed a consent form and completed an English learning questionnaire before they were given the test. During the test, the participants were asked to read a sentence and then select

Table 2. Non-native speaker participants' age, the age they started learning English, years of formal English instruction, years of residence in the USA, and English proficiency self rating scores (1 = minimum, 10 = near-native).

	N	Minimum	Maximum	Mean	S. D.
Age	10	27	38	31.30	2.983
Starting age	10	10	15	12.30	1.494
Years of formal instruction	10	8	20	12.80	4.077
Years of residence in USA	10	1	5	2.32	1.386
Self Rating: Speaking	10	4	8	6.20	1.398
Self Rating: Listening	10	5	9	7.00	1.155
Self Rating: Reading	10	6	9	7.60	.843
Self Rating: Writing	10	5	8	7.00	.943

one from among the four answers provided. The test materials contained sentences organized by word pairs. The following example, which served as an example in the test, illustrates what a test item looked like:

1 = Only 'rejected' is appropriate
2 = Only 'refused' is appropriate
3 = Both words are appropriate
4 = not sure

The Government ___2___ demands   least confident   most confident
last night from Sinn Fein to call   1   2   3   4 ⑤ 6   7   8   9   10
immediate all-party talks.

They were given as much time as they needed to complete the test. After they completed the sentences, they were also asked to rate the level of difficulty for them to distinguish these words on a 1-to-7 scale, and provide a brief written description, in Chinese, of the differences between the two members of the six pairs of words.

4.2   Results

The correct answer for each sentence was identified based on the results of the pre-test and was then used in judging the performance of the participants. Given the procedures taken in selecting the sentences, NSs were expected to be highly consistent among themselves in their answers both as a group or individually. This was indeed the case. Their average accuracy rate was 94%. No NSs had an error rate higher than 10%. No pair of words produced an error rate higher than 10% among NSs either. These results showed that the sentences adopted in the test provided a clear context for differentiating the test words. They also offered a baseline for measuring native-like meaning-related lexical performance in the test.

The Chinese ESL speakers' performance would be determined by the level of successful semantic development and restructuring. If substantial semantic development had occurred and they had successfully restructured their semantic structures, one expects them to maintain a high level of accuracy. Otherwise, they would make a considerable number of errors.

4.2.1 Difficulty ratings and written descriptions
The Chinese ESL speakers considered these pairs to be quite different in how difficult it was for them to distinguish. Their average rating score on a 7-point

scale for each pair is provided below, in ascending order (1=very easy, 7=very difficult): *doubt-suspect* (3.1), *insist-persist* (3.6), *safe-secure*(3.9), *accurate-precise*(4.2), *criterion-standard*(4.3), *complicated-complex*(4.8).

Their written descriptions generally failed to capture the differences. Out of a total of 60 cases (six pairs by 10 participants), there were 23 cases where they simply provided different translations for the pairs, without being able to further elaborate on the differences. The translations they provided could not show the semantic differences. There were five instances when they either wrote 'I don't know' or left the space blank. When they did try to describe the differences, their descriptions were usually not correct or sufficient to show the difference. For example, one participant described the difference between *complicated* and *complex* by saying the former had to do with thoughts and feelings and the latter had to do with matters. Another participant explained that *precise* was used with a meter and equipment and *accurate* was used to modify language and expressions. While this explanation is correct to some extent in itself, it is too simple to reveal the real differences between the two words. Still another considered *criterion* to be more formal than *standard*. In the small number of cases where correct descriptions were given, they were for *doubt-suspect* and *insist-persist*. Four participants were able to point out that the speaker was negative about the likelihood of the statement following *doubt*, but positive in the case of *suspect*. Two participants were able to explain that *insist* was related to one's opinion and attitude and *persist* was about action. A third participant was able to provide two Chinese expressions that showed the difference in the latter pair to some extent.

The participants' ratings and descriptions suggest two things. First, it is difficult for Chinese ESL speakers to verbally describe the differences of these words. Out of a total of 60 instances, only 7 successful descriptions were given. This difficulty confirms the selection of the right test words as I wanted to minimize the involvement of formal knowledge. Second, there are some variations among these pairs in terms of difficulty. Both the ratings and descriptions suggest *doubt-suspect* and *insist-persist* are easier than other pairs.

4.2.2 *Sentence completion scores*

In coding the NNSs' responses in the sentence completion test, a correct answer was first established based on NSs' performance. Any response that was different from the correct answer was considered an error, including the answer of 'not sure'. The incorrect responses were then collapsed across sentences of the same word pair. The number and percentage of incorrect responses for each word pair from the ten NNSs are presented in Table 3.

Table 3. Number and percentage of incorrect responses for six pairs of English words by ten advanced non-native speakers in the sentence completion test.

WORD PAIR	PARTICIPANTS										Total	%
	A	B	C	D	E	F	G	H	I	J		
insist persist (n=4)	0	0	2	1	2	0	0	0	0	2	7	18%
safe secure (n=3)	3	1	2	0	1	1	1	0	1	0	10	33%
doubt suspect (n=4)	1	3	1	0	3	2	2	0	0	2	14	35%
accurate precise (n=4)	1	1	0	1	2	3	1	0	1	4	14	35%
criterion standard (n=3)	0	1	1	2	3	2	1	0	1	2	13	43%
complicated complex (n=2)	0	2	1	2	2	2	0	2	1	0	12	60%
Total (n=20)	5	8	7	6	13	10	5	2	4	10	70	
%	25%	40%	35%	30%	65%	50%	25%	10%	20%	50%		35%

As is clear from Table 3, most Chinese ESL speakers did better than chance effect which would produce an error rate of 67% if they chose from the first three responses randomly. At the same time, their accuracy rate was far below the minimum of 90% accuracy of native English speakers. The overall accuracy rate was 65%, compared to NSs' 94%. Eight participants fell between 20% to 50% in error rate. One participant produced an error rate close to chance. Another participant, H, achieved a 90% accuracy.

An examination of the average error rate by word pair suggests a similar pattern. The error rates for most pairs were much lower than chance effect. At the same time, not a single pair of English words can be said to have been semantically acquired when one takes the ten NNSs' performance as a whole. The pair that received the highest accuracy rate, thus was the easiest, was *insist-persist*. The most difficult one was *complicated-complex*. Overall, the accuracy rates for the test words were in line with the difficulty rating scores provided by the same group of participants. They were correlated at .73, p=.05.

These findings are consistent with those from previous studies. Some level of semantic development seems to have occurred in these adult L2 learners. This is shown in this study in their better-than-chance accuracy rates. Because the test materials involved words that are not distinguished in their L1 and for which minimum explicit knowledge is available, one cannot attribute their performance to positive transfer or the involvement of explicit knowledge obtained from instruction or feedback. Thus, the observed accuracy level should be viewed as truly reflecting the level of semantic development that has occurred. On the other hand, with the exception of one person, these participants still have considerable difficulty in successfully distinguishing many of these words, which demonstrates the limitation of their semantic development. Furthermore, the lack of substantial semantic development does not seem to be related to a limited exposure to the target language. The average length of residence (LOR) of these participants was 2.3 years, which is not a short period of time. Furthermore, the four participants who had the longest LOR in the USA, C: 3 years, E: 4 years, G: 5 years, I: 3 years, did no better than those with a shorter LOR.

5.   What makes semantic development difficult?

What, then, makes semantic development so difficult? We can attempt to answer this question by first understanding what is needed for a learner to start the restructuring process. If we assume that an L2 word is first associated with an L1 translation or concept, as has been suggested by many researchers (Blum & Levenston 1978, Ellis 1997, Giacobbe 1992, Hall 2002, Jiang 2000, Ringbom 1983, Strick 1980,), at least the following two conditions have to be met in order for the semantic restructuring process to take place:

(1)   There is an indication of a mismatch between an L2 word and its L1 translation in meaning. Such an indication can be explicit, as in the form of overt correction from an instructor or interlocutor. Or it can be less direct, e.g. in an expression of confusion on the part of an interlocutor, or any other sign of unsuccessful communication.

(2)   Information is available regarding exactly how the L2 word is semantically different from the L1 concept. This information may come from direct correction and explanation, or from context.

However, the needed indication of semantic mismatch is often unavailable to an L2 learner for various reasons. The most important reason is perhaps that there is no semantic mismatch involved in the first place. While it is true that translation equivalents rarely share identical meanings, it is also true that they often share core meanings. Take the last five words in the preceding sentence for example. Their Chinese translations, *tameng* (they), *jinchang* (often), *fengxiang* (share), *hexing* (core), and *yishi* (meanings), have meanings very similar to those of the English words. One can replace these English words with the Chinese translations to form a Chinese sentence without changing much of its meaning.

As a result of such semantic overlap, an L2 word can often be successfully used with L1 meanings. We can further assume that a word is more often used with its core meanings than peripheral meanings. Thus, successful use of L2 words based on transferred L1 meanings may account for a majority of the instances of L2 word use.

Now imagine a situation in which some semantic mismatch is involved. Take one of the word pairs used in the present study for example. *Standard* and *criterion* share the same Chinese translation *biaozhun*. Thus, *biaozhun* refers to a broader concept covering the meanings of both English words. In this regard, *standard* or *criterion* does not match the meanings of *biaozhun* completely. In a Chinese ESL speaker's receptive use of English, each word will activate all its semantic elements contained in the broader L1 concept, making it difficult for a Chinese NS to notice any semantic differences. Because *biaozhun* has all the senses for the two English words, these L2 words are unlikely to cause mis-communication or comprehension difficulty. Thus, no indication of any semantic mismatch will come to the learner's attention.

In productive L2 use, it is likely that an L2 speaker may use such words incorrectly due to semantic mismatch, thus creating an error, an awkward sentence, or confusion. Such incorrect use of L2 words caused by L1 semantic transfer, even in advanced learners, is well documented in the SLA literature (e.g. Hyltenstam 1992, Lennon 1991, 1996, Martin 1984, Sonaiya 1991, Swan 1997). However, whether such misuses lead to a learner's conscious awareness of the semantic mismatch is another matter. Obvious word choice errors such as 'He bit himself in the *language*' (Ringbom 1983: 208) and 'I go to the *oven* in the morning to buy bread' (Zughoul 1991: 50) may trigger negative feedback. However, many other less dramatic errors may often be ignored. For example, the use of *criterion* in a context where *standard* is more appropriate may create an awkward sentence, but the meaning can be understood in context without much difficulty. Thus, L2 speakers may not always be made aware of such incorrect uses.

A further example of a semantic mismatch going unnoticed in L2 produc-tion can be found in the interesting semantic difference between the English word *meeting* and its Chinese equivalent *huiyi*. They differ in the number of people involved in the activity. Two people can have a meeting in English; but it takes at least three people to have a *huiyi* in Chinese; two people meet to have a *tianhua* (talk). A Chinese ESL speaker with a 'Chinese' understanding of the word *meeting* may use the expression 'have a talk' in place of 'have a meeting' without making any overt errors.

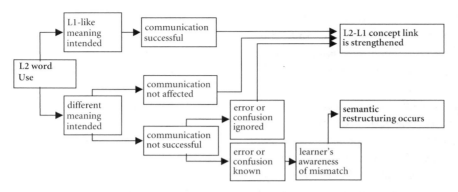

Figure 1. Different circumstances of L2 word use and their effect on semantic development.

The above examples and discussion show that in probably a majority of cases, L2 words can be used successfully based on transferred meanings, or used incorrectly, but without negative feedback provided to the L2 learner. Under such circumstances, L2 word use will only strengthen the connection between an L2 word and the transferred L1 meaning, contrary to the belief that increased L2 use will help semantic development, a point already made in Jiang (2000).

Semantic restructuring does occur, specially when an L2 learner is aware of a semantic mismatch between an L2 word and its transferred meaning and knows what the differences are. This can be the work of a powerful context. For example, the use of the word *meeting* to refer to a gathering of only two people will be a powerful example to demonstrate to an L2 listener the difference between this word and its Chinese translation and the nature of the difference. Semantic restructuring can also occur as a result of repeated exposure to L2 words in a differentiating context, in a process almost associative in nature. Multiple exposures to the use of *doubt* in a context that indicates a negative view of the likelihood of an activity will help differentiate it from *suspect* that is used in a positive context. However, the use of *meeting* to refer to two people may be hard to come by. Many exposures of contextualized use of *doubt* and *suspect* may be required before a learner finally picks up the difference. L2 learners may also differ in their ability to pick up such differences from context. Words may also differ in the extent such differentiating context is available, which may explain the variable accuracy rates on different test items in the present study. Context may be less helpful for differentiating words such as *complicated* and *complex.* Thus, semantic restructuring may be affected not only by the amount of exposure, but also by the quality of context, learner factors, and word factors. As a result, it can be slow and unpredictable. Figure 1 illustrates some circumstances that may contribute to the strengthening of initial L2-L1 concept mappings and semantic restructuring.

6.   Conclusion: importance of instructional intervention

The results of the present study and the previous ones reviewed earlier show that natural exposure alone may not provide enough impetus for semantic restructuring and development. I attempted to explain why this is the case in the preceding section. I'd like to argue in this context that instructional intervention has an important role to play in helping learners overcome plateaus in semantic development. However, effective semantics-oriented vocabulary instruction depends on a clear understanding of the similarities and differences between the two languages in terms of both individual words and the overall semantic/lexical system. At the word level, an instructor may not even realize the difficulty learners face in learning many L2 words such as *criterion* and *standard* without taking learners' L1 into consideration. Adequate knowledge of the cross-language differences between the English *meeting* and the Chinese *huiyi*, on the other hand, allows an instructor to develop effective materials that enable learners to see the difference in context.

On a macro level, system-wide differences may exist in the pattern of meaning lexicalization across languages. For example, there is an interesting difference between English and Chinese in the naming of concrete objects. Object names are lexicalized often following a functional principle in Chinese, i.e., objects that serve the same function often share the same name or word. In English, on the other hand, objects are often named by their shape. For example, Chinese has a single term *bi* to refer to all tools for writing, which in English can have different names such as *pen*, *brush*, *crayon*, and *marker*. Similarly, English has different words for a ruler, a tape measure, a yardstick, objects that are of very different shapes. But Chinese has a single term, *chi*, to refer to them all as they all serve the same function of measuring length. The same is true for *binocular* and *telescope* which are both called *wangyuanji* in Chinese, as they serve the same function. On the other hand, English often uses a single name for objects of the same shape, even though their functions are completely different. Thus, *rail* refers to a long, thin, and hard object, as train tracks or the object along staircases that people can hold on to. As the two objects serve different functions, they have different Chinese names, *tiegui* and *fushou* (literally 'iron track' and 'hold hand'), respectively. The same is true for the English word *tile*, which can be used to refer to different thin, rectangular- or square-shaped objects that serve different functions. But the Chinese translation, *wa*, only refers to the object that is used to cover the roof. Such analysis will no doubt help learners understand how concepts are lexicalized differently in different languages and thus facilitate their semantic restructuring process. In this sense, the old wisdom of contrastive analysis (e.g. Lado 1957) is still highly relevant in today's L2 vocabulary instruction.

Note

1. An effort was made to exclude sentences for which participants could identify the right word based on collocation rather than meaning. However, at least one sentence, Sentence 11 in the appendix, may be problematic in this regard. The blank in the sentence was followed by the preposition *on* which made *insist* a better choice than *persist* based on collocation knowledge. The presence of such sentences could have enhanced some participants' performance in the test, which means their level of semantic development could be lower than what their performance in the test indicated (if one does not consider collocation as related to semantic properties).

References

Blum, S., & Levenston, E. A. 1978. "Universals of lexical simplification". *Language Learning* 28: 399–415.

Bogaards, P. 2000. "Testing L2 vocabulary knowledge at a high level: The case of the Euralex French tests". *Applied Linguistics* 21: 490–516.

Brown, T. S., & Perry, F. L.Jr. 1991. "A comparison of three learning strategies for ESL vocabulary acquisition". *TESOL Quarterly* 25: 655–670.

Chun, D. M., & Plass, J. L. 1996. "Effects of multimedia annotations on vocabulary acquisition". *Modern Language Journal* 80: 183–198.

de Groot, A. M. B. 1992. "Bilingual lexical representation: A closer look at conceptual representations". In *Orthography, phonology, morphology, and meaning*, R. Frost & L. Katz (eds), 389–412. Amsterdam, Netherlands: North-Holland.

de Groot, A. M. B. 1993. "Word-type effects in bilingual processing tasks: Support for a mixed representational system". In *The bilingual lexicon*, R. Schreuder & B. Weltens (eds), 27–51. Amsterdam: John Benjamins.

Dufour, R. & Kroll, J. F. 1995. "Matching words to concepts in two languages: a test of the concept mediation model of bilingual representation". *Memory and Cognition* 23: 166–180.

Ellis, N. 1997. "Vocabulary acquisition: word structure, collocation, word-class, and meaning". In *Vocabulary: description, acquisition and pedagogy*, N. Schmitt, & M. McCarthy (eds), 122–139. Cambridge: Cambridge University Press.

Ellis, R. 1995. "Modified oral input and the acquisition of word meanings". *Applied Linguistics* 16: 409–441.

Fischer, U. 1994. "Learning words from context and dictionaries: an experimental comparison". *Applied Psycholinguistics* 15: 551–574.

Fraser, C. A. 1999. "Lexical processing strategy use and vocabulary learning through reading". *Studies in Second Language Acquisition* 21: 225–241.

Giacobbe, J. 1992. "A cognitive view of the role of l1 in the l2 acquisition process". *Second Language Research* 8: 232–250.

Goulden, R., Nation, P., and Read, J. 1990. "How Large Can a Receptive Vocabulary Be?". *Applied Linguistics* 11: 341–363.

Grace, C. A. 1998. "Retention of word meanings inferred from context and sentence-level translations: implications for the design of beginning-level call software". *Modern Language Journal* 82: 533–544.

Haastrup, K., and Henriksen, B. 2000. "Vocabulary acquisition: acquiring depth of knowledge through network building". *International Journal of Applied Linguistics* 10: 221–240.

Hall, C. J. 2002. "The automatic cognate form assumption: evidence for the parasitic model of vocabulary acquisition". *IRAL* 40: 69–87.

Henriksen, B. 1999. "Three dimensions of vocabulary development". *Studies in Second Language Acquisition* 21: 303–317.

Hogben, D., & Lawson, M. J. 1994. "Keyword and multiple elaboration strategies for vocabulary acquisition in foreign language learning". *Contemporary Educational Psychology* 19: 367–376.

Hudson, W. 1989. "Semantic theory and L2 lexical development". In *Linguistic perspectives on second language acquisition*, S. Gass & J. Schachter (eds), 222–238. Cambridge: Cambridge University Press.

Hulstijn, J. H. 1992. "Retention of inferred and given word meanings: experiments in incidental vocabulary learning". In *Vocabulary and Applied Linguistics*, P. J. L. Arnaud & H. Béjoint (eds), 113–125. London: MacMillan Academic and Professional Ltd.

Hulstijn, J. H., Hollander, M., and Greidanus, T. 1996. "Incidental vocabulary learning by advanced foreign language students: the influence of marginal glosses, dictionary use, and reoccurrence of unknown words". *Modern Language Journal* 80: 327–339.

Hyltenstam, K. 1992. "Non-native features of near-native speakers: on the ultimate attainment of childhood L2 learners". In *Cognitive processing in bilinguals*, R. J. Harris (ed), 351–390. Amsterdam, Netherlands: Elsevier Science Publishers B. V.

Ijaz, I. H. 1986. "Linguistic and cognitive determinants of lexical acquisition in a second language". *Language Learning* 36: 401–451.

Jiang, N. 2000. "Lexical representation and development in a second language". *Applied Linguistics* 21: 47–77.

Jiang, N. 2002. "Form-meaning mapping in vocabulary acquisition in a second language". *Studies in Second Language Acquisition* 24: 617–637.

Jiang, N. In press. "Semantic transfer and its implications for vocabulary teaching in a second language". *Modern Language Journal* 88 (3).

Kempe, V., & MacWhinney, B. 1996. "The crosslinguistic assessment of foreign language vocabulary learning". *Applied Psycholinguistics* 17: 149–183.

Lado, R. 1957. *Linguistics across cultures*. Ann Arbor: University of Michigan Press.

Laufer, B., & Nation, P. 1995. "Vocabulary size and use: lexical richness in l2 written production". *Applied Linguistics* 16: 307–322.

Laufer, B., & Hadar, L. 1997. "Assessing the effectiveness of monolingual, bilingual, and "bilingualised" dictionaries in the comprehension and production of new words". *Modern Language Journal* 81: 189–196.

Lennon, P. 1991. "Error and the very advanced learner". *IRAL* 29: 31–44.

Lennon, P. 1996. "Getting `easy' words wrong at the advanced level". *IRAL* 34: 23–36.

Martin, M. 1984. "Advanced vocabulary teaching: the problem of synonyms". *Modern Language Journal* 68: 130–137.

Meara, P. 1996. "The dimensions of lexical competence". In *Performance and competence in second language acquisition,* G. Brown, K. Malmkjaer, and J. Williams, (eds), 35–53. Cambridge: Cambridge University Press.

Moore, J. C., & Surber, J. R. 1992. "Effects of context and keyword methods on second language vocabulary acquisition". *Contemporary Educational Psychology* 17: 286–292.

Nation, I. S. P. 1990. *Teaching and Learning Vocabulary*. New York: Newbury House.

Paribakht, T. S., & Wesche, M. 1999. "Reading and "incidental" l2 vocabulary acquisition: an introspective study of lexical inferencing". *Studies in Second Language Acquisition* 21: 195–224.

Prince, P. 1996. "Second language vocabulary learning: the role of context versus translations as a function of proficiency". *Modern Language Journal* 80: 478–493.

Qian, D. D. 1999. "Assessing the role of depth and breadth of vocabulary knowledge in reading comprehension". *Canadian Modern Language Review* 56: 282–307.

Read, J. 1993. "The development of a new measure of L2 vocabulary knowledge". *Language Testing* 10: 355–371.

Richards, J. 1976. "The role of vocabulary teaching". *TESOL Quarterly* 10: 77–89.

Ringbom, H. 1983. "Borrowing and lexical transfer". *Applied Linguistics* 4: 207–212.

Rott, S. 1999. "The effect of exposure frequency on intermediate language learners' incidental vocabulary acquisition and retention through reading". *Studies in Second Language Acquisition* 21: 589–619.

Sanaoui, R. 1995. "Adult learners' approaches to learning vocabulary in second languages". *Modern Language Journal* 79: 15–28.

Schmitt, N., and Meara, P. 1997. "Researching vocabulary through a word knowledge framework: word associations and verbal suffixes". *Studies in Second Language Acquisition* 19: 17–36.

Schmitt, N. 1998. "Tracking the incremental acquisition of second language vocabulary: a longitudinal study". *Language Learning* 48: 281–317.

Segalowitz, N. 1995. "Automaticity and lexical skills in second language fluency: Implications for computer assisted language learning". *Computer Assisted Language Learning* 8: 129–149.

Segalowitz, S. J., Segalowitz, N. S., and Wood, A. G. 1998. "Assessing the development of automaticity in second language word recognition". *Applied Psycholinguistics* 19: 53–67.

Segalowitz, N., Watson, V., & Segalowitz, S. 1995. "Vocabulary skill: single-case assessment of automaticity of word recognition in a timed lexical decision task". *Second Language Research* 11: 121–136.

Selinker, L., and Lakshmanan, U. 1992. "Language transfer and fossilization: The multiple effects principle". In *Language Transfer in Language Learning*, S. Gass and L. Selinker (eds), 197–216. Amsterdam: John Benjamins.

Sonaiya, R. 1991. "Vocabulary acquisition as a process of continuous lexical disambiguation". *IRAL* 29: 273–284.

Strick, G. J. 1980. "A hypothesis for semantic development in a second language". *Language Learning* 30: 155–176.

Swan, M. 1997. "The influence of the mother tongue on second language vocabulary acquisition and use". In *Vocabulary: description, acquisition and pedagogy*, N. Schmitt, and M. McCarthy (eds), 156–180. Cambridge: Cambridge University Press.

Vermeer, A. 2001. "Breadth and depth of vocabulary in relation to L1/L2 acquisition and frequency of input". *Applied Psycholinguistics* 22: 217–234.

Weinreich, U. 1953. *Languages in contact: Findings and problems*. New York: Linguistic Circle of New York.

Wesche, M. B., and Paribakht, T. S. 1996. "Assessing second language vocabulary knowledge: depth versus breadth". *Canadian Modern Language Review* 53: 13–40.

Wolter, B. 2001. "Comparing the L1 and L2 mental lexicon: a depth of individual word knowledge model". *Studies in Second Language Acquisition* 23: 41–69

Zughoul, M. R. 1991. "Lexical choice: towards writing problematic word lists". *IRAL* 29: 45–59.

Appendix: Test materials used in the sentence completion test and correct answers*

1. COMPLICATED   2. COMPLEX   3. BOTH   4. NOT SURE

1. Please help us make a difference for the people of our community. Help us use this most powerful medium to probe the _____ issues, cultural developments and great opportunities of our changing society.

2. The "unfair dismissal and redundancy" legislation provides workers with extensive legal protection from routine managerial decisions making it more _____ and expensive to dismiss workers who are either incompetent or not needed, by giving the workers concerned special procedures for challenging those routine decisions.

1. CRITERIA   2. STANDARDS   3. BOTH   4. NOT SURE

3. The 1840 deal governing New Zealand's future was scarcely enlightened by today's _____.

4. Twain made his point explicit in two essays written about 1875. The essays raised questions about ethical _____ as well as about success.

5. We will never realize our full economic potential in this country until _____ of education and training match those of our competitors.

1. ACCURATE   2. PRECISE   3. BOTH   4. NOT SURE

6. Since few people know the _____ location of the Ashram, there are no drop-in visitors, no paparazzi, no autograph seekers.
7. What is the _____ relationship between the neurological abnormality and the learning problem?
8. Existing home buyers can often get limited warranties through realty brokers that offer one-year protection against major defects. The _____ terms and conditions vary, and typically there is a deductible if a claim is made.
9. Most outsiders had only the dimmest perception of how the firm worked, but most would have banked on Shell being a good corporate citizen. According to many, that description is _____. But environmental campaigners tell a different story.

1. INSISTED   2. PERSISTED   3. BOTH   4. NOT SURE

10. Opposition to these diversions _____ well after the end of the American Revolution.
11. He felt the films were arty trash and _____ on making his views known while they were being shown.
12. Kevin _____ that he had seen a document in which beneficial ownership had been transferred from the pension-fund manager to Robert Maxwell Group.
13. He had, at first, grossly misjudged the time and forces needed to expel the Iraqi invaders from Kuwait. His overestimation of the enemy's size and capability _____ to the last shot and beyond.

1. DOUBTED   2. SUSPECTED   3. BOTH   4. NOT SURE

14. He could never recall clearly how he had come to bring the girl home with him and he never saw her after that to ask. He _____ that he had drunkenly decided to do it after his money had run out.
15. The inquiry confirms what many had already _____: that while the secret services learnt of Saddam Hussein's covert military projects by talking to British businessmen exporting goods to Iraq, they routinely failed to pass on their knowledge to other departments.
16. Scotland Yard _____ direct involvement by the Libyan regime: "I think it is unlikely that a Libyan agent carried this out although I cannot rule out a political connection at this stage."
17. The test proposals were welcomed by education experts and campaign groups though some _____ if teachers were up to the job of preparing pupils.

1. SAFE   2. SECURE   3. BOTH   4. NOT SURE

18. The future of health care in this city is more _____ now than ever before. Your hospital is very different today than it was five years ago.
19. To keep that voice alive OSF must continue to build from within — not fall back on producing only the most popular, _____ plays.
20. After college, Hawthorne lived at home and trained to be a writer. Only when his first collection, *Twice-Told Tales*, made money did he feel _____ enough to marry Sophia Peabody and settle in the Old Manse in Concord, Massachusetts.

*Based on the native speaker's performance, the correct answers for the 20 sentences are 2, 1, 2, 2, 2, 2, 2, 1, 2, 1, 1, 2, 2, 2, 1, 1, 2, 1, 2.

CHAPTER 7

Individual differences in the use of colloquial vocabulary: The effects of sociobiographical and psychological factors

Jean-Marc Dewaele
Birkbeck College, University of London

Abstract

The present contribution examines some independent variables that are linked to the use of colloquial vocabulary. The first study, based on a corpus of conversations in French between the researcher and 29 Dutch L1 speakers who were learners of French, considers the effect of proficiency, frequency of contact with French, extraversion and gender on the use of colloquial vocabulary. The second study is based on a corpus of conversations in French between 62 native and non-native speakers of French who were students in the French department of Birkbeck College, London. Statistical analyses in the first study suggest that the use of colloquial words is linked to extraversion levels, frequency of contact with French and proficiency level in French. Similar effects were uncovered in the second study for extraversion and frequency of contact with French. It is argued that the extraverts' inclination to taking risks, combined with lower communicative anxiety, might explain the higher use of colloquial words. Proficiency seems to be a pre-requisite, but not the only factor, for actual use of colloquial vocabulary. Indeed, native speakers were found to use only marginally more colloquial words than non-native speakers.

1. Introduction

The relationship between the vocabulary research community and the mainstream Second Language Acquisition (SLA) researchers has not been easy, and yet collaboration is crucial if we want to build satisfactory models, argue Haastrup & Henriksen (2001). Paul Meara shares this point of view but strikes a more optimistic tone in a recent review article on the topic. According to him, the field of L2 vocabulary acquisition is growing in importance as lexical issues become more central to theoretical linguistics (Meara 2002a). We would like to argue that interest in lexical issues is also growing in a wide range of disciplines that are broadly referred to as 'bilingualism' research (cf. Pavlenko, Schrauf & Dewaele 2003). The present contribution will focus on the use of vocabulary that belongs to highly informal speech styles, namely colloquial vocabulary. It is widely used by French native speakers (NS) across the social spectrum. The so-called 'argot' has found its way into dictionaries and is perfectly appropriate in informal interactions. However, colloquial vocabulary is usually banned from textbooks for foreign learners of French (cf. Mougeon, Nadasdi & Rehner 2002) and it is generally avoided in classroom interactions. It is therefore not surprising that instructed learners of French use very few colloquial words (Dewaele & Regan 2001). There is relatively little research on this topic, probably due to the inherent difficulty of analysing something that is infrequent or absent in the data. As Labov (1972) pointed out, in order to carry out research on any variant, it must be present in sufficient numbers. It is also easier to explain why something is present in a corpus rather than absent. Is under representation of a feature in a user's interlanguage (IL) the result of conscious avoidance or of incomplete knowledge of the IL? Depending on the feature, one could argue in favour of either explanation, or even both. Very low frequency words might not yet have been acquired, but the absence of complex morphological forms, like some subjunctives in French, might be linked to the amount of effort needed to produce such a form. Moreover, the user would still have to overcome the uncertainty about the quality of the end-product. That uncertainty might prevent L2 users[1] from producing colloquial words which are not necessarily morphologically complex, but which might be either unknown, or insufficiently known to the user or perceived to present an unacceptable risk of loss of face. The question of avoidance has been considered in detail by Blum & Levenston (1978). They distinguish: (a) true avoidance, which presupposes choice, i.e., the learner knows the word or form being avoided, from (b) apparent avoidance, which is caused by lack of information; the learner simply does not know the lexical item. Recent research on avoidance in IL has been linked to differences and/or similarities between the L1 and the L2 (Dagut & Laufer 1985, Laufer & Eliasson 1993, Laufer 2000).

The relative infrequency of colloquial vocabulary in conversations of L2 users means that one needs enough comparable data to carry out analyses on interindividual variation. We will therefore base our analyses on two different corpora of conversations in French by NS and NNS. This amounts to a total of 91 speakers and a total of more than 100,000 words.

The present chapter will be structured as follows: in the first part we consider the theoretical background for the current investigation before focusing on the independent variables that might affect the use of colloquial vocabulary, i.e. proficiency, degree of extraversion, gender, age, social class, frequency of use of French, and native versus non-native status of the speaker. The second part presents the methodology of the first study on French IL from Dutch L1 students from the Free university of Brussels, followed by the methodology of the second study based on native French and French IL from mature students enrolled in Birkbeck College, University of London. Research hypotheses are then formulated. The third part focuses on the analyses from study 1 and study 2. Finally, in Part 4, the findings and their implications for vocabulary research are discussed.

2. Theoretical background

Variationist sociolinguists have investigated variation patterns among NS, quantifying the frequency of use of a particular linguistic variant (Labov 1972, Mougeon & Beniak 1991) and identifying both linguistic sources of variation (factors pertaining to the linguistic context in which the variants are used) and extralinguistic variables (gender, social class, group identity, situation, register). After a complete analysis of the data, a set of 'variable rules' would be formulated that would capture the probability of a particular variant appearing in a specific context.[2] Labov showed at the NWAVE 23 1994 conference in Stanford that sociolinguistic studies in the labovian tradition concentrate mainly on variation in the syntactical and, to a lesser extent, on phonological systems of speakers. Much less research has been done on synchronic lexical variation, i.e. the choice between variants that share the same meaning but belong to different registers like the French argot word *fric* versus the more formal variant *argent* (both words meaning 'money') (cf. Armstrong 1998).

Sociolinguistic research in SLA has grown exponentially in the last two decades (see for example Bayley 1994, Bayley & Preston 1996, Tarone 1988, 1997, Preston 1989, 2000, and Young 1999). This research focuses on the development of language learners' sociopragmatic competence, i.e. 'the social perceptions underlying participants' interpretation and performance of communicative action' (Kasper & Rose 2001: 2) and their sociolinguistic competence, i.e. 'the capacity to recognize and produce socially appropriate speech in context' (Lyster 1994: 263). The variation is thus the objective of the acquisition process. The focus of sociolinguists and sociopragmaticists in SLA is very different from that of SLA researchers interested in the development of morphology or syntax where variation has traditionally been conceived as transitory, as the sign that the system has not stabilized yet at a near-native level (unless it is fossilized, cf. Han 2003).

Variation patterns in the IL have been found to approximate NS-like variation but rarely reaching it. L2 users seem reticent in using non-standard variants, using higher proportions of formal variants instead (Mougeon *et al.* 2002).

2.1 Independent variables linked to synchronic variation in vocabulary choice

2.1.1 *Linguistic history*

Language learners do not move as freely on the continuum of speech styles as do NS. Learners' written academic discourse 'tends to reflect the spoken mode' (Bloor & Bloor 1991: 9), and yet their spoken discourse tends to be too explicit, a typical characteristic of written discourse (Dewaele 2001a, 2001b, 2002a). Hence the observation by Tarone & Swain (1995) that IL speakers tend to be monostylistic. They tend to use many features of formal speech styles and shun informal variants. The main reason for this is the type of input the learners are exposed to, and the type of output which they are expected to produce. Speech styles in classrooms tend to be rather formal, with a lot of written texts. Bijvoet (2002: 40) observes that language teaching is also traditionally more concerned with word phonology, morphology, lexico-syntax and denotative word meaning rather than with 'associative word meaning (consisting of connotations and stylistic properties'. She attributes the neglect of associative word meaning in classroom instruction firstly to the priority given to basic vocabulary learning, suitable for the widest possible range of social situations and, secondly, to the inherent difficulty in teaching the elusive associative aspect of lexical competence. While denotations are shared by large groups of speakers, connotations are shared by particular communities of practice and are much more dynamic. The narrowness of learners' lexical knowledge might not be too obvious as far as communication within the classroom on trivial matters is concerned: the speaker will not feel too personally involved in the topic. This might change completely however in topics where the speaker feels more involved. And topics of this type typically arise when L2 users engage in authentic informal communication with NS of their own age group, where vernacular styles are the norm (Blanco-Iglesias, Broner & Tarone 1995, Mougeon et al. 2002). While the learner could hide behind a non-specific group identity in the classroom, the issue of personal identity becomes crucial in authentic communication outside the classroom (i.e. when the learner becomes a legitimate L2 user) and the language socialization will develop at a higher rate (Kinginger 2000). Ochs (1996: 408) defined language socialization as 'the process whereby children and other novices are socialized through language, part of such socialization being a socialization to use language meaningfully, appropriately and effectively'.

We will now consider research that was carried out on the link between independent variables and the proportion of different types of words in IL, including emotional words, swearwords, and colloquial words.

Classroom input was found to affect the development of learners' vocabulary in subtle ways. Damen (1984) noticed that learners in English as a second language programmes learn more vocabulary having positive connotations and belonging to higher registers. As a consequence they often lack the means to express negative feelings (including colloquial expressions and swearwords). Even if the learners know more vernacular forms and negative words, they might still feel unsure about their appropriateness in certain situations (Blum-Kulka 1996). There might therefore be both a real, and a self-perceived, lack of sociopragmatic competence in the second language. While the real lack of competence is a matter of developing skills in the IL, the perceived lack depends much more on the personality of the learner (cf. Infra).
Dewaele & Pavlenko (2002) found that emotional words are underrepresented in IL corpora. They investigated the effect of five factors on the use of emotion vocabulary in 2 different IL corpora.

The first study considered the impact of language proficiency, gender, and extraversion on the use of emotion words in the advanced French IL of 29 Dutch L1 speakers.[3] The second examined the influence of sociocultural competence, gender, and type of linguistic material on the use of emotion vocabulary in the advanced English IL of 34 Russian L1 speakers. Combined, the results of the two studies demonstrated that the use of emotion words in IL is linked to proficiency level, type of linguistic material, extraversion, and, in some cases, gender of speakers (females using more emotion words). A multiple regression analysis in the first study revealed that gender and degree of extraversion were significant predictors for the proportion of emotion lemmas, a second regression analysis showed that gender and level of proficiency were strong predictors for the proportion of emotion word tokens. The finding that language proficiency does not influence the range of emotion lemmas used but does affect the frequency of use of emotion word tokens, with more advanced speakers using more emotion word tokens in their speech, was interpreted as an illustration of the detachment effect of the L2, i.e., words in the L2 seem to have less emotional resonance than their translation equivalents in the L1 (cf. Amati-Mehler, Argentieri & Canestri 1993, Harris, Ayçiçegi & Gleason 2003).

A study on self-reported language choice for swearing among 1039 multilinguals (Dewaele to appear a) revealed that multilinguals generally prefer to swear in their dominant language, though they might, using a conscious strategy, swear in a weaker language to soften the illocutionary force or to escape social conventions that prevent them from using swearwords in their L1. A separate study on the emotional force of swearwords and taboo words in multiple languages based on the same database revealed that participants perceive swearwords and taboo words in their L1 as having a stronger emotional resonance than in the languages learnt later in life (Dewaele to appear b). The context in which a language had been learned turned out to have a significant effect on both frequency of swearing in a language and perception of emotional force: languages that had been learned in a purely instructed context (as opposed to naturalistic or mixed learning) were used less frequently for swearing and the swearwords and taboo words in these languages were perceived to have a weaker emotional resonance. These results seem to confirm the finding by Blanco-Iglesias *et al.* (1995) that language learners might avoid colloquial words in their IL because they lack the expressive force of equivalent colloquial words in their L1. It also lends support to the finding by Toya & Kodis (1996) that L2 users find it difficult to be consciously rude in the L2. The researchers analysed the use of swearwords and the pragmatic use of rudeness in an L2 and found that expressiveness was clearly linked to the variety of registers in the input and to the confidence of the users. NS were found to be more expressive although the difference in reactions was smaller than expected. The authors suggest that the lower degree of expressiveness in the L2 could be linked to the more restricted input to which the learners had been exposed (there is little display of anger in the foreign language classroom) and the fact that learners have little confidence in using angry words.

A study on a part of the cross-sectional corpus of advanced oral French IL used in the present study, and on a longitudinal corpus of 6 Hiberno-Irish English L1 speakers, by Dewaele & Regan (2001), focused on the effect of contact and study abroad on the use of colloquial words. It was hypothesised that authentic interactions in the target language (TL), as well as total immersion in the TL culture for a prolonged period, and longer and more intense formal instruction in the TL would be linked to a more frequent use of colloquial vocabulary. Length of instruction was not found to be linked to the use of colloquial vocabulary. Only the amount of active authentic communication in the TL, especially in a total immersion context was found to be correlated with an increased use of colloquial vocabulary. The authors hypothesized that speakers of intermediate proficiency might ignore the existence of the colloquial words, or lack morphophonological information at the lexical level. It was also argued that incomplete semantic representation of the words could have prevented the production of colloquial words in more advanced speakers, and even highly fluent speakers might have gaps in their conceptual representations. Another possibility was that the semantic representation of the colloquial word might not have been linked to the TL concept (Pavlenko 1999, 2000, Dewaele & Pavlenko 2002). An English L2 user might, for example, have a semantic representation of the word *dog* that resembles that of a NS, but his/her conceptual representation might be different. While the latter might think of cute puppies as seen in TV commercials, the former might think of dogs as unclean animals, or food (Pavlenko 2000). A complete conceptual representation of a word would also imply that that word is integrated in culture-specific scripts. These 'scripts' are crucial in order to talk about various delicate and taboo subjects (Legrenzi, Girotto & Johnson-Laird 1993, Tomkins 1998). They are based on biological processes but they reflect the cultural environment (Tomkins 1998). It could be argued that the use of colloquial speech is also directed by specific scripts which are shared by NS (Kitayama & Markus 1994). These scripts are flexible and are adapted to the sociocultural and semiotic environment of the individual. Scripts which are used within one certain community of practice (Wenger 1998) are not necessarily shared by other groups but there is enough overlap in interpretive frames to coordinate practices and activities. Language learners probably quickly realize that their native scripts cannot be easily translated in the TL. Colloquial expressions that are perfectly acceptable in one culture can be totally out of place in another. One reason for this is that a word and concepts in one language rarely overlap completely with their translation equivalents in another language (Altarriba 2003, Panayiotou to appear).

It thus seems that to be able to use colloquial or emotional vocabulary appropriately (if at all), speakers must have not only a semantic but also a conceptual representation of a particular word, including a script where that word or expression might fit in. We briefly mentioned the effect of psychological variables, and will now focus on the main one, namely the extraversion-introversion dimension.

2.1.2 *Psychological variable: extraversion*

Studies on language and personality are relatively few in number (Furnham 1990, Dewaele & Furnham 1999, 2000). Moreover, a majority of studies on extraversion and language performed by linguists has focused on the effect of extraversion on language <u>learning</u> (Dewaele & Furnham 1999). Negative publicity for trait extraversion within the field of applied linguistics has resulted from one seriously flawed — but unchallenged- study by Naiman, Frohlich, Stern & Todesco (1978) on personality variables and language learning, where extraversion scores were found not to correlate with written language test results (Dewaele & Furnham 1999). Naiman et al's results echoed for two decades among applied linguists and this discouraged further research on the link between extraversion and other linguistic measures. Dewaele & Furnham 1999 argue that if Naiman et al. had used a wider variety of more sophisticated linguistic variables, covering not only written language but also natural communicative oral language, they might have found that the construct validity of the Eysenck Personality Inventory was not to blame for the lack of expected correlations. This is was what Dewaele & Furnham (2000) did using a corpus of French IL and testing a number of specific hypotheses. Correlational analyses between extraversion scores and six linguistic variables reflecting fluency and accuracy revealed that extravert L2 users are more fluent than introvert L2 users, especially in interpersonal stressful situations. It was argued that some cognitive and physiological characteristics associated with extraversion, such as superior short-term memory and resistance to stress, can explain the superior fluency of the extraverts' speech production (Dewaele & Furnham 2000, Dewaele 2002b).

The speakers' personality, especially their degree of extraversion, might affect their use of colloquial vocabulary. The first possible cause for the existence of this link could be the higher inhibition and social anxiety of introverts[4] (Cheek & Buss 1981, Fremont *et al.* 1976) combined with a higher overall language anxiety in IL speech production (MacIntyre & Gardner 1991, Dewaele 2002c). Dewaele (2002d) found that the position on the extraversion / introversion dimension significantly predicts foreign language anxiety in English (but not in French) in a population of 100 Flemish high school students. More extraverted students reported lower levels of foreign language anxiety. One possible linguistic consequence of the higher anxiety levels of introverts would be an avoidance of colloquial words out of fear that they might not be appropriate. A second possible cause for the introverts' preference for avoiding colloquial words might be related to the nature of extraversion / introversion. It has been established that introverts possess a higher level of arousal in the autonomous nervous system and in the cortex (Eysenck 1981, Matthews & Deary 1998). Introverts are over-aroused, extraverts are under-aroused. As any individual operates ideally with an optimal level of cortical arousal the more extraverted will be inclined to look for external stimulation to reach an optimal level whereas the more introverted people will try to avoid over-arousing situations. This means that certain stimuli received from the outside (specific situations or tasks) as well as from inside the organism (cognition), evoke stronger responses in introverts. One could argue that the use of emotional and colloquial words is the type of internal stimulus that might raise the level of arousal of a speaker beyond an optimal level (Dewaele & Pavlenko 2002).

As introverts have a higher level of cortical arousal, they might prefer to avoid use of particular colloquial words in order to keep their arousal levels under control. The extraverts on the other hand have lower levels of cortical arousal, which might allow them to use colloquial words more easily.

Eysenck & Eysenck (1985) suggest that the greater cognitive control of performance shown by introverts might prevent their high level of arousal from producing impulsive behavior. The authors also advance an alternative explanation, suggesting that it is the introverts' greater fear of punishment that may make them behave in a cautious manner. Both arguments seem complementary with regard to the use of colloquial vocabulary: higher cognitive control by introverts implies a closer monitoring of the use of non-standard words and their subsequent suppression before their articulation; the same suppression strategy could be used because the introverts fear disapproval from their interlocutor(s) and thus prefer words from more formal registers.

2.1.3   Social variables: gender, generation and social class

The traditional factors of gender, generation and social class could also affect the use of colloquial words. Sociolinguistic research typically reports that women, adults and speakers from higher social classes tend to use fewer non-standard phonological and syntactical forms than men, teenagers and speakers from lower social backgrounds (Labov's 'Principle 1') (Labov 1972, 1990, Tagliamonte 1998).

Although much less research has been carried out into variation in lexical variants, traditional gender, generational and social patterns have also emerged in native speech vocabulary (Armstrong 1998). No such clear-cut pattern emerges in IL. Mougeon *et al.* (2002) reviewed studies on sociolinguistic markers in French L2 that included the social and the gender variable and they report gender effects in some studies, with females using more standard variants, while no such effect was found in other studies. Studies where a gender effect was discovered usually included participants living in a francophone area where more frequent contacts with NS from both sexes were possible. The patterns for social class seem equally blurred. Some studies on French immersion populations — but not all — found that students from higher social classes use fewer stigmatised variants than students from lower social classes. Mougeon *et al.* (2002) speculate that gender and social effects may occur when participants have inferred the sociostylistic value of certain variants through explicit instruction in the variation patterns. They could then transfer their preference for informal or formal variants from their L1 to their L2. The effect of age or generation on sociolinguistic variation in French IL is equally unclear because of the concurrent effect of educational context. Lyster & Rebuffot (2002) report an overgeneralization of the informal address pronoun *tu* in the speech of young Canadian learners in French immersion classes while Dewaele (2002e) reports an overuse of the formal address pronoun *vous* in the speech of adult learners of French in London, UK. The absence of *vous* in the Canadian study might have been linked to the absence of that form in the oral and written input as teachers usually prefer *tu* for addressing the students, or use an indefinite *tu*, and the pedagogical material does not address this choice explicitly.

3.   Hypotheses

These considerations have been hypothesized as follows for our two studies:

Hypothesis 1: More extraverted speakers use more colloquial words than more introverted speakers (studies 1 and 2).

Hypothesis 2: More proficient speakers use more colloquial words than less proficient IL speakers (study 1 only).

Hypothesis 3: Speakers from higher social background will use less colloquial words than IL speakers from lower social background (study 1 only).

Hypothesis 4: Female speakers will use fewer colloquial words than male speakers (studies 1 and 2).

Hypothesis 5: Younger speakers will use more colloquial words than older speakers (study 2 only).

Hypothesis 6: NS will use more colloquial words than NNS (study 2 only).

Hypothesis 7: Frequent speakers of French will use more colloquial words than those who use French rarely (study 1 and 2).

4.   Methodology

4.1   Study 1

4.1.1 *Participants*

Twenty-nine university students, 10 female and 19 male, aged between 18 and 21 (Mean = 19.5 years, SD = 1.4 years), participated in the experiment. They had taken French at a high school level (3 to 5 hours a week) for 6 to 8 years and had been following advanced courses in French with the researcher at the language institute of the Free University of Brussels. These courses included sections on colloquial vocabulary through songs, cartoons and texts. Both the participants and the researcher were trilinguals (Dutch-French-English) although the participants' French was weaker. Their French could be described as an 'pre-advanced to advanced IL' (Bartning 1997). All participants were highly fluent in English which they had studied for at least 6 years, including an intensive course of 150 hours in the previous academic year. Teacher and students communicated usually in French but the students knew that the teacher had native competence in Dutch. The participants were administered the English version of the Eysenck Personality Inventory (Eysenck & Eysenck 1984) in order to determine their degree of extraversion.[5] Participants with a score on the extraversion scale that varied within one standard deviation around the mean: 11.2, SD 3.3; Normative score: 11) were labelled 'ambiverts' (n=20), those with scores outside this range were labelled either 'introverts' (n=3) or 'extraverts' (n=6). Participants also completed a sociobiographical questionnaire. Three groups of participants were created according to the amount of contact they reported with French: 13 reported little or no contact with French outside the classroom, 9 reported occasional contact and 7 reported frequent use of French.

Morpholexical accuracy rates were used to determine the speakers' level of proficiency (Dewaele 1994). These morpholexical accuracy rates were found to correlate positively and significantly with speech rate measured as average number of words produced per minute (Dewaele 1998) and negatively with the proportion of filled pauses (Dewaele 1996). As high accuracy has been linked with high fluency and these two aspects are generally considered to be the main components of 'proficiency' in IL (Alderson, Clapham & Steel 1997), the first variable was used to divide the speakers into three proficiency levels. The first group, labelled 'low proficiency', contained 4 participants with mean morpholexical accuracy rates that were more than one standard deviation (2.86) below the group mean (93.3%). The second and largest group, 'medium proficiency', contained 19 participants whose mean accuracy scores lie within one standard deviation above and under the group mean. The third group, labelled 'high proficiency', consisted of 6 participants with mean accuracy rates that were more than one standard deviation above the group mean. The social class of the speaker was determined through the education level of the parents. Given the small size of the sample, we opted for a distinction between 'high' (n = 13), i.e. at least one of the parents had obtained a higher degree after finishing secondary education, and 'low' (n = 16), i.e. none of the parents had obtained a degree after secondary education (cf. Preston 1989).

4.1.2 *Linguistic material*

The effect of the formality of the situation on linguistic variables is considerable (Dewaele & Furnham 2000). We therefore restricted our analysis to conversations recorded in an informal situation where colloquial words were most likely to occur. The first corpus is thus based on one-to-one conversations between the researcher and 29 subjects in a relaxed atmosphere. They were told that the purpose of the conversation was merely to have a relaxed informal chat about their studies, hobbies, politics etc. Efforts were made to make the interviewees feel at ease, and to this end it was stressed that the content more than the form of their speech was important. Errors were not corrected and a coherent and spontaneous discussion was thus maintained. There was no time-restriction. The recordings were transcribed by the researcher into orthographical French (34,787 words of learners). These transcriptions were then coded at the word level according to their grammatical nature and possible lexical or morphological errors.

4.2   Study 2

4.2.1 *Participants*

Sixty-two university students, 35 female and 27 male, aged between 22 and 65 (Mean = 35.5 years, SD = 10.8 years), contributed to the second corpus. They were enrolled in the BA French program at Birkbeck College, University of London, and had had between 5 and 11 years of instruction in French. They had been following advanced language courses in French with the researcher. These courses also focused on colloquial vocabulary through songs, cartoons and texts. Their French could be described as 'pre-advanced to advanced' (Bartning 1997).

The participants were administered the Eysenck Personality Inventory (Eysenck & Eysenck 1984) in order to determine their degree of extraversion. Participants with a score on the extraversion scale that ranged from 9 to 18 were labelled 'ambiverts' (n = 22); those with scores outside this range were labelled either 'introverts' (n = 11) or 'extraverts' (n = 10). Participants also completed a questionnaire concerning their linguistic history. Twenty-nine participants reported that they rarely spoke French outside college, 13 reported that they did so occasionally and 20 reported that they did so frequently. Nine participants were NS of French who had lived in London for at least 4 years; 53 participants had different L1s. L1 speakers of English formed the largest sub-group (n = 29), followed by Spanish (n = 5), Mauritian Creole (n = 5), Italian (n = 4), Arabic (n = 3). Other participants were NS of Dutch, Farsi, Gouro, Lingala and Turkish. French was the L2 of 40 participants, English was the L2 of 13 participants. Other L2s included Armenian, German, Mandarin Chinese, Gaelic, Italian, Dutch, Spanish and Punjabi.

4.2.2 *Linguistic material*

This second corpus is based on one-to-one audio-recorded conversations between the 62 participants including the researcher. One participant had two conversations with different interlocutors. Conversations were based on a list of 12 topics ranging from personal to more general. They included the composition of the family, motivation to study French, political beliefs, likes and dislikes in music, literature, food, danger of death experiences, best and worst holidays, and experience with muggings or burglaries. Participants assumed the role of interviewer or interviewee and changed roles after about 10 minutes. The transcribed interviews amount to 67,968 words.

4.3   Statistical design

Means and standard deviations were computed for all the groups in study 1 and study 2. The differences in means between the different groups were tested with two-sample Kolmogorov-Smirnov tests as nonparametric alternatives to t-tests. Kruskal-Wallis tests were used as nonparametric equivalents to one-way ANOVAs, because of small sample sizes and a sampling distribution that was not always normal. In study 2, we used a nonparametric Spearman Rho analysis to check the relationship between the proportion of colloquial words and participants' age. We used the same technique in study 1 to analyse the relationship between proficiency levels and levels of frequency of use.

Words with a colloquial value were coded using stylistic indications in the French monolingual dictionary *Le Petit Robert* (1979). As the focus of our research is on interindividual varation, we calculated individual rates for proportions of colloquial words at token level. The most frequent colloquial words in the two corpora are *hein* (interjection), *ben* (interjection), *truc(s)* 'thing(s)', *copains* 'friends', *fric* 'money', *bosser* 'work', *merde* 'shit', *sympa* 'nice', *chichis* 'fuss', *bouquin(s)* 'book(s)', *macho* 'macho', *mec* 'guy', and *super* 'super'.

4.4   Results

4.4.1   *Study 1*

The first corpus contains 196 colloquial words, which represents .56% of the total number of word tokens produced. The average of individual proportions of colloquial words in the corpus is .52% (SD = .49). The large standard deviation is linked to the fact that 7 participants did not use any colloquial words. Despite the high skewness value (.72) the distribution of the data is normal (Kolmogorov-Smirnov Z = .83, p = ns). The distribution can be seen in Table 1.

In this section we will analyse the link between proportion of colloquial words and extraversion, proficiency, frequency of contact, gender and social

Table 1. Distribution of participants in frequency classes according to use of colloquial words (study 1).

Frequency class	Number of participants
0%	7
. 001%–.5%	9
. 501%–1.0%,	8
1.001%–1.5%,	3
more than 1.501%	1

background (hypotheses 1, 2, 3, 4 and 7). A Kruskal-Wallis test showed that extraversion level (introvert, ambivert, extravert) was significantly linked to the proportion of colloquial words: Chi-Square=8.2, df=2, p<.016. As can be seen in Figure 1, the extravert group (n=6) uses more colloquial words than both the ambivert (n=20) and introvert (n=3) groups, who obtain very similar values.

A Kruskal-Wallis test with proficiency level (high n=6, medium n=19, low n = 4) as main independent variable and proportion of colloquial words as dependent variable shows a significant effect: Chi-Square=12, df=2, p<.002. Figure 3 shows a linear relation between proficiency and proportion of colloquial vocabulary. More proficient speakers use more colloquial vocabulary.

A Kruskal-Wallis test with frequency of contact (rarely n = 13, sometimes n=9, regularly n=7) as main independent variable and proportion of colloquial words as dependent variable reveals a significant effect: Chi-Square= 14.1, df=2, p<.001. Here also a linear relationship emerges with more frequent users of French using more colloquial vocabulary in that language (see Figure 2).

A two-sample Kolmogorov-Smirnov test revealed that the difference in proportion of colloquial words between the 16 participants from 'lower' social class and the 13 participants from 'higher' social class was not significant (Kolmogorov-Smirnov Z=.81, p=ns). A two-sample Kolmogorov-Smirnov test revealed a non-significant difference in proportion of colloquial words (Kolmogorov-Smirnov Z=.72, p=ns) between the 9 female and the 20 male participants.

To sum up, the results show that degree of extraversion, frequency of contact and level of proficiency are strongly linked to the use of colloquial words in the first corpus of advanced French IL. Gender and social class, on the other hand, do not have a significant effect on the use of colloquial words. In other words, more extraverted, more frequent and proficient speakers of French use a higher proportion of colloquial vocabulary. It must also be acknowledged that there is a positive correlation between proficiency levels and levels of frequency of use (Spearman Rho(28)=.54, p<.01); but this relationship lies outside the scope of the present chapter. These findings fully support hypothesis 1 and 2 and reject hypothesis 3 and 4.

4.4.2   Study 2

There are 324 colloquial words in the second corpus, which represent .48% of the total number of word tokens produced. The average of individual

Table 2. Distribution of participants in frequency classes according to use of colloquial words (study 2).

Frequency class	Number of participants
0%	21
.001%–.5%	21
.501%–1.0%,	12
1.001%–1.5%,	4
more than 1.5%	4

proportions of colloquial words in the corpus is .51% (SD=.89%). The large standard deviation suggests that the data are not normally distributed. A one-sample Kolmogorov-Smirnov test shows that this is indeed the case: $Z=2.24$, $p<.0001$. Table 2 offers a view of the distribution of the results along 5 frequency categories. It is striking that 21 participants (33.9% of the total and all NNS) do not use a single colloquial word during their exchange and that as a consequence the distribution is heavily skewed towards the lower end of the scale (skewness value=3.1, Standard Error=.30).

In this section we will analyse the link between proportion of colloquial words and extraversion, gender, age, native speaker status and frequency of speaking French (hypotheses 1, 4, 5, 6 and 7).

A Kruskal-Wallis test showed that extraversion level (introvert, ambivert, extravert) is significantly linked to the proportion of colloquial words: Chi-Square=9.5, df=2, $p<.009$. The introvert group ($n=11$) has the lowest proportion of colloquial words, the ambivert group ($n=22$) occupies an intermediate position and the extravert group ($n=10$) has the highest proportion of colloquial words (see Figure 1).

A two-sample Kolmogorov-Smirnov test revealed a non-significant difference in proportion of colloquial words (Kolmogorov-Smirnov $Z=.92$, $p=$ns) between the 35 female participants (Mean=.34 %, SD=.49%) and the 27 male participants (M=.73%, SD=1.21%). A Spearman correlation analysis revealed a significant negative correlation between age of the participants and their proportion of colloquial words (Rho (61)=−.27, $p<.034$). In other words, younger speakers used more colloquial words.

A two-sample Kolmogorov-Smirnov test revealed a marginally significant difference in proportion of colloquial words (Kolmogorov-Smirnov $Z=1.31$, $p<.063$) between the 9 NS and the 53 NNS. A look at the range shows that NS vary between .07% and 2.36% proportion of colloquial words, while the NNS vary between 0% and 4.47%.

A Kruskal-Wallis test with frequency of speaking French as main independent variable and proportion of colloquial words as dependent variable shows a significant effect: Chi-Square=14.9, df=2, p<.001. This shows that those who rarely speak French (n=29) use fewer colloquial words than those who use it sometimes (n=13), while those who use it regularly (n=20) have the highest proportion of colloquial vocabulary.

To sum up, the findings of study 2

(1) support hypothesis 1 (more extraverted participants use more colloquial words)
(2) reject hypothesis 4 (male speakers do not use significantly more colloquial words than female speakers)
(3) support hypothesis 5 (younger speakers use more colloquial words than older ones)
(4) partially support hypothesis 6 (NS tend to use more colloquial vocabulary than NNS)
(5) support hypothesis 7 (regular users of French use more colloquial words than those who don't use French regularly).

5. Discussion

The advantages of using two corpora of comparable data produced by different populations and investigating the effects of similarly defined dependent and independent variables are clear in the present investigation. Research on individual differences in applied linguistics often relies on small samples because of the time-consuming nature of the data collection, transcription and analysis. Relationships between independent and dependent variables in small single corpora can often be obscured by the presence of outliers (making them either stronger or weaker than they really are). By combining two corpora, one gets a much clearer view and the probability that an apparently strong effect due to a single outlier becomes much smaller. Three such cross-corpus comparisons were carried out, and the three independent variables were found to have similar effects on the proportions of colloquial words.

The effect of extraversion on the use of colloquial words was significant in both corpora as can be seen in Figure 1. More introverted speakers use fewer colloquial words than their more extraverted peers, which fits with introverts' profile of being more cautious, more anxious, more inhibited and suffering from a greater fear of punishment. An analysis of the means for the three groups (introverts, ambiverts and extraverts) in study 1 reveals however that the values are not linear. Ambiverts use even fewer colloquial words than the introverts, but the extraverts use clearly more of these words than the two other groups. However, study 2 shows a linear relation between the proportion of colloquial words of the introverts, ambiverts and extraverts. As the groups are bigger in study 2, one can assume that the unexpected order at the lower end of the extraversion dimension in study 1 was a mere coincidence. The global image that emerges is that differences are limited between ambiverts and introverts but that the extraverts stand out. They use many more colloquial words which could be the result of their lower levels of foreign language anxiety, less inhibition, and less fear of punishment.

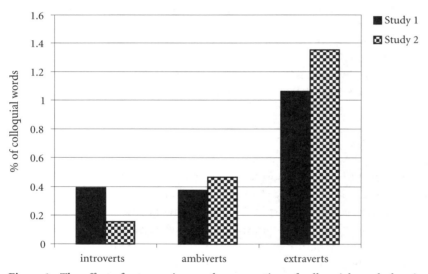

Figure 1. The effect of extraversion on the proportion of colloquial vocabulary in the two studies (*study 1:* introverts n = 3, ambiverts n = 20, extraverts n = 6; *study 2:* introverts n = 11, ambiverts n = 22, extraverts n = 10).

Frequency of contact with French also shows similar significant effects on the use of colloquial words in both corpora. This confirms earlier findings on the effect of the year abroad and regular contact with NS (Regan, to appear, Dewaele & Regan 2001, 2002, Dewaele 2002a). The studies showed that after their stay abroad or after prolonged contact with NS the L2 users approximated roughly — though not exactly — to the NS norm on a range of sociolinguistic variables. It seems thus 'that living abroad for an extended period does something to the learners' usage which classroom input does not' (Regan, to appear).

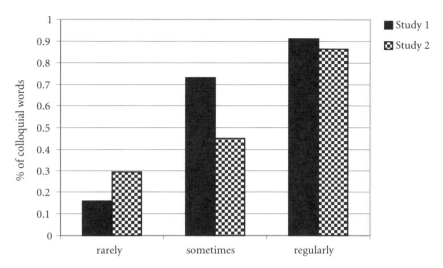

Figure 2. The effect of frequency of use on the proportion of colloquial vocabulary in the two studies (*study 1:* rarely n=13, sometimes n=9, regularly n=7; *study 2:* rarely n=29, sometimes n=13, regularly n=20).

As mentioned before, the amount of contact with French is correlated with morpholexical accuracy. It is therefore not surprising to find a similar positive relationship between morpholexical accuracy and proportion of colloquial words. Morpholexical accuracy was also found by Dewaele & Pavlenko (2002) to be linked to the frequency of use of emotional lemmas and word tokens: more proficient speakers (i.e. speakers with higher rates of morpholexical accuracy) used more emotional word tokens and tended to use a wider variety of emotional lemmas than less proficient speakers. The authors argued that the low frequency of emotional words in the spontaneous conversations of IL speakers might be due to the fact that they have not yet developed detailed scripts to deal with the general topic of 'expressing emotions in the IL'. Less proficient speakers use only basic scripts. This means that the difference between more proficient and less proficient speakers is based not so much at the lexical and semantic level, but it is different at the conceptual level (i.e. presence or absence of scripts on emotion) (Dewaele & Pavlenko 2002). It is very likely that similar scripts exist that reinforce the expressive power of communicative intentions through the use of colloquial words. An important factor in the decision of the less proficient speakers to avoid colloquial words is undoubtedly their uncertainty of lexical nuance (Hyltenstam 1988, Preston 1996, Dewaele & Regan 2001, Bijvoet 2002). All the speakers in both our studies had

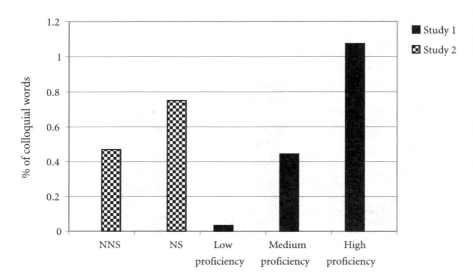

Figure 3. The effect of proficiency and NS/NNS status on the proportion of colloquial vocabulary in the two studies (*study 1:* proficiency: low n = 4, medium n = 19,
high n = 6; *study 2:* NS n = 9, NNS n = 53).

been taught an estimated 150 colloquial words. Many participants had little
chance of using these words in authentic communication. This lack of 'active'
sociopragmatic and stylistic skills in French may have convinced them to stay
clear of words carrying the label 'vernacular' in their mental lexicon. This
strategy would allow them to hide the deficiencies in their communicative
competence. The similarity in patterns for proficiency and NS/NNS status can
be seen in Figure 3.

Several researchers have pointed out that the nature of lexical knowledge
and its acquisition in an L2 is complex and multifaceted (Hulstijn 2001, Meara
2002b, Nation 2001). There are different levels of word knowledge (e.g. the
distinction between productive and receptive knowledge) and the learning of
vocabulary items in the L2 can be either incidental or intentional. The present
study does not allow us to go beyond mere speculation about the reasons why
L2 users use so few colloquial words. Were they avoiding them? Did they have
purely receptive knowledge, or no knowledge at all about these words? What
the findings do show is that the decision to use, or not to use, colloquial
vocabulary seems to be the result of a complex interaction of psychological,
situational, linguistic and sociobiographic variables. The present study thus
adds yet another facet to existing research on IL vocabulary. It also raises one

important caveat about the link between proficiency and use of colloquial words. The fact that the difference between NS and NNS in study 2 was only marginally significant shows the limitations of the predictive value of proficiency in the use of colloquial words. There can be no doubt about the NS' mastery of colloquial vocabulary, as all indicated that French was still their dominant language. Their decision not to use much colloquial vocabulary could indicate that they considered the interaction to be of an academic nature, where a vernacular register would be inappropriate. In other words, the proportion of colloquial vocabulary in IL is not a better indicator of sociopragmatic or sociolinguistic competence than Mean Length of Utterance is for syntactic competence (cf. Dewaele 2000). NS and NNS may be capable of producing vernacular speech and long utterances, but they might also decide to avoid colloquial words and produce short sentences. In other words, they are capable to move along different registers.

The absence of a link between gender and social class and the use of colloquial words might be seen as evidence that the participants have not yet perceived variation patterns linked to gender and social class in French. It is probably difficult to discover these patterns in a classroom context, where more formal speech styles dominate and where colloquial words might be an object of study but not an instrument of communication. We would therefore expect that gender and social class might gradually gain in predictive power once the speakers gain mastery of more vernacular speech styles in French. Learners might gradually conform with the scripts used by certain communities of practice they identify with in the target language and culture (Wenger 1998). The finding that younger speakers in study 2 used more colloquial vocabulary might be related to the general phenomenon that younger speakers use more slang (Tagliamonte 1998), but could also be associated with another factor, namely the recency of a study abroad period. Several younger speakers had spent a couple of months in a francophone country during the previous academic year. It is possible that the increased use of colloquial words was an after-effect. Regan (2002) has shown a similar pattern for *ne* deletion in her corpus of Irish learners, a year after their home-coming.

6.   Conclusion

These results both confirm and expand findings in recent sociolinguistic research in SLA (Preston 2000) that the use of sociolinguistic variants are determined by a variety of psychological and sociobiographical variables. The frequency of use of colloquial words in IL seems to be linked both to the presence and the completeness of semantic and conceptual knowledge. This knowledge varies according to frequency and type of contact speakers have had with French, and their resulting proficiency in that language. As such it could be argued that the use of colloquial words is a criterion of a certain acquisition level, probably situated between pre-advanced and advanced levels (Bartning 1997).

The personality of the speaker also plays a crucial role. More introverted speakers tend to avoid colloquial words, more extraverted speakers use them more freely. It was suggested that this is linked to the nature of extraversion itself, ranging from the over-aroused, cautious, anxious introvert, to the under-aroused, impulsive, confident extravert.

Our findings also show that 'more' is not always 'better' or 'more native-like' as far as the use of non-standard sociolinguistic variants are concerned. Once L2 users reach the advanced level and master colloquial vocabulary, they need to become aware of its appropriate use, developing specific scripts in different registers and mimicking native variation patterns.

Notes

1. The word "L2 user" refers "to a person who knows and uses a second language at any level. One motivation for this usage is the feeling that it is demeaning to call someone who has functioned in an L2 environment for years a "learner" rather than a "user". A person who has been using a second language for twenty-five years is no more an L2 learner than a fifty-year-old monolingual native speaker is an L1 learner" (Cook, 2002: 4).

2. However, the concept of variable rules has been criticized on both theoretical and technical grounds by several authors (e.g. Fasold 1990). It is noteworthy that in L1 variationist articles, authors no longer attempt to formulate variable rules; they merely report frequency differences and associated factor effects.

3. The corpus that is also used in the present study.

4. Eysenck (1981) states that: "the anxiety dimension, as measured by tests such as the Manifest Anxiety Scale (Taylor, 1953), lies within the (...) space defined by introversion-extraversion (...), correlating approximately +0.3 to 0.4 with the introversion end of introversion-extraversion dimension" (p. 167).

5. The researcher provided linguistic assistance with a few queries about the exact meaning of words.

References

Alderson, J. C., Clapham, C., and Steel, D. 1997. "Metalinguistic knowledge, language aptitude and language proficiency." *Language Teaching Research* 1 (2): 93–121.

Altarriba, J. 2003. "Does cariño equal 'liking'? A theoretical approach to conceptual non-equivalence between languages." In *New directions in the study of bilingual memory*, A. Pavlenko, R. Schrauf and J.-M. Dewaele (eds), Special issue of the *International Journal of Bilingualism* 7 (3): 305–322.

Amati-Mehler, J., Argentieri, S. and Canestri, J. 1993. *The Babel of the unconscious: Mother tongue and foreign languages in the psychoanalytic dimension*. Madison, CT: International Universities Press.

Armstrong, N. 1998. "La variation sociolinguistique dans le lexique français." *Zeitschrift für Romanische Philologie* 114 (3): 462–495.

Bartning, I. 1997. "L'apprenant dit avancé et son acquisition d'une langue étrangère. Tour d'horizon et esquisse d'une caractérisation de la variété avancée." *AILE Acquisition et Interaction en Langue Etrangère* 9: 9–50.

Bayley, R. 1994. "Interlanguage variation and the quantitative paradigm: Past-tense marking in Chinese-English." In *Research Methodology in Second-language Acquisition*, E. Tarone, S. Gass and A. Cohen (eds), 157–181. Hillsdale, NJ: Lawrence Erlbaum.

Bayley, R. and Preston, D. (eds). 1996. *Variation in Second Language Acquisition*. Amsterdam and Philadelphia: John Benjamins.

Bijvoet, E. 2002. "Near nativeness and stylistic lexical competence in Swedish of first and second generation Finnish immigrants to Sweden." *The International Journal of Bilingualism* 6 (1): 39–51.

Blanco-Iglesias, S., Broner, J. and Tarone, E. 1995. "Observations of language use in Spanish immersion classroom interactions." In *The Current State of Interlanguage*, L. Eubank, L. Selinker and M. Sharwood Smith (eds), 241–254. Amsterdam and Philadelphia: John Benjamins.

Bloor, M. and Bloor, T. 1991. "Cultural expectations and socio-pragmatic failure in academic writing". In *Socio-cultural issues in English for academic purposes*, P. Adams, B. Heaton and P. Howarth (eds), 1–12. London: Macmillan.

Blum, S. and Levenston, E. A. 1978. "Universals of lexical simplification." *Language Learning* 28: 399–415.

Blum-Kulka, S. 1996. "Introduccion a la pragmatica del interlenguaje". In *La competencia pragmatica. Elementos linguisticos y psicosociales*, J. Cenoz and J. Valencia (eds), 155–175. Bilbao: Universitat del Pais Vasco.

Cheek, J. M. and Buss, A. H. 1981. "Shyness and sociability." *Journal of Personality and Social Psychology* 41 (2): 330–339.

Cook, V. 2002. (ed) *Portraits of the L2 user*. Clevedon: Multilingual Matters.

Dagut, M. and Laufer, B. 1985. "Avoidance of phrasal verbs: a case for contrastive analysis." *Studies in Second Language Acquisition* 7: 73–79.

Damen, L. 1984. "Overcoming the Pollyanna Syndrome." *Cross-Currents* 11: 59–63.

Dewaele, J.-M. 1994. "Variation synchronique des taux d'exactitude. Analyse de fréquence des erreurs morpholexicales dans trois styles d'interlangue française." *International*

Review of Applied Linguistics 32: 275–300.

Dewaele, J.-M. 1996. "Les phénomènes d'hésitation dans l'interlangue française: analyse de la variation interstylistique et interindividuelle." *Rassegna Italiana da Linguistica Applicata* 28: 87–103.

Dewaele, J.-M. 1998. "Speech rate variation in 2 oral styles of advanced French interlanguage." In *Contemporary Approaches to Second Language Acquisition in Social Context*, V. Regan (ed), 113–123. Dublin: University College Academic Press.

Dewaele, J.-M. 2000. "Saisir l'insaisissable ? Les mesures de longueur d'énoncés en linguistique appliquée." *International Review of Applied Linguistics* 38: 31–47.

Dewaele, J.-M. 2001a. "Une distinction mesurable: corpus oraux et écrits sur le continuum de la deixis." *Journal of French Language Studies* 11: 179–199.

Dewaele, J.-M. 2001b. "Interpreting the maxim of quantity: interindividual and situational variation in discourse styles of non-native speakers." In *Cognition in Language Use: Selected Papers from the 7th International Pragmatics Conference*, Vol. 1, E. Németh (ed), 85–99. Antwerp: International Pragmatics Association.

Dewaele, J.-M. 2002a. "Using sociostylistic variants in advanced French IL: the case of nous/on." In *EUROSLA Yearbook 2*, S. Foster-Cohen, T. Ruthenberg, M. L. Poschen (eds), 205–226. Amsterdam/Philadelphia: John Benjamins.

Dewaele, J.-M. 2002b. "Individual differences in L2 fluency: The effect of neurobiological correlates." In *Portraits of the L2 user*, V. Cook (ed), 219–250. Clevedon: Multilingual Matters.

Dewaele, J.-M. 2002c. "The effect of multilingualism and socio-situational factors on communicative anxiety of mature language learners." In J. Ytsma and M. Hooghiemstra (eds), *Proceedings of the Second International Conference on Trilingualism* (CD Rom).

Dewaele, J.-M. 2002d. "Psychological and sociodemographic correlates of communicative anxiety in L2 and L3 production." *The International Journal of Bilingualism* 6: 23–39.

Dewaele, J.-M. 2002e. "Variation, chaos et système en interlangue française. In *Appropriation de la variation en français langue étrangère*, J.-M. Dewaele and R. Mougeon (eds), Special issue of *AILE Acquisition et Interaction en Langue Etrangère* 17: 143–167.

Dewaele, J.-M. (to appear a) "Blistering Barnacles! What language do multilinguals swear in?!" In *Bilingualism and emotions*, J.-M. Dewaele and A. Pavlenko (eds), Special issue of *Estudios de Sociolinguistica* 5 (2004).

Dewaele, J.-M. (to appear b) "The emotional force of swear words and taboo words in the speech of multilinguals." In *Languages and Emotions: A crosslinguistic perspective*. J.-M. Dewaele and A. Pavlenko (eds), Special issue of *Journal of Multilingual and Multicultural Development* 25 (2004).

Dewaele, J.-M. and Furnham, A. 1999. "Extraversion: the unloved variable in applied linguistic research." *Language Learning* 49 (3): 509–544.

Dewaele, J.-M. and Furnham, A. 2000. "Personality and Speech Production: A pilot study of second language learners." *Personality and Individual Differences* 28: 355–365.

Dewaele, J.-M. and Pavlenko, A. 2002. "Emotion vocabulary in interlanguage." *Language Learning* 52: 265–324.

Dewaele, J.-M. and Regan, V. 2001. "The use of colloquial words in advanced French interlanguage." In *EUROSLA Yearbook 1*, S. Foster-Cohen and A. Nizegorodcew (eds),

51–68. Amsterdam / Philadelphia: John Benjamins.

Dewaele, J.-M. and Regan, V. 2002. "Maîtriser la norme sociolinguistique en interlangue française: le cas de l'omission variable de 'ne'." *Journal of French Language Studies* 12: 123–148.

Eysenck, H. J. and Eysenck, M. W. 1985. *Personality and Individual Differences. A Natural Science Approach.* New York and London: Plenum Press.

Eysenck, H. J. and Eysenck, S. B. G. 1984. *Manual of the Eysenck Personality Inventory.* London: Hodder and Stoughton.

Eysenck, M. W. 1981. "Learning, Memory and Personality." In *A Model for Personality,* H. J. Eysenck (ed), 169–209. Berlin: Springer Verlag.

Fasold, R. 1990. *The Sociolinguistics of Language.* Oxford: Basil Blackwell.

Fremont, T., Means, G. H., and Means, R. S. 1976. "Anxiety as a function of task performance feedback and extraversion-introversion." *Psychological Reports* 27: 455–458.

Furnham, A. 1990. "Language and Personality." In *Handbook of Language and Social Psychology,* H. Giles and W. P. Robinson (eds), 73–95. Chichester: John Wiley and Sons.

Haastrup, K. & B. Henriksen 2001. "The interrelationship between vocabulary acquisition theory and general SLA research." In *EUROSLA Yearbook 1,* S. Foster-Cohen and A. Nizegorodcew (eds), 69–78. Amsterdam / Philadelphia: John Benjamins.

Han, Zh. 2003. "Fossilization: From simplicity to complexity." *International Journal of Bilingual Education and Bilingualism* 6 (2): 95–128.

Harris, C. L., Ayçiçegi, A. and Gleason, J. B. (2003) "Taboo words and reprimands elicit greater autonomic reactivity in a first than in a second language." *Applied Psycholinguistics* 24: 561–579.

Hulstijn, J. 2001. "Intentional and incidental second-language vocabulary learning: A reappraisal of elaboration, rehearsal and automaticity". In *Cognition and Second Language Instruction,* P. Robinson (ed), 258–286. Cambridge: Cambridge University Press.

Hyltenstam, K. 1988. "Lexical characteristics of near-native second-language learners of Swedish. *Journal of Multilingual and Multicultural Development* 9 (1–2): 67–84.

Kasper, G. and Rose, K. R. 2001. "Pragmatics in Language Teaching." In *Pragmatics in Language Teaching,* K. R. Rose and G. Kasper (eds), 1–9. Cambridge: Cambridge University Press.

Kinginger, C. 2000. "Learning the pragmatics of solidarity in the networked foreign language classroom." In *Second and foreign language through classroom interaction.* J. K. Hall and L. S. Stoops Verplaetse (eds), 23–46. Mahwah, NJ: Erlbaum.

Kitayama, S. and Markus, H. R. 1994. "Introduction". In *Emotion and Culture. Empirical studies of mutual influence,* 1–19. S. Kitayama and H. R. Markus (eds), Washington: American Psychology Association.

Labov, W. 1972. *Sociolinguistic Patterns.* Pennsylvania: University of Pennsylvania Press.

Labov, W. 1990. "The intersection of sex and social class in the course of linguistic change." *Language Variation and Change* 2: 205–254.

Laufer, B. 2000. "Avoidance of idioms in a second language: the effect of L1-L2 similarity." *Studia Linguistica* 54 (2): 186–196.

Laufer, B. and Eliasson, S. 1993. "What causes avoidance in L2 learning: L1-L2 difference, L1-L2 similarity?" *Studies in Second Language Acquisition* 15: 35–48.

Legrenzi, P., Girotto, V. and Johnson-Laird, P. N. 1993. "Focussing in reasoning and decision making." *Cognition* 49: 37–66.

Lyster R. 1994. "The effect of functional-analytic teaching on aspects of French immersion students' sociolinguistic competence." *Applied Linguistics* 15 (3): 263–287.

Lyster, R. and Rebuffot, J. 2002. "Acquisition des pronoms d'allocution en classe de français immersif." In *Appropriation de la variation en français langue étrangère*, J.-M. Dewaele and R. Mougeon (eds), Special issue of *AILE Acquisition et Interaction en Langue Etrangère* 17: 51–72.

MacIntyre, P. D. and Gardner, R. C. 1991. "Methods and results in the study of anxiety in language learning: a review of the literature." *Language Learning* 41: 85–117.

Matthews, G. and Deary, I. 1998. *Personality Traits*. Cambridge: Cambridge University Press.

Meara, P. 2002a. "Review article: The rediscovery of vocabulary". *Second Language Research* 18 (4): 393–407.

Meara, P. 2002b. Vocabulary acquisition research group archive (VARGA) available at www. swan.ac.uk/cals/calsre/varga.

Mougeon, R. and Beniak, E. 1991. *Linguistic consequences of language contact and restriction: The case of French in Ontario*. New York / Oxford: Oxford University Press.

Mougeon, R., Nadasdi, T. and Rehner, K. 2002. "État de la recherche sur l'appropriation de la variation par les apprenants avancés du FL2 ou FLE." In *Appropriation de la variation en français langue étrangère*, J.-M. Dewaele and R. Mougeon (eds), Special issue of *AILE Acquisition et Interaction en Langue Etrangère* 17: 7–50.

Naiman, N., Frohlich, M., Stern, H. H. and Todesco, A. 1978. *The Good Language Learner*. Toronto: Ontario Institute for Studies in Education.

Nation, P. 2001. *Learning Vocabulary in Another Language*. Cambridge: Cambridge University Press.

Ochs, E. 1996. "Linguistic resources for socialising humanity." In *Rethinking linguistic relativity*, J. Gumperz and S. Levinson (eds), 407–437. Cambridge: Cambridge University Press.

Panayiotou, A. to appear. "Bilingual Emotions: The Untranslatable Self." In *Bilingualism and emotions*, J.-M. Dewaele & A. Pavlenko (eds), Special issue of *Estudios de Sociolinguistica* 5 (2004).

Pavlenko, A. 1999. "New approaches to concepts in bilingual memory." *Bilingualism: Language and Cognition* 2 (3): 209–230.

Pavlenko, A. 2000. "What's in a concept? *Bilingualism: Language and Cognition* 3 (1): 31–36.

Pavlenko, A., Schrauf, R. and J.-M. Dewaele (eds) 2003. *New directions in the study of bilingual memory*. Special issue of the *International Journal of Bilingualism* 7 (3).

Preston, D. 1989. *Variation and Second Language Acquisition*. Oxford: Blackwell.

Preston, D. 1996. "Variationist linguistics." In *Handbook of Second Language Acquisition*, W. C. Ritchie and T. K. Bhatia (eds), 229–265. San Diego and London: Academic Press.

Preston, D. 2000. "Three kinds of sociolinguistics and SLA: A psycholinguistic Perspective." In *Social and Cognitive Factors in Second Language Acquisition. Selected Proceedings of the 1999 Second Language Forum*, B. Swierzbin, F. Morris, M. E. Anderson, C. A. Klee and E. Tarone (eds), 3–30. Somerville, MA: Cascadilla Press.

Regan, V. 2002. "Le contexte d'acquisition : La variation du groupe et de l'individu." *AILE. Acquisition et Interaction en Langue Etrangère* 17 : 123–141.

Regan, V. to appear. "From speech community back to classroom: what variation analysis can tell us about the role of context in the acquisition of French as a foreign language". In *Focus on French as a Foreign Language: Multidisciplinary Approaches,* J.-M. Dewaele (ed.). Clevedon: Multilingual Matters.

Rey, A. and Rey-Debove, J. 1979. *Le Petit Robert.* Paris: Société du nouveau Littré.

Tagliamonte, S. 1998. "Was/were variation across the generations: View from the city of York." *Language Variation and Change* 10: 153–191.

Tarone, E. 1988. *Variation in interlanguage.* London: Edward Arnold.

Tarone, E. 1997. "Analyzing IL in natural settings: A sociolinguistic perspective on second-language acquisition." *Communication and Cognition* 30: 137–149.

Tarone, E. and Swain, M. 1995. "A sociolinguistic perspective on second language use in immersions classrooms." *Modern Language Journal* 79: 166–178.

Tomkins, S. S. 1998. "Script theory: Differential magnification of affects." In *Human Emotions. A reader,* J. M. Jenkins, K. Oatley and N. L. Stein (eds), 209–218. Oxford: Blackwell.

Toya, M. and Kodis, M. 1996. "But I don't want to be rude: On learning how to express anger in the L2." *JALT Journal* 18: 279–295.

Wenger, E. 1998. *Communities of practice: learning, meaning and identity.* Cambridge: Cambridge University Press.

Young, R. 1999. "Sociolinguistic approaches to SLA." *Annual Review of Applied Linguistics* 19: 105–32.

CHAPTER 8

Second language lexical inferencing: Preferences, perceptions, and practices

David D. Qian
The Hong Kong Polytechnic University

Abstract

Unknown words often create obstacles to comprehension in second language reading. In order to find what English as a second language (ESL) learners do when encountering a new word, a survey was conducted with a group of university students with a Korean or Chinese linguistic background. Information gathered from the respondents indicates that the top-down approach to reading was popular among the learners surveyed and many respondents claimed that they frequently guessed unknown words from contexts. A subsample from the group was later invited to participate in a reading experiment focusing on lexical inferencing. Follow-up individual interviews were also conducted. The data from the interviews showed that these learners' actual lexical inferencing practices were significantly different from the self-reported strategies they had indicated in the questionnaire.

1. Introduction

For ESL learners, unknown words in texts often create obstacles to their comprehension (Nation 1990, 1993, 2001). When encountering an unfamiliar word, learners can resort to different resources to deal with the problem, such as using dictionaries, seeking help from the teacher or a peer, or attempting to determine the meaning of the word by guessing its meaning from the context (Harley & Hart 2000). According to O'Malley & Chamot's (1990) taxonomy of L2 learning strategies, asking a teacher or a peer for help belongs to the social or affective category and guessing the meaning of the word from the context is a cognitive strategy. In Schmitt's (1997) taxonomy of strategies for L2 vocabulary learning, lexical guessing is referred to as a discovery strategy. In his survey with a sample of about 600 Japanese learners of English and focused on the perceived usefulness of a taxonomy of vocabulary learning strategies, Schmitt found referring to dictionaries an important strategy used by the respondents. Harley & Hart (2000), in a study with 35 secondary school learners of French in Canada, discovered that L2 vocabulary strategies popular with these learners included guessing word meanings from contexts, using bilingual dictionaries, and asking teachers or friends for help. They also found that few learners among this group frequently used monolingual French dictionaries when encountering a new word.

While there are a number of ways of dealing with unknown words, informed lexical guessing, or inferencing, is often seen as a popular and useful approach to text processing in L2 reading (Bensoussan & Laufer 1984, Carton 1971, dos Santos & Sanpedro Ramos 1993, Fan 2003, Haastrup 1991, Harley & Hart 2000, Morrison 1996, Qian 1998, 1999). Basing on the results of a study with 1,067 ESL learners in Hong Kong, Fan (2003) reports that lexical guessing was among the most frequently used strategies by tertiary level learners of English there. In an investigation with about 850 university-level ESL learners, Gu and Johnson (1996) also found that contextual guessing of unknown words was a popular learning strategy, whose frequency of use was positively, and highly, correlated with language proficiency. Lexical inferencing involves making informed guesses of the meaning of an unknown word with the help of all available linguistic cues as well as other sources of knowledge the learner can resort to. Carton (1971: 45) notes that inferencing 'is intended to refer to a process of identifying unfamiliar stimuli... In inferencing, attributes and contexts that are familiar are utilized in recognizing what is not familiar'.

One thing to bear in mind, however, is that the density of unfamiliar words in a text often plays a significant role in the success or failure in this type of guessing. The higher the density of unknown words, the more challenging the guessing task will be (Nation 2001). Haastrup (1991) assumed that inferencing at the text level and at the word level bear a close relationship and therefore inferencing can be considered a comprehension process. Research on strategies for lexical guessing has been influenced by theoretical models of L2 reading (Qian 1998), among which, top-down models (Goodman 1967, 1968, 1981, Smith 1971) and interactive models (Rumelhart 1977, Stanovich 1980) have a particular bearing. Due to the influence of these theories, ESL teachers and learners generally believe that lexical inferencing mainly involves top-down processing. In lexical guessing, clues can be available at different levels, ranging from lower-level ones, such as orthographical, morphological and phrasal, to mid-level ones such as sentential and inter-sentential, and then to more global-level clues from a whole paragraph or a whole text. In addition to linguistic cues, clues relating to world knowledge are often useful.

2. The present study

The present study was designed to investigate learners' approaches to dealing with unknown words while reading English texts: What approaches learners would claim they preferred, what approaches learners would think they followed, and what approaches learners would actually adopt in lexical inferencing. The study was conducted in order to find out what strategies are popular with young adult ESL learners and to also determine whether the top-down approach to reading comprehension was indeed a critical factor influencing lexical inferencing strategies. The following research questions were addressed in the study:

(1) What resources or help do young adult ESL learners usually use when they encounter unknown words in an English text?

(2) What are the most favoured lexical inferencing practices as perceived and reported by young adult ESL learners?

(3) What are actual lexical inferencing practices of young adult ESL learners in their reading comprehension?

(4) Do the lexical inferencing practices of young adult ESL learners match the lexical inferencing approaches as they have perceived and reported they often use?

2.1 Method

2.1.1 *Participants*
The data were generated from

(1) a survey of 61 respondents, who were all international students having recently arrived in Canada and were attending intensive ESL programmes at two universities in southern Ontario, and

(2) the interviews of a sub-sample of the questionnaire respondents, who were

invited to first participate in a reading experiment, which included guessing the meaning of unknown words in context, before the interview sessions.

The participating students were all from the Korean or Chinese language background with an average age of about 24.

2.1.2 *Instruments*

The questionnaire, which was developed to explore eight learner behaviours related to dealing with unknown words in English texts, contains the following two general questions for structured responses:

(1) How often do you do each of the following when you meet an unfamiliar word in reading an English text?

(2) What kind of information do you use when trying to guess the meaning of an unfamiliar word in an English text?

Under the first question, which was modelled after Part 1 of the Questionnaire used in a Harley & Hart (2000) study, eight ways of dealing with a new word were described. For the second question, six strategies were described for making use of various levels and aspects of one's knowledge to deal with an unknown word in comprehending a text. The respondents were provided with four choices of time frequency to indicate how often they resort to each option in the situation described in the above questions. The frequency choices were: *often, sometimes, rarely* and *never* (see Appendix for the complete questionnaire).

A one-page text on greenhouses was prepared for the reading experiment. The text contained 10 highlighted words (*greenhouse, feature, indispensable, edible, irrespective, permanent, functional, conduct, devices, free-standing*), which were presumed unknown to the participants and accounted for about 7% of the total number of words of the text. Except for the word *greenhouse*, which appeared three times, all the other target words appeared only once in the text. Four experienced ESL teachers, including two native English speakers and two non-native English speakers, were invited to evaluate the suitability of the experimental text, in order to ensure that the contextualized meanings of the target words were indeed inferable and that helpful clues, beyond the morphological cues contained in the target words, were available at different levels for inferring the meanings of most target words. Only one target word, *free-standing,* appeared to be without obvious clues beyond the word itself. However, it was agreed that this word contained helpful morphological information for meaning-inferencing, and it was useful to have a target word of this type.

A pilot study was also carried out with four learners of different English proficiency levels to ensure that learners of intermediate or high-intermediate level would not normally know these words but would be able to infer the meaning of some of these items with the help of clues from the text.

Questions for individual interview sessions were developed based on the following generic questions:

(1)   Please can you summarize the main idea of this passage?
(2)   How do you explain this sentence in your own words?
(3)   What is the meaning of word X (an unknown word) in this sentence?
(4)   Why did you think this was the meaning of the word here?
(5)   Did you consider other meanings before deciding on this one?
(6)   You have indicated you did not know this word. So how did you work out the meaning of this word?
(7)   What information helped you understand this sentence?
(8)   Is there anything else that helped you understand this sentence?

2.1.3   *Procedure*

The investigation was carried out in two phases. In the first phase, the questionnaire was administered to all potential participants. The second phase was focused on the reading experiment and the follow-up individual interviews with some respondents.

The questionnaire on dealing with new words during reading was first administered to over 100 students in the Intensive ESL Programmes described above, with the help of their ESL instructors. In total, 61 students responded to the questionnaire. Two weeks after the collection of the questionnaires, a sub-sample of 12 respondents was randomly selected and invited to participate in a reading experiment, which lasted about one hour. Each participant attended the experimental reading session individually. At the reading session, the participant was first asked to underline all the new words they encountered in the experimental text. Then they were instructed to read through the experimental text and work out the meanings of the underlined words independently and without resorting to dictionaries. All words underlined by the participant became stimuli, which often included some or most of those originally highlighted words.

Upon the completion of the reading task, each participant went through a one-hour interview, during which questions were asked about how the participant inferred the meanings of the unknown words in the experimental text and why they did it that way. Questions were also asked about some non-target words underlined by interviewees, when the interviewer suspected that these words could hinder their comprehension of the target words. Coming from high-intermediate English level classes, most participants spoke fluent English, except two, who preferred to be interviewed in their L1. As a precaution, those interviewed in English were informed beforehand that they could also write down the meaning of the target words in L1 in addition to their oral explanations if needed. All interviews were tape-recorded and transcribed later. As an example, an excerpt from the interviews is provided below, together with the keyword coding used for the data analysis.

Relevant text: There is a greenhouse to suit every requirement, heated or unheated, small or large, permanent or portable, decorative or functional.

Interviewer:	*Now what does 'permanent' mean here?*
Student:	*Permanent … I think it is opposite to portable.*
Interviewer:	*So what word would you use if I take out 'permanent' from this sentence?*
Student:	*Ah… fixed.*
Interviewer:	*Fixed? So what words helped you to figure out this meaning?*
Student:	*Permanent?*
Interviewer:	*Yeah.*
Student:	*Portable.*
Interviewer:	*Why?*
Student:	*Because in other things, like 'small or large' [coding: syntagmatic cue], they have opposite meanings.*

In this inferencing attempt, the learner mainly used as clues the meaning of other words in the sentence containing the target word *permanent*. Phrases such as 'small or large' gave her the direction that the meaning of *permanent* should be 'opposite to portable'. Therefore, she chose 'fixed' as the meaning for *permanent* in this context, and successfully accomplished the inferencing task.

2.2 Data analysis

The questionnaire data from the survey were analysed quantitatively and the rank-orders of all options were computed. The interview data, as exemplified by the excerpt above, were first examined qualitatively using content analysis. A set of key words indicating linguistic and other relevant categories emerged during the analysis. These key words were later used as the guidelines to group different inferencing strategies that appeared during the data analysis (see

Tables 4 and 5 for the broad categories representing each inferencing strategy). Frequencies of the use of each strategy were computed based on the results of the qualitative analysis.

2.3   Results

2.3.1   *How learners approach unknown words*
The purpose of the first question was to identify the participants' perceptions of their most frequent behaviours when they encountered unknown words. Table 1 summarizes the questionnaire responses from the 61 respondents. As Table 1 shows, guessing meaning from context was reported as the most frequent and popular behaviour among the respondents. About 62.3% of the sample indicated that they *often* guessed word meaning from the context. Another 34.4% stated that they *sometimes* guessed the meaning of an unknown word from the context.

The participants also reported looking up an unknown word in a bilingual dictionary as a frequent behaviour. About 41% of the sample noted that they would *often* consult an English-Korean or English-Chinese dictionary when

Table 1. Frequency of learners' self-reported behaviours in dealing with unknown words while reading (n = 61)

Behaviour	Number (%) of learners			
	Often	Some-times	Rarely	Never
a) Look up the word in an English-Korean/ Chinese dictionary	25 (41.0)	21 (34.4)	10 (16.4)	5 (8.2)
b) Look it up in an English-only dictionary	20 (32.8)	26 (42.6)	9 (14.8)	6 (9.8)
c) Guess its meaning from the context	38 (62.3)	21 (34.4)	2 (3.3)	0 (0)
d) Ignore the word	6 (9.8)	35 (57.4)	18 (29.5)	2 (3.3)
e) Ask the teacher for assistance	6 (9.8)	19 (31.1)	27 (44.3)	9 (14.8)
f) Ask a friend if they know the word	7 (11.5)	21 (34.4)	21 (34.4)	12 (19.7)
g) Look for clues to meaning in the word itself	14 (23.0)	30 (49.2)	13 (21.3)	4 (6.6)
h) Make a note of the word (i.e. write it down)	18 (29.5)	29 (47.5)	7 (11.5)	7 (11.5)

they encountered an unknown word. Another 34.4% indicated that they *sometimes* used an English-Korean or English-Chinese dictionary to get the meaning of an unknown word. With regard to using monolingual English dictionaries for this purpose, about 32.8% of the sample acknowledged that they *often* sought help from an English-only dictionary for the meaning of an unknown word, and 42.6% indicated they *sometimes* consulted an English-only dictionary for a word meaning.

Making a note of unknown words while reading English texts was also a popular practice among the participants. About 29.5% of the sample reported *often* doing this, and another 47.5% acknowledged *sometimes* doing this. Another noteworthy finding was the proportion of respondents who indicated that they looked for the meaning of an unknown word from clues within the word. About 23% of the sample stated that they *often* did this, and 49.2% indicated that they *sometimes* did this. In addition, about 9.8% of the sample acknowledged that they would *often* ignore an unknown word in a reading process, and as high as 57.4% of the respondents reported *sometimes* doing so. These two groups make up over 67% of the sample.

In comparison, the other two strategies, i.e. asking the teacher for assistance and asking a friend for assistance, were infrequently employed. Only 9.8% of the sample indicated they *often* asked the teacher for assistance when encountering an unknown word. About 31.1% reported they *sometimes* did so. As for getting a friend's help in understanding an unfamiliar word, only about 11.5% indicated that they *often* did so, and about 31.1% of the respondents indicated that they *sometimes* would resort to this approach. These two approaches, therefore, appeared to be the most infrequently used ones.

Table 2. Ranking of frequencies of learners' self-reported behaviours in dealing with unknown words while reading (n = 61)

Rank	Behaviour		Mean Ranking	SD
1	1c.	Guess its meaning from the context	3.59	.56
2	1a.	Look up the word in an English-Korean/Chinese dictionary	3.08	.95
3	1b.	Look up the word in an English-only dictionary	2.97	.95
4	1h.	Make a note of the word	2.95	.94
5	1g.	Look for clues to meaning in the word itself	2.89	.84
6	1d.	Ignore the word	2.74	.68
7	1f.	Ask a friend if they know the word	2.38	.93
8	1e.	Ask the teacher for assistance	2.36	.86

When a scale of four points is assigned to the four frequency categories (*often* = 4, *sometimes* = 3, *rarely* = 2, and *never* = 1), a mean ranking of self-reported behaviours emerges. Table 2 shows that when the 61 learners encountered an unknown word in an English text, they would most likely try to work out the meaning of the word by guessing from the context, their next most likely approach was checking out the meaning of the word in a bilingual (English-Korean/Chinese) dictionary or a monolingual English dictionary, and the least likely was to ask a friend or a teacher for a solution.

2.3.2 *How learners infer the meaning of unknown words in context*
The second research question asks about the most favoured lexical inferencing practices as perceived and reported by young adult ESL learners. For this purpose, mean ranking by the entire sample and by the sub-sample were both computed for each strategy in the questionnaire (Tables 3 and 4). The ranks of the perceived strategies and the frequencies of actual use of these strategies are compared in Table 5.

The results reported in Table 3 indicate that the participants in the survey believed that their lexical inferencing strategies were mainly top-down, as

Table 3. Results of survey of the whole sample: ranking of students' preferred lexical inferencing strategies perceived (n = 61)

Item	Rank	Strategy	Short Name	Mean Ranking (Max 4)
2f	1	I make use of the meaning of the paragraph or text as a whole to guess the meaning of the unknown word	Global meaning	3.64
2c	2	I use my background knowledge of the topic of the text to guess the meaning of the unknown word	World knowledge	3.59
2b	3	I use the meaning of other words in the same sentence to help me guess the meaning of the unknown word	Syntagmatic cues	3.36
2e	4	I examine the unknown word to see if any part of it is familiar in meaning	Morphological cues	3.21
2d	5	I look for grammatical clues in the surrounding sentence to help me guess the meaning of the unknown word	Sentence grammar	2.98
2a	6	I examine the unknown word to see if it contains any grammatical clues to tell me what part of speech it belongs to	Word class	2.95

Table 4. Results of survey of the sub-sample: ranking of students' preferred lexical inferencing strategies perceived (n = 12)

Item	Rank	Strategy	Short Name	Mean Ranking (Max 4)
2f	1	I make use of the meaning of the paragraph or text as a whole to guess the meaning of the unknown word	Global meaning	3.83
2c	2	I use my background knowledge of the topic of the text to guess the meaning of the unknown word	World knowledge	3.75
2e	3	I examine the unknown word to see if any part of it is familiar in meaning	Morphological cues	3.17
2b	4	I use the meaning of other words in the same sentence to help me guess the meaning of the unknown word	Syntagmatic cues	3.08
2d	5	I look for grammatical clues in the surrounding sentence to help me guess the meaning of the unknown word	Sentence grammar	2.92
2a	6	I examine the unknown word to see if it contains any grammatical clues to tell me what part of speech it belongs to	Word class	2.83

evidenced by the fact that the top two categories of their perceived strategies (*global meaning* and *world knowledge*) were both the most top-down in nature among the six options provided in the questionnaire.

The results of the analysis of the data from the sub-sample (see Table 4) also indicate a similar trend, except that this time the ranks of the top two categories stand out more saliently (3.83 and 3.75) than their ranks (3.64 and 3.59) with the entire sample. In Table 3, the difference between the second rank (3.59) and the third rank (3.36) is 0.23, whereas in Table 4 that difference has increased to 0.58 between the second ranked *world knowledge* and the third ranked *morphological cues*.

The third research question aims to identify actual lexical inferencing practices of young adult ESL learners in their reading comprehension. Research Question 4 was proposed to determine whether the lexical inferencing practices of young adult ESL learners match the lexical inferencing approaches they have reported they often use. Table 5 provides comparisons of all results. It is surprising to note that the most popular strategies as perceived by the participants, i.e., *global meaning* and *world knowledge*, have now descended to the 5th and 3rd ranks respectively when it comes to actual use. Instead, *Syntagmatic cues*, which ranked the 3rd with the entire sample and the 4th with

Table 5. Comparing perceptions and actual applications of lexical inferencing strategies

Rank of Perceived Strategies (n = 61)	Rank of Perceived Strategies (n = 12)	Strategy	Frequency of Actual Use (n = 12)	Rank of Actual Use (n = 12)
1	1	Global meaning	6	5
2	2	World knowledge	16	3
3	4	Syntagmatic cues	23	1
4	3	Morphological cues	21	2
5	5	Sentence grammar	7	4
6	6	Word class	5	6

Note. The Frequencies of Actual Use were calculated according to the actual total number of times participating learners used, or tried to use, a contextual clue deemed to belong to a specific category of knowledge source corresponding to the inferencing strategy listed in Table 5.

the sub-sample, has now ascended to the top rank. Similarly, the most bottom-up strategy, *morphological cues,* which ranked 4th with the entire sample and 3rd with the sub-sample, has now become the 2nd ranked strategy in terms of the frequency of actual use.

3. Discussion

This study has produced some unexpected, yet interesting, findings. The results indicate that when encountering an unknown word in an English text, ESL learners reported that they would often try to work out its meaning by guessing from the context. The results also show that, while making use of a monolingual or bilingual dictionary to find out word meaning may also be a likely behaviour among these learners, the frequencies of this behaviour, as reflected in Tables 1 and 2, are somewhat lower than that of lexical guessing. Also surprisingly, these learners' least likely behaviour when they encounter an unknown word would be to ask a friend or a teacher for help. These findings only partially corroborate findings from previous research (e.g. Gu & Johnson 1996, Harley & Hart's 2000, Schmitt 1997). Although these studies have all found lexical inferencing and using bilingual dictionaries to be popular strategies with L2 learners, participants in the Harley and Hart study, however, did report using monolingual French dictionaries as an infrequent behaviour, whereas the present study found a high mean ranking (3rd among eight options) for using monolingual English dictionaries by young adult ESL learners with a Chinese or Korean background. Another difference is that asking help from a teacher or a peer was perceived as a favoured behaviour among learners in Harley and Hart's study, whereas in the present study these two strategies were reported as the least used ones. Lexical guessing was perceived as an important strategy by learners in Gu & Johnson's (1996) survey and the present investigation. In Schmitt's (1997) study, however, this strategy was not regarded as being popular by his survey respondents.

However, since results of the present study have demonstrated that what the learners perceived and reported they did when inferring lexical meanings are fairly different from what they actually did in the inferencing processes, it now becomes a question whether or not learners' judgments should be deemed reliable based on their reports on their own reading behaviours when encountering unknown lexical items in texts. In other words, we should be concerned about to what extent we can rely on research results purely generated from survey data.

A further comparison between findings from the present study and from the Harley & Hart (2000) study reveals that, while both studies were conducted in Ontario, Canada, Harley & Hart's investigation used a sample of grades 9 and 11 local English-speaking students in French language programmes. However, the participants in the present study were university-age international students, who were attending intensive English programmes and who spoke Chinese or Korean as their first language. Since the age ranges and the cultural and linguistic backgrounds of the samples in the two studies were different, it is possible that the differences in the findings of the two studies were due to the differences in the participants' demographic and linguistic backgrounds. Another possibility is that English-speaking Canadian students and Asian students may perceive their own learning styles and achievements differently due to cultural differences, as demonstrated by the results of Laufer & Yano's (2001) study.

With reference to lexical inferencing, in the present study, the participants relied heavily on the immediate semantic context (*syntagmatic cues*) and the forms of unknown words *per se* (*morphological cues*) to obtain the meanings of the unknown words, but made very light use of clues from the *global meaning* of the text, *word class*, and *sentence grammar*. These results suggest that the participants' actual approaches to processing the meaning of a general academic English text were not as top-down as they themselves had perceived. However, without further investigation, it is difficult to explain why this discrepancy has emerged, although it is likely that the discrepancies may be related to learners' metacognitive strategies for L2 learning (O'Malley & Chamot 1990). Another possible reason for the discrepancies could be that learners were often told to use top-down strategies by their teachers, who nowadays mostly subscribe to integrative or top-down reading approaches. Because of this influence, learners now believed they were already doing it this way. It is also possible that the discrepancies were, to some limited extent, caused by the way some target words appeared in the experimental text so that inferencing strategies could not be applied equally on every occasion. For example, participants were able to use only clues within the target word *per se* in inferring the meaning of *free-standing*, while other target words had more global clues for the participants to access. Also, some clustering of target words in a couple of sentences may have increased the difficulty level for lexical inferencing for some participants although, in reality, none of them had more than two unknown words in any single clause. Further exploration, especially in-depth interview, is highly desirable in order to uncover the reasons why learners perceived their lexical inferencing strategies as more top-down than they actually were.

The present results also appear to suggest that vocabulary learning research purely based on survey data is precarious. As shown in this paper, survey data on learners' perceived learning strategies do not always reliably reflect what strategies learners actually adopt. This may have a practical implication for frontline ESL teachers. In learning English vocabulary, students might not always do what they believe or say is right for them. Their actual practices may deviate significantly from what they perceive they often do. It would therefore be helpful if teachers would factor in this possible deviation when teaching new vocabulary or planning and organizing learning activities.

References

Bensoussan, M., and Laufer, B. 1984. "Lexical guessing in context in EFL reading comprehension". *Journal of Research in Reading*, 7: 15–32.

Carton, A. S. 1971. "Inferencing: A process in using and learning language". In *The psychology of second language learning*, P. Pimsleur, and T. Quinn (eds), 45–58. Cambridge: Cambridge University Press.

dos Santos, V. M. X., and Sanpedro Ramos, S. R. M. 1993. "Guessing and its pedagogical implications for reading comprehension". Paper presented at the 10th AILA World Congress, Amsterdam.

Fan, M. Y. 2003. "Frequency of use, perceived usefulness, and actual usefulness of second language vocabulary strategies: A study of Hong Kong Learners". *Modern Language Journal*, 87: 222–241.

Goodman, K. S. 1967. "Reading: A psycholinguistic guessing game". *Journal of the Reading Specialist*, 6: 126–135.

Goodman, K. S. (ed.) 1968. *The psycholinguistic nature of the reading process*. Detroit: Wayne State University Press.

Goodman, K. S. 1981. "Miscue analysis and future research directions". In *Learning to read in different languages*, S. Hudelson (ed.), ix-xiii. Washington, DC: Center for Applied Linguistics.

Gu, Y. and Johnson, R. K. 1996. "Vocabulary learning strategies and language learning outcomes". *Language Learning*, 46: 643–697.

Haastrup, K. 1991. *Lexical inferencing procedures or talking about words: Receptive procedures in foreign language learning with special reference to English*. Tübingen: Gunter Narr.

Harley, B., and Hart, D. 2000. "Vocabulary learning in the content-oriented second language classroom: Student perceptions and proficiency". *Language Awareness*, 9: 78–96.

Laufer, B., and Yano, Y. 2001. "Understanding unfamiliar words in a text: Do L2 learners understand how much they don't understand?" *Reading in a Foreign Language*, 13 (2): 549–566.

Morrison, L. 1996. "Talking about words: A study of French as a second language learners' lexical inferencing procedures". *Canadian Modern Language Review*, 53: 41–75.

Nation, I. S. P. 1990. *Teaching and learning vocabulary*. New York: Newbury House.

Nation, I. S. P. 1993. "Vocabulary size, growth, and use". In *The bilingual lexicon*, R. Schreuder, and B. Weltens (eds), 115–134. Amsterdam/ Philadelphia, PA: John Benjamins.

Nation, I. S. P. 2001. *Learning vocabulary in another language*. Cambridge: Cambridge University Press.

O'Malley, J. M. and Chamot, A. U. 1990. *Learning strategies in second language acquisition*. Cambridge: Cambridge University Press.

Qian, D. D. 1998. *Depth of vocabulary knowledge: Assessing its role in adults' reading comprehension in English as a second language*. Unpublished PhD thesis, University of Toronto.

Qian, D. D. 1999. "How ESL learners use their knowledge sources in reading comprehension". Paper presented at TESL Ontario Conference, Toronto, Canada.

Rumelhart, D. E. 1977. "Toward an interactive model of reading". In *Attention and performance, VI*, S. Dornic (ed.), 573–603. Hillsdale, NJ: Lawrence Erlaum.

Smith, F. 1971. *Understanding reading*. New York: Holt, Reinhart and Winston.

Schmitt, N. 1997. "Vocabulary learning strategies". In *Vocabulary: Description, acquisition and pedagogy*, N. Schmitt and M. McCarthy (eds), 199–227. Cambridge: Cambridge University Press.

Stanovich, K. E. 1980. "Toward an interactive-compensatory model of individual differences in the development of reading fluency". *Reading Research Quarterly*, 16: 32–71.

APPENDIX

QUESTIONNAIRE ON READING STRATEGIES

Dear Student,
People have different ways of dealing with new words in a second language. There is no 'right' way or 'wrong' way. This questionnaire asks you what you actually do, not what you think you should do, in reading an English text. Please complete it to help me understand how you deal with words you don't know.

1. How often do you do each of the following when you meet an unfamiliar word in reading an English text? (Please check **one** box for each item.)

	often	sometimes	rarely	never
a) Look up the word in an English-Korean/Chinese dictionary	[ ]	[ ]	[ ]	[ ]
b) Look up the word in an English-only dictionary	[ ]	[ ]	[ ]	[ ]
c) Guess its meaning from the context	[ ]	[ ]	[ ]	[ ]
d) Ignore the word	[ ]	[ ]	[ ]	[ ]
e) Ask the teacher for assistance	[ ]	[ ]	[ ]	[ ]
f) Ask a friend if they know the word	[ ]	[ ]	[ ]	[ ]
g) Look for clues to meaning in the word itself	[ ]	[ ]	[ ]	[ ]
h) Make a note of the word (i.e. write it down)	[ ]	[ ]	[ ]	[ ]
i) Other (specify) _____	[ ]	[ ]	[ ]	[ ]

2. What kind of information do you use when trying to guess the meaning of an unfamiliar word in an English text: (Please check **one** box for each item.)

	often	sometimes	rarely	never
a) I examine the unknown word to see if it contains any grammatical clues to tell me what part of speech it belongs to	[ ]	[ ]	[ ]	[ ]
b) I use the meaning of other words in the same sentence to help me guess the meaning of the unknown word	[ ]	[ ]	[ ]	[ ]
c) I use my background knowledge of the topic of the text to guess the meaning of the unknown word	[ ]	[ ]	[ ]	[ ]
d) I look for grammatical clues in the surrounding sentence to help me guess the meaning of the unknown word	[ ]	[ ]	[ ]	[ ]
e) I examine the unknown word to see if any part of it is familiar in meaning	[ ]	[ ]	[ ]	[ ]
f) I make use of the meaning of the paragraph or text as a whole to guess the meaning of the unknown word	[ ]	[ ]	[ ]	[ ]

Thank you very much for your help.

TESTING

The relation between lexical richness and vocabulary size in Dutch L1 and L2 children

Anne Vermeer
Tilburg University

Abstract

Most measures of lexical richness in spontaneous speech data, based on the distribution of, or the relation between types and tokens, appear to be neither reliable nor valid. This chapter describes an alternative, the MLR (*Measure of Lexical Richness*), that measures lexical richness on the basis of the degree of difficulty of the words used, as measured by their (nine levels of) frequency in daily language input. The MLR is calculated by means of a semi-automatic computer program, and is meant for the analysis of texts of (pupils in) primary education, with a vocabulary size of up to about 25,000 different lemmas. To validate the MLR, spontaneous speech data of 16 native Dutch children with Dutch as their first language, and 16 ethnic minority children with Dutch as a second language in grade 2 (age 7/8) were gathered (about 200 utterances from each child) and analysed with the MLR. The children's MLR scores were compared with their scores on a Receptive Vocabulary task (giving an indication of the size of vocabulary), with their scores on a Definition task, and with various type/token based measures. The outcomes of the validation study showed that the MLR differentiates significantly between the two groups with obvious differences in vocabulary (Dutch L1 and Dutch L2 children), shows high and significant correlations with vocabulary tasks administered to the same children, and is independent of syntactic abilities (MLU) and text length (number of types and utterances). Thus, the MLR seems to be a more valid measure of lexical richness in spontaneous speech data for children than type/token based measures, and it has the added advantage of providing an estimate of the absolute size of a child's productive vocabulary.

1.   Introduction

The purpose of this chapter is to propose a valid measure of lexical richness. Measures of lexical richness attempt to quantify the degree to which a varied and large vocabulary is used in spoken or written texts (Laufer & Nation 1995: 307). The best known, but also the worst, measure of lexical richness is undoubtedly the Type Token Ratio (TTR), in which 'types' (V) are the number of different words, and 'tokens' (N) the total number of words. Those measures are, however, less successful than was initially supposed, as pointed out by Malvern & Richards (1997). Most measures of lexical richness are, like the TTR, based on the distribution of, or the relation between, types and tokens. The main problem with these measures is that this relation varies as proficiency develops, and if a relation between two measures is dependent on development, a stable measure cannot be found. For example, 'Ideal weight', measured with 'length' and 'weight' as values, will never be a stable measure for all people, because from age 1 to 18, people are growing in length, but after 18 no more (and after 80 they will even shrink a bit). The same holds for a type/token based measure: it is supposed to change (from low to high) but it does not, because V develops in another way and speed as N, dependent on state of development (as with length of people). If there is a linear relation between the increases in the number of types and tokens (produced during a certain activity) over time, the TTR (V/N), for example, will have a constant value, and no development will be measured. In a curvilinear relation, where the number of tokens increases relatively faster than the types, the TTR will decrease in value. However, depending on the stage of acquisition, an irregular pattern is also possible. Imagine a learner having just acquired the function words *a* and *the* at a certain stage of acquisition. Only these two types will account for a strong increase in the number of tokens, because *a* and *the* are very frequent. The denominator (N variants) outnumbers the numerator (V variants), which produces a *de*creasing curve, although it is clear that the learner has made progress in language acquisition (see also Vermeer 1992: 151–153). In addition to this problem, type/token based measures are heavily dependent on text length and on the number of topics discussed. For an annotated bibliography, see Richards & Malvern (1997).

Not surprisingly thus, research shows that type/token based measures are neither reliable nor valid (cf. Laufer & Nation 1995, Malvern & Richards 1997, Tweedie & Baayen 1998, Vermeer 2000, Jarvis 2002). Often, they do not discriminate between groups with obvious differences in vocabulary, and they

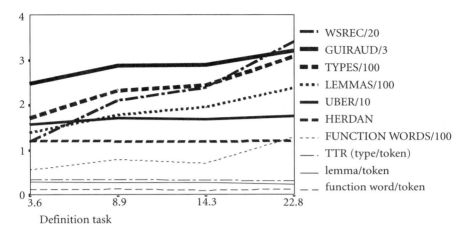

Figure 1. Scores on different lexical measures in spontaneous speech data collected from four groups of children, based on the Definition task (from: Vermeer 2000)

often show no increase in vocabulary growth in longitudinal studies. Figure 1 (from Vermeer 2000) shows the outcomes of various type/token based measures of four groups with different levels of vocabulary.

On the basis of their scores on a Definition task, 150 elementary school children between 4 and 7 years old were divided into four groups with mean scores (see Figure 1) of 3.6; 8.9; 14.3; and 22.8, corresponding to mean receptive vocabulary sizes of about 1,500 words, 3,000 words, 4,500 words, and 6,000 words, respectively. They also performed a receptive vocabulary test (WSREC). In addition to the two vocabulary tasks, for each child, 200 utterances of free speech were analysed and the mean scores on various measures of lexical richness were calculated. These are graphically displayed in Figure 1 (some means have been divided in order to display them in one figure, see the legend). As can be seen, the mean number of TYPES and LEMMAS increases steadily over the four groups. GUIRAUD (V/√N) remains about the same for groups 2 and 3, as does the number of FUNCTION WORDS. The other measures, such as UBER $(logN)^2/(logN-logV)$ and HERDAN (logV/logN), and the last two measures (LEMMA/TOKEN and FUNCTION WORDS/TOKEN), do not increase over the four groups. Thus, simply counting the number of types or lemmas seems to be the best measure of lexical richness, but it is unclear whether in that case it is also syntactic enrichment or Mean Length of Utterance that is measured.

Language development goes along with increasing length of constituents and sentences, in which function words take over the role of juxtaposition of sentences (which occurs when a person reaches the 3,000– to 4,500–word stage). However, a distinction between function and content words does not lead to better and more reliable results for the lexical measures (cf. Richards 1987: 207). Moreover, the variance in the frequency of words shows a distribution in which the first 1,000 most frequently used words of a language are very frequent and the other words very infrequent, known as 'the law of Zipf' (frequency multiplied by rank has a constant value), and graphically displayed as a hyperbola (cf. Alekseev 1984). For that reason, all compound measures show irregular patterns. Both developments (increasing length of sentences and variance in word frequency) make any measure based on a relation between types and tokens in a growing vocabulary very complicated. However, Malvern & Richards (1997, 2000, 2002, McKee, Malvern & Richards 2000) claim to have found a way to use mathematical modelling to overcome the influence of variable text length. Their measure is calculated in two steps. First, a curve of the TTR against tokens is produced by randomly sampling words from the text. Next, the software (*vocd*) finds the best fit between this empirical curve and theoretical curves calculated from the model by adjusting the value of a parameter. Jarvis' (2002) analysis shows that this parameter, D, provides accurate curve-fitting models of lexical diversity, but his Tables 4 and 5 also show that D does not discriminate very well between groups with obvious differences in vocabulary, and his Tables 6 and 7 show low or moderate correlations of D with both vocabulary test scores and holistic ratings (Jarvis 2002: 73–79), indicating a low concurrent validity. Thus, despite Malvern & Richards' parameter D, the conclusion holds that type/token based measures provide no valid measures of lexical richness.

My major objection to type/token-based measures is that they do not take into account the *difficulty* of a word. Whether a word is difficult or not, these measures just count how many types and tokens appear in the data. However, there is a relation between the difficulty of a word and acquisition order. Words are not learned in an arbitrary order. Genus terms or prototypes like *bird* or *chair* are more frequently heard and used in everyday speech than super categories (*animal* or *furniture*) or subcategories (*blackbird* or *swivel chair*) and are, therefore, also learned at an earlier stage (Van der Vliet 1997: 69). Huttenlocher *et al.* (1991) found that the relative frequency of words from the parents' input is strongly related to the order of acquisition of those words by their children. High frequency words are better known than low frequency ones (Kibby 1977, Nation 1990: 77, Brown 1993: 277, Vermeer 2001). In the latter study

(2001: 229), I found high correlations between children's word knowledge and frequency of occurrence of those words in the frequency corpus of Schrooten & Vermeer (1994): for 4-year-olds, .67 (for native Dutch children with Dutch as their first language: DL1) and .77 (for ethnic minority children with Dutch as a second language: DL2), and for 7-year-olds, .53 (DL1) and .60 (DL2). For information on the effects of word frequency and age of acquisition in recognition and recall, see also Dewhurst, Hitch & Barry (1998), and Gerhard & Barry (1998).

Since the frequency of a word is related to acquisition order, a more valid measure of lexical richness might be to relate the words in spontaneous speech data to their frequency (or frequency classes) in a corpus, such as that of Francis & Kučera (1982). This is comparable to a procedure in the Lexical Frequency Profile (LFP, Laufer & Nation 1995) for written texts, in which four levels are distinguished, or the measure for Advanced Lexical Richness (ALR, Treffers-Daller & Van Hout 1999) for spoken texts, in which two frequency levels are distinguished. Moreover, it makes an indication of absolute vocabulary size possible, in the same way as is done by extrapolating scores on some vocabulary tests (cf. the Vocabulary Levels Test, Laufer & Nation 1999). It should be noted, however, that the relation between word frequency and acquisition order is more complex for adults than it is for children. Firstly, adults know more words, and, after the most frequent 12,000 words, enormous numbers of words have approximately the same frequency (see Hazenberg 1994), so it is difficult to establish a rank order. Secondly, the relation does not hold for many academic words, in particular for adult L2 learners, because of their interlingual roots and international use. For that reason, presumably, in Laufer (1998), the LFP (in which the third of four levels consists of academic words only) decreases with augmenting vocabulary in tenth and eleventh grade ESL classes: the students' knowledge of English academic words does not reflect their knowledge of English vocabulary. For children in primary education, however, word frequency in daily input is strongly related to acquisition order (see above), and word frequency can be used as an operationalization of the degree of difficulty of a word. In my opinion, the *difficulty of words*, as measured by their frequency (or frequency classes) in daily input in children, must be the starting point in measuring lexical richness. It is not only more transparent (the relation between 'an infrequent word' and 'a difficult word' is clear and easy to understand), but it is also independent of text length and syntactic abilities.

2.   Towards an alternative measure of lexical richness

In this section, I will describe an alternative lexical measure of spontaneous speech data, the MLR (*Measure of Lexical Richness*), based on the degree of difficulty of the words used, measured by calculating their relative frequency in daily language input. To establish the difficulty of a word, I distinguished nine categories of frequency classes (the geometric means of the frequencies) in the word list of Schrooten & Vermeer (1994), representing nine categories of difficulty. The geometric mean (see Van Hout & Vermeer 1992) covers aspects of both word frequency and variation between different corpora. In Schrooten & Vermeer (1994) nearly 2 million words (tokens) were collected in schools (Kindergarten and grades 1 to 6) — yielding a total of 26,000 lemmas — from both oral and written language input in primary-education teachers' instructions, picture books, readers, and language, arithmetic, and social studies textbooks. Using the MLR, we measured the relative distribution of the words in texts, over these nine categories of difficulty.

To validate the MLR, spontaneous speech data collected from 16 native Dutch children (DL1) and 16 ethnic minority children (DL2) in grade 2 (age 7/8) were gathered (about 200 utterances from each child) and analysed. The children's MLR scores were compared with their scores on a Receptive Vocabulary task and a Definition task. In the following section, I will describe the procedure and some important points in establishing the MLR score. Next, in a description of a validation study, the following questions will be answered:

(1)   Does the MLR differentiate between the two groups (DL1 and DL2), which show obvious differences in vocabulary?
(2)   What is the concurrent validity of the MLR?
(3)   Is the MLR independent of the number of types and utterances, and of Mean Length of Utterance?

3.   MLR procedure

First, a computer program was developed that automatically modified the spontaneous speech data of each child in such a way that every word was transformed to its lemma form ('dictionary entry'), followed by all possible meanings of that lemma. See Example 1.

Example 1:   Input/output of the first MLR program

input: **Was dit haar bank?** (was this her bank?)

output:	example (translation)

Was/zijn_kww*5#   copula, past tense (I *was* ill)
zijn_hww*5#   auxiliary verb, past tense (I *was* taken to Leiden)
zijn_bevinden*5#   verb, past tense (Maxima *was* here)
was_wasgoed#   Ik doe de *was* (I do the *laundry*)
was_kaars#   De *was* van een kaars (the *wax* of a candle)
wassen_schoon#   Ik *was* me (I *wash* myself)
afwassen#   Ik *was* af (I *do the dishes*)

dit/dit

haar/haar_bez.vnw.#   *Haar* fiets (*her* bike)
haar_pers.vnw.#   Ik zag *haar* (I saw *her*)
haar_N#   Het *haar* op mijn hoofd (the *hair* on my head)

bank?/bank_zitten#   Ik zit op een *bank* (I sit on a *couch*)
bank_geld#   Een lening van de *bank* (a loan of the *bank*)

Thus, in the example, *Was dit haar bank,* the first word '*was*' is read by the computer as it were a word with seven possible meanings: as conjugation of the three different Verbs *zijn,* as Nouns with two different meanings, as the conjugation of the Verb *wassen,* or as part of the Verb *afwassen.* The most frequent alternative of these seven meanings in the Word list of Schrooten & Vermeer (1994) is always the first alternative given. Note that, in contrast to the Lexical Frequency Profile (Laufer & Nation 1995) where word families form the basis, here lemmas are counted as 'words'. If a person knows one word of a word family, it does not imply that he knows all the other members of that family (see also Bogaards 2001). On the basis of this output, in which the first alternative is taken as the meaning of the word, the MLR1 score is calculated. However, in this example, the speaker meant a financial *bank,* and not a couch to sit on. To get the intended meaning, the correct alternative has to be placed manually in the first position, for instance, by removing *bank_zitten.* In addition to deciding which alternative is the correct one in the context, removal of proper names, and linking the parts of expressions and collocations together (such as *the_cold_war*) have to be done by hand. See Example 2 for the output after manual disambiguation.

Example 2:   Output of the first MLR program, after disambiguation by hand

zijn_kww*5#	(copula, past tense)
dit	
haar_bez.vnw.#	(poss. pronoun)
bank_geld#	(financial institute)

On the basis of this manually corrected output, MLR2 is calculated.

Another computer program matches the lemmas in the output with those in the nine frequency classes of the word list of Schrooten & Vermeer (1994). See Table 1. This program is based on a modified version of VocabProfile (Nation & Heatley 2002; I thank Paul Nation for making an uncompiled version available for me).

As can be seen in the third column in Table 1, the first list (voclist 1) consists of the one thousand lemmas that have the highest (geometric) mean of frequency, in other words, the thousand most frequent words in daily input in elementary school. The second list consists of the one thousand lemmas that follow, et cetera. Voclists 6 and 7 consist of about 1,500 / 1,600 lemmas, voclist 8 has about 4,500 lemmas, and the ninth list more than 13,000 lemmas. The first one thousand lemmas in the first voclist account for no less than 85.3 % of the tokens in the entire corpus, as can be seen in the fourth column, the second list with one thousand lemmas covers 6% of the corpus. In line with Zipf's law, only a few lemmas are very frequent, whereas the 13,000 least frequent words account for less than one percent of all tokens in the corpus.

To calculate the MLR, the relative distribution of the token coverage in the Schrooten & Vermeer corpus in the fourth column is taken as 'model'. This

Table 1. Number of tokens, lemmas, and token coverage in each word list in Schrooten & Vermeer (1994)

word list	tokens per voc list	lemmas per voc list	token coverage	cumulative lemmas	cumulative coverage
voclst1.dat	1.669.651	1.000	85.3	1.000	85.3
voclst2.dat	117.031	1.000	6.0	2.000	91.3
voclst3.dat	51.222	1.000	2.6	3.000	93.9
voclst4.dat	29.718	1.000	1.5	4.000	95.4
voclst5.dat	19.196	1.000	1.0	5.000	96.4
voclst6.dat	19.002	1.500	1.0	6.500	97.4
voclst7.dat	13.348	1.613	0.7	8.113	98.1
voclst8.dat	20.340	4.577	1.0	12.690	99.1
voclst9.dat	18.470	13.890	0.9	26.580	100
Total	1.957.978	26.580			

corpus is considered indicative of the language input in elementary school. In other words, if the relative distribution of the words of an analysed text over the nine lists is the same as those in the fourth column in Table 1, then the MLR score is considered to match with a vocabulary of about 26,000 words. If a person uses relatively more words from the first four lists, then her/his score is lower. If someone with a very small vocabulary uses words from the first list only, his MLR score is 1 (indicating a vocabulary size of about 1,000 words). The MLR score is calculated by adding up each quotient of the text coverage of the text of the child, and the 'model' coverage of Schrooten & Vermeer ('token coverage' in Table 1) of each voclist x. Each quotient is multiplied by the number of lemmas (and divided by 1,000) in that voclist x, as indicated in column 3 in Table 1. Voclist 2 and higher have a weighted multiplication factor in the denominator to compensate for the fact that most texts under investigation have not two million, but only about one thousand tokens. A huge corpus has relatively more hapaxes, and relatively higher coverage percentages in the lower frequency ranges. The multiplication factor in the denominator ranges from 1.25 (voclist 2) to 9 in voclist 9. In Example 3, for one text a concrete example is shown how the MLR score is calculated.

Example 3

voclist	tokens/%	'model'	(cov %/ (model*weight))*nlemmas/1,000		
1	832/89.5	85.3	(max/85.3) *	1,000/1,000	=1.00
2	43/4.6	6.0	(4.6/(6.0*1.25)) *	1,000/1,000	=0.61
3	11/1.2	2.6	(1.2/(2.6*1.75)) *	1,000/1,000	=0.26
4	7/0.8	1.5	(0.8/(1.5*2)) *	1,000/1,000	=0.27
5	6/0.6	1.0	(0.6/(1.0*3)) *	1,000/1,000	=0.20
6	15/1.6	1.0	(1.6/(1.0*4)) *	1,500/1,000	=0.60
7	4/0.4	0.7	(0.4/(0.7*4)) *	1,600/1,000	=0.23
8	6/0.6	1.0	(0.6/(1.0*6)) *	4,600/1,000	=0.46
9	6/0.6	0.9	(0.6/(0.9*9)) *	13,800/1,000	=1.02
not in the lists	41			MLR-score total	=4.65
total	971–41=930 words		indicated productive vocabulary size		=4,650

There were 971 tokens in the speech data of this child, of which 41 were not in the lists (in particular names of children). In the second column is shown how many of these tokens were found in the nine voclists, and the percentages. For example, this child produced 43 tokens, or 4.6%, that were found in voclist 2. As the 'model coverage' of voclist 2 is 6.0% (column 3), the score of the child on this voclist is 4.6/(6.0*1.25)= 0.61. For voclist 2 and higher, a multiplication factor is added in the denominator. The outcome of each quotient is multiplied by the number of lemmas in that voclist (e.g. 1,000 in voclist 2, 1,500 in voclist 6, 4,600 in voclist 8) and divided by 1,000.

Because the MLR score is related to the Schrooten & Vermeer corpus, it can give, like an extrapolated score on a vocabulary test related to a dictionary, an indication of a person's vocabulary size. Thus, a total score of 2 indicates a vocabulary size of about 2,000 words, a score of 5 indicates a vocabulary size of about 5,000 words. In Example 3, the child has an indicated productive vocabulary of about 4,650 words.

4.   Validation study

4.1   Subjects

To validate the MLR, direct (spontaneous speech) and indirect (vocabulary tests) language data were gathered for 16 Dutch native and 16 ethnic minority children in grade 2 (mean age 7;11, sd 0;7). The Dutch children had Dutch as their first language (DL1). The minority children (mostly from Turkish or Moroccan backgrounds) had Dutch as a second language (DL2), and primarily spoke their native languages at home. All the children had their primary socialization in the Netherlands. The minority children belonged to the second generation of immigrants who came to the Netherlands over the past few decades. All the children (DL1 and DL2) came from lower Socio-Economic Status groups (working-class families, with lower vocational education).

4.2   Instruments

Spontaneous speech data were gathered in a 30- to 45-minute individual interview with the experimenter, which took place in a separate room. The children were asked to tell a story from a picture book and were interviewed on various topics, such as friends, television, and holidays. The number of topics in each interview was — in so far as possible — held constant. The recorded interviews were transcribed and analysed. For each child, a corpus of 150 to 200 T-units is available, leaving out *yes, no*, interjections and direct imitations of the experimenter. The following variables were counted in the corpus of each child: the number of utterances, tokens, types, and lemmas, on the basis of which

Mean Length of Utterance (MLU) and Guiraud (V/√N) were calculated.
In addition to the direct data (spontaneous speech), the children's Dutch
language proficiency was evaluated by using ten subtasks of the Revised Dutch
Language Proficiency Test (*Taaltoets Alle Kinderen*), a standardized discrete-
point test for the assessment of oral proficiency in Dutch as L1 and L2 for four-
to ten-year-olds (Verhoeven & Vermeer 2001). Two of the ten tasks, which
were all individually administered, related to vocabulary. These were the Receptive Vocabulary Task and the Definition Task. In the Receptive Vocabulary
Task, the child had to point to one picture (out of four), being the correct
referent of an orally presented word, as in the Peabody Picture Vocabulary
Test. The task is related to the language corpus of Schrooten & Vermeer (1994)
in such a way that it is possible to give an indication of the absolute size of the
receptive vocabulary of the children (cf. Nation 1993, Laufer & Nation 1999).
In the Definition Task, the child had to explain or describe the meaning of a
given word; descriptions were scored dichotomously as correct (1), or incorrect (0), by means of comparison to model answers. Both tasks are reliable,
with Cronbach's alphas of .95 and .90, respectively. With respect to concurrent
validity, both tasks have high (r>.60) and significant (p<.001) correlations
with teachers' ratings and spontaneous speech data (cf. Vermeer 1999).

4.3   Procedure

To examine the validity of the MLR, means and standard deviations of the
various vocabulary measures (tokens, types, lemmas, Guiraud, MLR1, and
MLR2) and the two vocabulary tasks were calculated separately for DL1 and
DL2 children, and t-tests were used to find out whether they reflected differences in vocabulary in Dutch. In order to further study the concurrent validity,
correlations were calculated between the various measures for the whole population. Finally, the vocabulary size, based on the extrapolation of the score on
the Receptive Vocabulary Task, was compared to the indicated vocabulary size
based on the MLR2 score.

5.   Results

In Table 2, the means and standard deviations on various measures are displayed, separately for Dutch L1 and L2 children. In the last column, t-values
show whether the scores of these two groups differed significantly or not. On the

two vocabulary tasks, Dutch L1 and L2 children obtained significantly different scores. Of the type/token based measures of lexical richness, only the number of lemmas showed barely significant (t=−1.91, Sig t=.065) differences between the two groups. For the DL1 children, the score on MLR2 was somewhat higher than on MLR1, because they also used more infrequent meanings of words, which is clear only after disambiguation of the text. The scores of the DL2 children on MLR2 was somewhat lower than MLR1, because some words, in particular the names of children (e.g. 'Koen', which means, as an infrequently used adjective, *brave*; or 'Bob', also *sledge*), were counted as words before disambiguation (in MLR1), whereas all proper names were left out in MLR2. The score of MLR1, based on the first, sometimes not intended, meaning of a word, discriminated almost significantly (t=−1.953, Sig t=.060) between the two groups, whereas MLR2 (based on the correct meaning in the context), discriminated significantly (t=−2.48, Sig t=.019). Therefore, the MLR2 score seems to be a better measure than the type/token based measures, because it discriminates between two groups with obvious differences in vocabulary in Dutch.

The indicated sizes of vocabulary are shown at the bottom of Table 2. Extrapolation of the mean scores of the Receptive Vocabulary Task shows an indicated size of vocabulary of 5,020 words for Dutch L1 children, and 4,040 words for Dutch L2 children. The MLR2 based sizes of productive vocabulary (associated with spontaneous speech data, and thus, vocabulary use) are about 1,000 words lower: 3,750 words for Dutch L1 children, and 3,040 words for Dutch L2 children.

Table 2. Means and standard deviations by Measure and Student group

	Dutch L1 (n=16)		Dutch L2 (n=16)		DL1 vs DL2
	Mean	sd	Mean	sd	t-test, df=30 t / Sig t
Utterances	197.4	46.3	192.8	45.9	−.35 / .732
MLU	5.6	0.6	5.5	1.4	−.24 / .814
tokens (N)	1121.0	313.3	1024.9	381.8	−.78 / .443
types (V)	395.9	191.6	350.1	193.8	−.67 / .506
lemmas	314.1	58.2	272.3	65.3	−1.91 / .065
Guiraud (V/ N)	11.7	4.7	10.6	4.9	−.65 / .523
MLR1	3.62	.73	3.17	.57	−1.95 / .060
MLR2	3.75	.97	3.04	.60	−2.48 / .019
Definition Task	25.8	5.6	15.1	3.6	−6.52 / .000
Rec Voc Task	83.2	12.7	64.5	11.1	−4.49 / .000
voc size RecVT	5,020		4,040		
voc size MLR2	3,750		3,040		

Table 3. Correlations between different lexical measures
(all children, n=32, ** = p< .01, * = p< .05)

	MLR2	type	lemma	Guir	Def	RecV	MLU	N utterances
MLR1	.93**	−.05	.24	−.04	.61**	.45**	.07	−.01
MLR2		−.01	.18	.00	.71**	.50**	.11	−.03
types			.64**	.97	.12	.13	.63**	.26
lemmas				.50**	.25	.34*	.61**	.66**
Guiraud					.15	.17	.50**	.08
Def Task						.67**	.07	−.11
RecV Task							.09	.18
MLU								.12

In Table 3, correlations between different lexical measures and vocabulary tasks are displayed for all children (n = 32). As can be seen, high and significant correlations were found between both MLR scores and the Definition Task (for MLR1, r=.61, and for MLR2, r=.71, both p<.01) and the Receptive Vocabulary Task (for MLR1, r=.45, and for MLR2, r=.50, both p<.01), showing the concurrent validity of the MLR. The correlations of both MLR scores with the Number of utterances and Mean Length of Utterances were all very low (r=−.01, −.07, −.03, .11), indicating that the MLR is independent of text length or syntactic abilities. Of the type/token based measures of lexical richness, only the number of lemmas showed a moderately significant correlation (r=−.34, p<.05) with the Receptive Vocabulary Task. However, the number of lemmas also had high and significant correlations with Mean Length of Utterances (r=.61, p<.01) and Number of utterances (r=.66, p<.01). Thus, the number of lemmas is associated with syntactic abilities and text length, whereas both MLR scores show concurrent validity with the Vocabulary tasks, and almost no correlations with MLU and text length. The MLR is thus a valid measure of lexical richness, independent of text length.

6. Conclusions and discussion

Variance in word frequency ('the law of Zipf': frequency multiplied by rank has a constant value), and the fact that language development goes along with increasing length of constituents and sentences make any lexical measure of spontaneous speech data based on a relation between types and tokens very problematic. Such measures are also dependent on syntactic abilities and text length. Moreover, they do not take into account the *difficulty* of a word. As the frequency of a word in daily input is, at least in children's language, related to the degree of difficulty of that word, a more valid lexical measure is to relate the words to their degree of difficulty as measured by calculating their frequency in daily input. The results of this study show that the MLR (*Measure of Lexical Richness*), based on the degree of difficulty measured using nine categories of frequency classes in a reference corpus,

(1)   differentiates significantly between groups with obvious differences in vocabulary (DL1 and DL2)
(2)   shows high and significant correlations with vocabulary tasks administered to the same children
(3)   is independent of syntactical abilities (MLU) and text length (number of types and utterances).

Moreover, for both groups of children (DL1 and DL2), the MLR score can indicate a productive vocabulary size, of 3,750 words (DL1) and 3,040 words (DL2), which is, for the two groups respectively, 1,230 and 1.000 words lower than the estimated receptive vocabulary size, based on the extrapolation of scores on the Receptive Vocabulary Task

So far, the results seem to be promising, but further research is necessary. First, it is not clear whether the MLR discriminates between groups with higher vocabulary levels. As indicated, the MLR is linked to a frequency corpus recorded in primary education, and thus is only suitable for these age groups. The reference corpus has 26,000 lemmas, but this might not be enough for children in the higher grades. Children in the higher grades use more rare words, especially compound nouns, which are used very productively in Dutch to form new words (e.g. *balletschoenenlaatjes*, ballet-shoes-drawer-DIM-PLUR). Since these will not be in the lists, the MLR will be less reliable. Moreover, because the frequencies in voclists 8 and 9 are quite low in the reference corpus, the reliabilities are low, too, and it is unclear whether the words in voclist 9 represent a higher level of difficulty than those in voclist 8. Secondly, an acceptable minimum number of tokens and utterances for a corpus has to be worked out in order to obtain a reliable MLR. It is unlikely that a corpus of only 50 tokens produces a reliable outcome. What is an acceptable minimum number of tokens? 100? 300? In this study, the highest number of tokens was 1733, the lowest, 516; the highest number of utterances was 200, the lowest, 109. Although low correlations between the MLR and the number of utterances or tokens have been found, a minimum number of tokens and utterances is required. The same holds for the number of topics discussed. A corpus, in which a child talks about only one topic, presumably produces a lower MLR score than a corpus of the same child talking about 101 topics. It is advisable to keep the number of topics constant, in so far as that is possible.

The major disadvantage of the MLR is that the procedure is time consuming, because disambiguation has to be done manually. MLR1, obtained without disambiguation of the output, does not differentiate significantly between the two groups. On the other hand, correlations between MLR1 and MLR2 (after disambiguation), and the correlations of MLR1 with the vocabulary tasks, are high. The use of children's names, in particular, caused an overestimation of MLR1; simply leaving out proper names in the spontaneous speech data might go a long way to overcoming this problem. More research into different speech data has to be done to see whether these differences between MLR1 and MLR2 are acceptable.

The MLR procedure is also suitable for indicating levels of difficulty of a particular written text for primary school children by calculating the relative number of known/unknown tokens and/or lemmas in a text ('text coverage'; see, e.g. Carver 1994, Laufer 1989). The percentage of text coverage can indicate the degree of difficulty of a text for a reader. As the precise relationship between text coverage and text comprehension is dependent on various factors — for example, knowledge of the world, the subject matter, the number of cognates, the style, the text type -, for reasonable comprehension of a text, a token coverage of 95–96% is considered to be a threshold, or a lemma coverage of about 87% (cf. Hazenberg 1994). In the MLR procedure, percentages of token and lemma coverage are calculated automatically for children with a vocabulary size of 3,000, 5,000, and 8,000 words.

Finally, from both theoretical and empirical perspectives, the MLR procedure, in which lexical richness is based on the difficulty of the words used in a text, seems to be a far better measure of lexical richness in spontaneous speech data for children than type/token based measures, and it has the added advantage of providing an estimate of the absolute size of a child's productive vocabulary.

References

Alekseev, P. M. 1984. *Statistische Lexikographie*. Bochum: Brockmeyer.
Bogaards, P. 2001. "Lexical units and the learning of foreign language vocabulary". *Studies in Second Language Acquisition* 23 (3): 321–343.

Brown, C. 1993. "Factors affecting the acquisition of vocabulary: Frequency and saliency of words". In *Second language reading and vocabulary learning*, Th. Huckin, M. Haynes and J Coady (eds), 263–286. Norwood, NJ: Ablex.

Carver, R. 1994. "Percentage of unknown vocabulary words in text as a function of the relative difficulty of the text: Implications for instruction". *Journal of reading behavior* 26 (4): 413–438.

Dewhurst, S., Hitch, G. and Barry, Chr. 1998. "Seperate effects of word frequency and age of acquisition in recognition and recall". *Journal of Experimental Psychology* 24 (2): 284–298.

Francis, W. and Kučera, H. 1982. *Frequency analysis of English usage*. Boston, MA: Houghton Mifflin.

Gerhard, S. and Barry, Chr. 1998. "Word frequency effects in oral reading are not merely age-of-acquisition effects in disguise". *Journal of Experimental Psychology* 24 (2): 267–283.

Hazenberg, S. 1994. *Een keur van woorden [A pick of words]*. PhD thesis. Amsterdam: Free University.

Huttenlocher, J., Haight, W., Bryk, A., Seltzer, M. and Lyons, Th. 1991. "Early vocabulary growth: Relation to language input and gender". *Developmental Psychology* 27 (2): 236–248.

Jarvis, S. 2002. "Short texts, best-fitting curves and new measures of lexical diversity". *Language Testing* 19 (1): 57–84.

Kibby, M. W. 1977. "Note on relationship of word difficulty and word frequency". *Psychological Reports* 41: 12–14.

Laufer, B. 1989. "What percentage of text-lexis is essential for comprehension?" In *Special language: From humans thinking to thinking machines*, C. Laurèn and M. Nordmann (eds), 316–323. Clevedon: Multilingual Matters.

Laufer, B. 1998. "The development of passive and active vocabulary in a second language: Same or different?" *Applied Linguistics* 19, 2: 255–271.

Laufer, B. and Nation, I. 1995. "Vocabulary size and use: Lexical richness in L2 written production". *Applied Linguistics* 16 (3): 307–322.

Laufer, B. and Nation, I. 1999. "A vocabulary-size test of controlled productive ability". *Language Testing* 16 (1): 33–51.

Malvern, D. and Richards, B. 1997. "A new measure of lexical diversity". In: *Evolving models of language*. A. Ryan and A. Wray (eds), 58–71. Clevedon: Multilingual Matters.

Malvern, D. and Richards, B. 2000. "Validation of a new measure of lexical diversity". In: *From sound to sentence: Studies on first language acquisition*, M. Beers, B. Van de Bogaerde, G. Bol, J. de Jong and C. Rooijmans, (eds), 81–96. Groningen: Centre for Language and Cognition.

Malvern, D. and Richards, B. 2002. "Investigating accomodation in language proficiency interviews using a new measure of lexical diversity". *Language Testing* 19 (1): 85–104.

McKee, G., Malvern, D. and Richards, B. 2000. "Measuring vocabulary diversity using dedicated software". *Literary and Linguistic Computing* 15: 323–337.

Nation, I. S. P. 1990. *Teaching and Learning Vocabulary*. Boston: Heinle and Heinle.

Nation, P. 1993. "Using dictionaries to estimate vocabulary size: Essential, but rarely followed, procedures". *Language Testing* 10 (1): 27–40.

Nation, P. and Heatley, A. 2002. RANGE: a program for vocabulary analysis. Available at http://www.vuw.ac.nz/lals/staff/paul-nation/nation.aspx

Richards, B. 1987. "Type/Token Ratios: What do they really tell us?" *Journal of Child Language* 14: 201–209.

Richards, B. and Malvern, D. 1997. *Type-Token and Type-Type measures of vocabulary diversity and lexical style: An annotated bibliography*. Reading: University of Reading (also available on www at: http://www.rdg/ac/uk/~ehsrichb/home.html)

Schrooten, W. and Vermeer, A. 1994. *Woorden in het basisonderwijs. 15.000 woorden aangeboden aan leerlingen [Words in primary education, 15,000 words offered to pupils]*. Tilburg: Tilburg University Press. (also available on www via: http://www.annevermeer.com: "woordenlijst").

Treffers-Daller, J. and Van Hout, R.1999. "De meting van woordenschatrijkdom in het Turks van Turks-Duits tweetaligen" [Measurement of lexical richness in Turkish of Turkish-German bilinguals]. In: *Artikelen van de derde sociolinguïstische conferentie*, E. Huls and B. Weltens (eds), 428–440. Delft: Eburon.

Tweedie, F. and Baayen, R. H. 1998. "How variable may a constant be? Measures of lexical richness in perspective". *Computers and the Humanities* 32: 323–352.

Van der Vliet, H. 1997. *Dingen onder woorden: conceptuele semantiek voor een computerlexicon [Things into words: Conceptual semantics for a computer lexicon]*. PhD thesis University of Amsterdam, Amsterdam: IFOTT.

Van Hout, R. and Vermeer, A. 1992 Frequenties van woorden en het geometrisch gemiddelde. [Frequencies of words and the geometric mean]. *Gramma/Tijdschrift voor Taalen Tekstwetenschap* 1, 2, 125–132.

Verhoeven, L. and Vermeer, A. 2001. *Taaltest Alle Kinderen.[Language Test for All children]*. Cito, Arnhem.

Vermeer, A. 1992. "Exploring the second language learner lexicon". In: *The construct of language proficiency*, L. Verhoeven and J. DeJong (eds), 147–162. Amsterdam/Philadelphia: John Benjamins.

Vermeer, A. 1999. "Pygmalion in de klas? Onderzoek naar de bevooroordeeldheid van leraren bij de inschatting van de taalvaardigheid van hun autochtone en allochtone leerlingen" [Pygmalion in the classroom? Biases of teachers in evaluating language proficiency of DL1 and DL2 children]. In: *Artikelen van de derde sociolinguïstische conferentie*. E. Huls and B. Weltens (eds), 487–495. Delft: Eburon.

Vermeer, A. 2000. "Coming to grips with lexical richness in spontaneous speech data". *Language Testing* 17 (1): 65–83.

Vermeer, A. 2001. "Breadth and depth of vocabulary in relation to L1/L2 acquisition and frequency of input". *Applied Psycholinguistics* 22: 217–234.

CHAPTER 10

The construction and validation of a deep word knowledge test for advanced learners of French

Tine Greidanus, Paul Bogaards, Elisabeth van der Linden, Lydius Nienhuis, Tom de Wolf
Vrije Universiteit Amsterdam, Universiteit Leiden, Universiteit van Amsterdam, Universiteit Utrecht, Universiteit van Amsterdam

Abstract

This chapter describes the construction and validation of a deep word knowledge test for advanced learners of French as a second language. The present version of the test was developed in three successive stages. The pilot version and the first and second versions were all administered to groups of Dutch university students of French at two levels. The test was validated with several groups of native speakers of French of corresponding age and schooling. The results of the Dutch students on the second test were compared with their results on a test of breadth of word knowledge, and with a test of depth of word knowledge. The section Discussion and conclusion addresses three questions: the evaluation of certain characteristics of the test format, the responses given by the French native speakers, and the relationship between depth and breadth of vocabulary knowledge.

1. Introduction

The distinction between breadth and depth of lexical knowledge is rapidly becoming a common one. There are a great number of test formats that evaluate the breadth of word knowledge, *i.e.* the number of words known. Tests evaluating the depth of word knowledge, *i.e.* the extent to which a given word is known, are still rare. Read (1993) and Read (1998) developed two formats of a *Word Associates Test*, and Wesche & Paribakht (1996) presented a *Vocabulary Knowledge Scale*. In our paper we present a study measuring aspects of deep word knowledge of Dutch university students of French at an advanced level. Read (this volume) defines three aspects of deep word knowledge: precision of meaning, comprehensive word knowledge, and network knowledge. The test we developed addresses essentially the network type of knowledge of French words. The format adopted is that of Read (1993).

Since the creation of this format, the word associates test has been used in a number of studies. The base form of an item consists of a target word followed by a number of words, half of which have a relationship with the target word, and half of which do not. Participants have to indicate whether there is a relationship between the target word and the response words or not. Read (1993) gives the following example:

> *edit*
> arithmetic   film   pole   publishing
> revise   risk   surface text

The correct association words are *film, publishing, revise* and *text*. The studies that used the format differ in certain respects:

(1)   the language of the test is either the L1 of the participants, or a L2. Read (1993) and Greidanus and Nienhuis (2001) used the test with L2 participants; Schoonen and Verhallen (1998), Verhallen, Özdemir, Yüksel, & Schoonen (1999), and Beks (2001) with L2 and L1 participants.

(2)   the vocabulary tested. Schoonen & Verhallen (1998), Verhallen *et al.* (1999) and Greidanus & Nienhuis (2001) used basic vocabulary; Read (1993) academic words; Beks (2001) less frequent words.

(3)   the number of possible responses. Read (1993) had eight possible responses, all the other studies six.

(4)   the number of correct responses. This number is fixed in most studies, always half of the possible responses; in Beks (2001) the number of correct responses (fixed or not) is an independent variable.

(5)   the nature of the distracters. In Read (1993) and Beks (2001) distractors have no relationship with the target word; in Schoonen & Verhallen (1998), and Verhallen *et al.* (1999) there is a certain relationship between the distractors and the target word, but it is looser than the relationship between the target word and the associates; in Greidanus & Nienhuis (2001) this constitutes an independent variable.

The relative proliferation of the format suggests that it is a useful one for research on vocabulary knowledge. It has various advantages:

(1) a word associates test is efficient in use, compared with other methods of deep word knowledge testing, for example definition and description tasks, or a test such as the *Vocabulary Knowledge Scale.*

(2) it is independent of the mother tongue of the participants, which makes it interesting in a teaching environment.

The psychometric data resulting from the experiments in the above-mentioned studies are good. The test can be used to assess deep word knowledge, but it can also be used for studies on the vocabulary acquisition process.

In the present study we did both. We will first present the different stages of the construction and validation of the deep word knowledge test we developed;[1] Section 3 compares the results of the test with those of two other word knowledge tests; in our Discussion and Conclusion we will evaluate certain characteristics of the test format, make some remarks on the responses given by the French native speakers, and address the question of the relationship between depth and breadth of vocabulary knowledge.

2. Development of the test

2.1 Form and construction of the test

Our test was a word associates test based on Read (1993). It shared a certain number of characteristics with the above-mentioned studies. It contained a series of test items, each with a stimulus word and six possible responses which did or did not have a clear relationship with the stimulus word. The association words (the correct responses) could have various relationships with the stimulus word: they were paradigmatic (synonyms, antonyms, superordinates, subordinates), syntagmatic (collocations) and analytic (the association word can enter in the definition of the stimulus word, or it has a means-end or a part-whole relationship with the stimulus word). The choice of the type of relationship was determined by the possibilities offered by each stimulus word; the types were not equally spread over each item.

The distractors were words that did not belong to the semantic or syntactic network of the French stimulus word. Some of them belonged to the network of the Dutch equivalent of the stimulus word.[2]

Most of the above-mentioned studies on word associates tests have an equal number of correct and incorrect responses. In our test we chose to vary the number of correct responses between two and four. We did this because, if there were always three correct responses, the participants could make their choice by elimination. With a variable number of correct responses they had to determine each time whether the response word belonged to the network of the stimulus word.

All the words used in the test came from the frequency list of Juilland, Brodin & Davidovitch (1970), which contains 5,083 words. By 'words' we mean lexical items, not word families. These words are arranged in three sublists according to usage, frequency, and dispersion. We used the usage sublist. Usage is a measure that takes account of frequency and dispersion (cf. Juilland *et al.*1970: LVII-LXI). As it is a term for corrected frequency, we will henceforth use the term 'frequency'. The Juilland list is based on a corpus of written prose texts of 500,000 words (plays, novels and short stories, essays, texts from periodicals, and scientific and technical texts).[3] The stimulus words were chosen from the five subsequent ranges of 1,000 words, including concrete as well as abstract words (nouns, verbs, and adjectives). The association words and the distractors belonged to the same range as the stimulus word, or were more frequent. The first version of our test contained 455 words (65 stimulus words and 390 association words and distractors); the second contained 441 words (63 stimulus words and 378 association words and distracters).[4] Our ultimate aim is to construct a test consisting of 50 items, 10 items in each of the five frequency ranges. The first two versions of the test had 12 till 17 items in each frequency range. We did this in order to be able to chose the items that were found to be the best after a thorough analysis of all the available items.

All test items were arranged in alphabetical order, as were the responses to each test item. The test was preceded by detailed instructions (one page) which addressed the different types of relationships between the stimulus word and the association words, followed by an example item with comments. The participants were asked to answer all test items. The instructions specified that the number of cases to tick off (= the correct responses) varied per item. One point was awarded for each correctly recognised or rejected relationship. The maximum score for each item was therefore six. Two examples of items (with our comment) are shown below. The first example (*jeune*) has a monosemous item as target word, whereas the target word of the second one (*défense*) is polysemous.

jeune (young)	■ *âge* (age)	(in definition)
	□ *blanc* (white)	
	■ *fille* (girl)	(collocation)
	□ *livre* (book)	
	□ *oiseau* (bird)	
	■ *vieux* (old)	(antonym)
défense (defence; prohibition; tusk)	□ *balle* (ball)	
	□ *coq* (cock)	
	■ *éléphant* (elephant)	(part-whole)
	■ *interdiction* (interdiction)	(synonym)
	■ *légitime* (legitimate)	(collocation)
	■ *ministère* (ministry)	(collocation)

2.2 First version of the test

A pilot version of our deep word knowledge test (DWK test) was administered to various small groups of Dutch university students and to two groups of French-speaking participants: university students at the 'Maîtrise' level (fourth-year university students studying 'French as a foreign language'), and sixth-grade secondary school pupils. The test was improved on the basis of the results of this pilot.

The first version of the DWK test consisted of 65 items. There were 22 items with two correct responses, 34 items with three correct responses, and 9 items with four correct responses. It was administered in 1999 to Dutch-speaking first- and third-year students studying French language and literature at four Dutch universities, and French-speaking participants studying economics at an IUT (Institut Universitaire de Technologie) in Lille (France). Before entering university, the Dutch participants had a secondary education with an average of 2 or 3 hours of French a week over a period of 6 years. They were therefore advanced (first-year university students) and very advanced (third-year university students) learners of French. The first purpose of this test was to ascertain whether the items of the five frequency levels differentiated between the groups. The data are shown in Table 1.

An *ANOVA* with Group (on three levels) as the independent variable and Score on the frequency groups as dependent variable showed that the mean total scores and the mean scores for the frequency ranges 2, 3, 4 and 5 differed significantly ($p < .0001$) for each of the three levels of language proficiency. In frequency range 1 (the most frequent words) only the mean of the first-year students differed significantly from that of the other two groups.

Table 1. Mean scores and standard deviations of the three participant groups for the items of the five frequency ranges of Juilland et al. (1970) (max. = 78[1]), and of the whole test (max. = 390).

	French. IUT stud. n = 25		Dutch stud. third year n = 33		Dutch stud. first year n = 67	
	M	SD	M	SD	M	SD
Freq. 1	72.1	3.3	70.4	3.5	63.4*	5.1
Freq. 2	68.3*	4.6	60.9*	4.2	55.5*	4.2
Freq. 3	69.3*	3.2	65.6*	4.0	56.8*	5.3
Freq. 4	67.5*	4.5	60.3*	4.2	50.7*	5.0
Freq. 5	68.7*	3.8	61.1*	5.6	51.8*	2.9
Total	345.9*	15.3	318.3*	17.6	278.2*	16.7
	89%		81%		71%	

Note. Freq. 1 = words from rank 1–999, Freq. 2 = words from rank 1000–1999, etc.
[1] The test had 65 items. These items were not equally distributed over the five frequency classes. The scores given in the table have been recalculated so as to be easily comparable, that is on the basis of an equal distribution over the frequency classes.
* $p < .05$

The table shows clearly that the mean scores for each of the five frequency ranges descend fairly regularly, with comparable differences from left to right. The scores of the groups are fairly homogeneous, as is shown by the standard deviations.

We calculated the reliability of the test as internal consistency, *i.e.* as Cronbach's α.[5] The figures were: .89 for the IUT students, .88 for the third-year students and .84 for the first-year students. With 65 items, a fairly large number, this level of reliability is reasonable, but not surprising.

The French-speaking participants had a mean score of 89% of the maximum score. The fact that they did not come closer to the maximum score can be due to errors in the test. But it is also possible that some responses demanded a maximum knowledge of the French language that not all French native speakers have. A comparison between the three groups of French-speaking participants *i.e.*, the two groups of French native speakers in the pilot study and the IUT group, showed that the test differentiated surprisingly well between the groups of native speakers, the order being: Maîtrise students > IUT students > secondary school pupils. The first and third group are particularly suitable for comparison because they took an identical test. Their mean scores were found to differ considerably; a *t* test showed that the mean scores of these two groups differed significantly at a $p < .001$ level. The difference between the mean of the Maîtrise students and that of the IUT students was fairly small. As these two

Table 2. Mean scores and standard deviations of three groups of native speakers of French (max. = 390)

	Maîtrise students n = 19		IUT students n = 25		Secondary school pupils n = 89	
	M	SD	M	SD	M	SD
Total score	352.7	15.4	346.1	15.3	319.4	15.8

groups were not given exactly the same test, we could not run a *t* test in order to see if the difference was significant. The data appear in Table 2.

We decided to focus mainly on the scores of the IUT students in working up to an improved version of the test. They represent the knowledge of the French language of educated native speakers of the age of our students; they have not yet achieved the near-maximum proficiency that Maîtrise students are credited with.

In improving the test, we concentrated in particular on the item analysis of the *p* and *a* values[6] and of the discrimination indices, the R_{it} values, of the IUT students. For the *p* and *a* values of the responses we set a limit that they had to be greater than .80 (= 80% correct responses) and less than .20 (= 20% incorrect responses, *i.e.* marked distractors), while the R_{it} values had preferably to be greater than .30, as is customary. We adapted items and/or responses that did not conform to these criteria; when adaptation proved scarcely possible, we eliminated these items and replaced them with others. It was evident that the extent to which an item and/or response contributed to the differentiation between the level groups was an important criterion for the improvement of the test. Thus we obtained the version of the test that will be discussed in the next section.

2.3   Second version of the test

The second version of the test had the same form and was based on the same principles as the first test. It had 63 items. There were 21 items with two correct responses, 31 items with three correct responses, and 11 items with four correct responses. This version was administered to three different-level groups of Dutch-speaking university students of French and to four different-level groups of French-speaking participants, secondary school pupils and university students. Table 3 shows the results of the Dutch-speaking participants.

We observed that the means diminished neatly from third-year students through second-year students to first-year students, and that this occurred for

Table 3. Means and standard deviations of first-, second- and third-year Dutch university students for the items of the five frequency ranges of Juilland et al.(1970) and of the whole test (max. = 360[1])

	Dutch students third year n = 23		Dutch students second year n = 22		Dutch students first year n = 69	
	M	SD	M	SD	M	SD
Freq. 1	63.6	2.2	61.6	3.4	57.4*	5.3
Freq. 2	56.6	3.2	55.5	4.2	51.8*	4.4
Freq. 3	62.3	3.2	59.6	3.1	53.3*	5.7
Freq. 4	58.7**	4.5	54.9	4.2	48.6*	6.5
Freq. 5	55.0	3.9	52.4	4.4	47.8*	4.7
Total	296.2**	12.6	284	14.6	258.9*	22.8
	82%		79%		72%	

Note. Freq. 1 = words from rank 1–999, Freq. 2 = words from rank 1000–1999, etc.
[1] The test had 63 items. Frequency classes 1–4 had 12 items, frequency class 5 had 15. The scores of this last category were recalculated so as to give a score for 12 items. We did this in order to be able to compare the scores for the five frequency classes. Thus the maximum score for the whole test is 360.
* $p < .05$; ** $p < .01$.

all five frequency levels. As the number of subjects was quite low and the number of different aspects quite high, it was impossible to run a *MANOVA*. So it was decided to run for the items of frequency levels 1–5 and for the total scores six separate *ANOVA's* with group as independent variable and scores as dependent variable. The results were significant in all cases ($p < .001$). Post-hoc Newman-Keuls tests indicated a significant difference ($p < .05$) between first-year students on the one hand, and second- and third-year students on the other. There was equally a significant difference ($p < .01$) between the total scores of the third-year students on the one hand and the first- and second-year students on the other. For the items of frequency level 4, there was a significant difference between the scores of the third-year students and those of the other two groups ($p < .01$). The reliability of the test was satisfactory in all cases: $a = .78$ for third-year students, .82 for second-year students and .92 for first-year students. These results show that the test has a good discriminatory power, at least between first-year students and the groups at the other two levels.

A comparison with the results of the first version of the test showed that the means corresponded nicely: 81% and 82% correct responses respectively for the third-year students and 71% and 72% correct responses respectively for the first-year students. There were no second-year students in the first version.

In order to validate the test, we also administered it to native speakers of French of the same educational level and age as our students or a bit younger.

Table 4. Mean scores and standard deviations of four groups of young native speakers of French of the items with words from the five different frequency ranges of Juilland *et al.*(1970) and of the whole test (max. =360[1])

	Univ. students third year n = 20		Univ. students second year n = 23		Sec. school 5th grade n = 27		Sec. school 4th grade n = 27	
	M	SD	M	SD	M	SD	M	SD
Freq. 1	63.6	7.8	62.4	5.0	63.5	3.4	62.0	7.2
Freq. 2	63.1*	4.4	61.0	4.9	61.3	3.8	59.1	5.1
Freq. 3	66.4	4.0	64.7	3.7	63.2	2.7	62.2	4.9
Freq. 4	64.0	4.9	61.6	4.3	62.5	2.7	61.7	7.2
Freq. 5	65.8**	4.9	62.8	3.9	60.7	3.1	60.6	5.2
Total	322.9	24.0	312.5	18.6	311.2	12.5	305.6	27.1
	90%		87%		86%		85%	

Note. Freq. 1 = words from rank 1–999, Freq. 2 = words from rank 1000–1999, etc.
[1] The test had 63 items. Frequency classes 1–4 had 12 items, frequency class 5 had 15. The scores of this last category were recalculated so as to give a score for 12 items. We did this in order to be able to compare the scores for the five frequency classes. Thus the maximum score for the whole test is 360.
* $p < .05$; ** $p < .01$.

In total there were four different groups: two groups of university students, second- and third-year students reading French language and literature, and two groups of secondary school pupils, mean age 17 and 16 respectively. Table 4 gives the results of these four groups.

We noticed that the means for the total scores diminished gradually from the highest level group to the lowest. The same methodology was applied for the native speaker groups as for the student groups. For the items of frequency classes 2 and 5 an *ANOVA* indicated a significant difference between third-year students on the one hand and the three other groups on the other ($p < .05$ and $p < .01$ respectively). For the items of the other frequency classes and the total score no two groups differed significantly. Reliability was highly satisfactory in all cases: $\alpha = .95$ for the third-year university students, .92 for the second-year university students, .85 for the fifth-graders and .95 for the fourth-graders.

In improving the first version of the test, we decided that, for a final version of the test, the p and a values of the scores of the native speakers of French of the same age as our students had to be greater than .80. The total scores of the four French groups were satisfactory in this respect, being equal to or greater than .85.

When we compared the results of the French and the Dutch groups we saw that the means of the total scores, once more, diminished steadily from one level group to the next, which was satisfactory.

Although the overall results of the second version of the test were good, there were still items and/or responses that did not conform to our requirements (p and a values $> .80$ and $< .20$, and R_{it} values $> .30$). We will remove or correct those items in future research.

3.   The DWK test and two other word knowledge tests

Did our DWK test succeed in measuring word knowledge of a different nature than other word knowledge tests? In order to answer this question, we administered two other tests of French word knowledge to two of the three Dutch groups who participated in the second version of the DWK test:

- – a traditional word knowledge test that evaluated broad word knowledge,
- – another test measuring relationships between words.

The participants in this experiment were two of the three groups of Dutch students who took the second version of the DWK test, discussed in Section 2.3. The first-year students were given a traditional test of broad word knowledge, the so-called IKAF test; the third-year students took another type of qualitative word knowledge test, the word relation test (WRT test) (Bogaards 2000).

3.1   The broad word knowledge test (IKAF test)

The IKAF word knowledge test is a thoroughly pretested test, designed in the 1970s as a diagnostic test for Dutch first-year university students of French language and literature. The item words are chosen from the Savard & Richards (1970) list, containing the 3,300 French words that are used most frequently. We administered the test to our first-year students only, believing that it would be too easy for third-year students and would therefore lead to a ceiling effect. The version we used consisted of two parts, each with 25 items. The first part evaluated receptive knowledge. It was a multiple choice test in which the participants had to choose the correct definition. An example is shown below:

Je le *plains* beaucoup.   (I *pity* him a lot.)

J'éprouve un sentiment de   1. respect   (respect)
                                 2. crainte   (fear)
                                 3. pitié   (commiseration)
                                 4. affection   (affection)

The second part tested productive knowledge. It was a completion test, in which the French equivalent of a Dutch word had to be inserted in a context, for example:

Est-ce que tu .... te promener seul la nuit ?   (durf)
(Do you .... to walk alone at night?)   (dare)

The test performance was lower than we had expected: the number of correct answers just exceeded 50% (mean 26.3, SD 9.9). However, the correlations between the IKAF test, the entire test as well as the two parts, and the DWK test were reasonable or high (n = 69): DWK – IKAFa (receptive) $r = .70^{**}$; DWK – IKAFb (productive) $r = .81^{**}$; DWK – IKAF (entire test) $r = .79^{**}$ ($^{**} p<.01$).

It appears therefore that our word knowledge test measured to a certain extent the same knowledge as the broad IKAF word knowledge test. This was what we expected. Indeed, broad word knowledge is indispensable in order to develop deep word knowledge. It is obvious that a relationship exists between the two. We presumed at the same time that both tests did not exactly evaluate the same type of knowledge. A deep word knowledge test, in fact, does not only ask for knowledge of meanings of words but, more precisely, for knowledge of the relationship between words. A one-to-one relationship between the two is not to be expected. All in all, the observed correlations seemed satisfactory. We will return to this point in Section 4.

3.2   The word relations test (WRT test)

The word relations test is described by Bogaards (2000). It represents the final state in the development of a series of tests based on the *Euralex French Tests (EFT)*, a format developed by Meara (1992). Objective of the *Word Relations Test (WRT)* is to evaluate the word knowledge of advanced learners. The test has 70 items, each consisting of two words. The test included frequent as well as infrequent words.[7] Many of the items contain infrequent words. The students were asked to mark the items in which there was an obvious connection between the two words. Thus, in order to respond correctly to the test, the students needed to have a broad vocabulary knowledge (they had to know the less frequent words), as well as a deep vocabulary knowledge (they had to know if there was a relationship between the two words in the item). The instruction listed the possible relationships, as in the DWK test: synonyms, antonyms, hyperonyms, hyponyms, definitions and collocations. An example of three items is shown below:

■ bateau: mouche   (boat – fly)   (collocation)
□ bâtisse: bébé   (building – baby)
■ cabrer: cheval   (to rear – horse)   (collocation)

This test, which was assumed to be too difficult for our first-year students, was presented to the third-year students. As in the case of the IKAF test, the number of correct answers just exceeded 50% (mean 36.0, SD 6.8). Thus, this test too appeared to be somewhat difficult for these students. This may be attributed to the fact that the students did not know the less frequent words or because they did not know the relationship between the words in the item. It is also possible that some students adopted the wrong strategy and assumed that the distribution between correct and incorrect answers in the test was 50% — 50%. In reality, this distribution was 70% — 30%. By adopting this strategy, students may have marked fewer responses than they should have done.

The correlation between the WRT and the DWK was not high: .46 (n = 23, not significant). This is partly to be expected. Indeed, a large number of items of the WRT contains infrequent words, whereas the DWK only has items with frequent or rather frequent words. Thus, the tests may measure the same thing, but at different levels of proficiency. The low correlation can, however, also have been caused by the relatively small size of the group (23 students). The greater homogeneity of this group (third-year students perform more homogeneously than first-year students) can also explain this low correlation. Anyhow, we cannot conclude that DWK and WRT measure the same thing.

4.   Discussion and conclusion

In this section we will first discuss matters concerning the test format itself, then make some remarks pertaining to the responses of the French native speakers, and finally address the question of the relationship between the breadth and depth of vocabulary knowledge.

The main difference between our test and the other deep word knowledge tests mentioned in the *Introduction* is that the number of association words, i.e. the correct responses, was not fixed. Beks (2001) investigated this question of a fixed versus a variable number of correct responses. She found that in her four groups of participants (two groups of Dutch university students and two groups of French university students) there was a significant difference only for one French group, the group of the third-year students, in favour of the version with a fixed number of associates. So, this issue does not seem very relevant. A great technical advantage of a variable number of association words is that it makes items easier to construct. Indeed, it is not always possible to find three correct association words for a given word. If one can make a test item with two or even one association word, this increases the range of testable words.

This leads us to a disadvantage of the Read (1993) format. Not every word has the right properties to function as a stimulus word. Some words simply do not have syntagmatic associations, or clear paradigmatic or analytic associations such as to be usable in a test. A fair number of our initial 5,000 words had to be excluded for some reason.

John Read himself had another objection to this first format of the *Word Associates Test*. He reports 'a willingness to guess responses to stimulus words that were either not known or partially known' (1993: 365). In fact, this guessing was a careful process of elimination, at least for the more proficient learners. The learners 'who were willing to guess were often quite successful at selecting the correct responses — and in fact they were by no means guessing blindly' (1993: 366). The primary reason was that the associates had semantic connections between themselves. This finding made him change the format of the original version in the format presented in Read (1998), although he remarks himself 'that, frequently, the ability to select correct responses is based on a combination of good vocabulary knowledge and a certain resourcefulness in seeking possible associates, as well as the confidence to make guesses' (1993: 367). But, as Bogaards (2000: 496) observes:

> 'It is questionable whether these reservations disqualify this test format. If its only purpose is to measure how well the selected target items are known, then the test may not do a very good job. But one could be interested also in more general qualitative knowledge of the lexicon. In that case it would be interesting to be able to make a difference between learners who are successful in identifying two or three associates even without knowing the stimulus word, and those who were not struck by any meaningful relationship between the nine words given in each item. Moreover, 'resourcefulness in seeking possible associates' and 'confidence to make guesses' may be seen as negative when one wants to know whether selected relationships are recognized by the learner or not. But in a more general way, such strategies seem to be helpful in normal language use and learners who exploit these means may be said to have richer vocabularies than those who do not.'

In all events, the possibility to vary the number of associates makes guessing less attractive and keeps the participant alert. Moreover, the risk of semantic connections between the associates is lower when there are fewer associates.

We remarked above that it was not always easy to find three acceptable associates for a given target word. The original Read (1993) format even had four associates for each item word. It is probably significant that all subsequent studies had three.

Although there is still room for improvement, the DWK test turned out to be a valid, reliable and useful tool for measuring specific aspects of lexical knowledge.

As for the responses of the French native speakers, it clearly appeared that differences exist between groups of French native speakers of a higher level. This difference in word knowledge between groups of native speakers poses an interesting problem for designers of a test demanding native-like language proficiency. If, in test construction, one has to choose native proficiency as a reference and maximal score, the norm appears to be variable; thus there are various possible choices. This issue manifests itself concretely when one has to decide whether or not to exclude certain responses apparently known by a majority of one group of native speakers, but not yet by an (often younger) group. For further details on this subject, see Nienhuis *et al.* (2000).

The fact that the scores of the French native speakers on the DWK test were not 100% correct may have been due to flaws in our test. There is also another possibility: the words we used were frequent words. There were three types of relationship that the selected associates could have with the stimulus word: paradigmatic, analytic and syntagmatic. In paradigmatic and analytic relationships there is a relationship with another word. But in syntagmatic relationships we may have two words forming in fact one lexical unit. *Léger* (light) and *coeur* (heart) are frequent words, known certainly by all the French participants. But a collocation like *le coeur léger* (light-hearted) has a meaning of its own, and the frequency of this collocation is unknown. It is not inconceivable that certain French participants did not know this expression, or did not think of it. The *p* values of the responses of the four French groups on this item were .95, .65, .63 and .63 respectively. The frequency of the lexicalised expression as a whole seemed to play a role. For *troisième âge* (senior citizens) we found the following *p* values: .80, .83, .96 and .96 (here the younger participants performed better than the older ones), for *âge d'or* (golden age), a less frequent expression, they were .60, .52, .22 and .07 respectively. Greidanus & Nienhuis (2001) and Beks (2001) investigated the question of the type of association and found that the scores for the syntagmatic associations were significantly lower than those for the paradigmatic and analytic associations for the two Dutch groups in the first study and for the two Dutch groups and the two French groups in the second study. A closer analysis of the answers of the French participants concerning the different types of relationship, and the syntagmatic associations in particular, may shed more light on this issue.

We found a significant correlation between our DWK test and the IKAF test, a broad knowledge test. Qian (1999) found a comparable positive correlation (.82) between a broad word knowledge test and a deep word knowledge test. He drew the conclusion that 'learners' scores on the depth and breadth dimensions of vocabulary knowledge are also closely, and positively, associated, which leads us to believe that development of the two dimensions is probably interconnected and interdependent' (1999: 299). He remarks that the high correlation between the scores on the two tests may be due to 'partial construct overlap of the two measures':

> 'The VS [the broad vocabulary knowledge test] measures primary meaning of words, while the DVK [the deep vocabulary knowledge test] measures knowledge of synonymy, polysemy, and collocation. Although the DVK tests more and deeper aspects of vocabulary knowledge than the VS, primary meaning is, in certain cases, part of synonymy and polysemy, and knowledge of word meaning sometimes has an impact on knowledge of collocation.' (1999: 299)

Our DWK test and the IKAF test had a similar overlap. Qian's DVK test was nevertheless found to have made 'a significant and unique contribution to the prediction scores on academic reading comprehension beyond the prediction provided by scores on vocabulary size' (1999: 299).

Nurweni & Read (1999) report on a research study conducted in an Indonesian university to estimate the English vocabulary knowledge of first-year students. The tests used evaluated the breadth and depth of the lexical knowledge of the participants. It was found that the relationship between breadth and depth of vocabulary knowledge depended on the students' proficiency level. For students with a relatively high proficiency, there was a strong correlation between the two tests, whereas for those with low proficiency (the majority) the correlation was low.

Vermeer (2001) found strong correlations between the breadth measures he used and the depth measures. This finding prompted him to state: 'Thus, it would seem that measuring breadth matches up very much to measuring depth: if one knows more words, one can describe a stimulus word in greater depth' (2001: 225). Vermeer's participants were young children, L1 and L2 speakers of Dutch, whose lexical knowledge was obviously limited. We submitted the DWK test to native speakers of French, secondary school pupils and university students. The mean scores of these participants were certainly high, but they were not 100% correct, a result one would expect if there is no distinction between depth and breadth: all the words used in the test came from a list of the 5,000 most frequently used French words. Obviously, the knowledge of our native speaker participants largely exceeded this number. Apparently, a native speaker may know the two words, but fail to see a relationship between them when confronted with them in a test.

In conclusion, we might say that there is, indeed, a strong relationship between depth and breadth, but we would not go as far as Vermeer when he claims that 'there seems to be no conceptual distinction between breadth and depth' (2001: 222). As long as we do not have a theoretical model on the nature of lexical knowledge and the lexical acquisition process, such a definite statement is premature.

Acknowledgments

We wish to thank Danièle Flament-Boistrancourt, Dominique Fattier et Driss Ablali (Université de Paris X) and Georges Sentis (Lycée de la Madeleine, Lille), who administered the different versions of the test to the French participants. We would also like to thank John Read for his comments on an earlier draft of this paper.

Notes

1. We reported on previous stages of our study in Nienhuis *et al.* (2000) and Van der Linden *et al.* (2001).

2. In the item *coude* (elbow), for example, the distractor *travailler* (to work) is based on the Dutch expression *met z'n ellebogen werken* (use one's elbows, litt. work with one's elbows).

3. The Juilland corpus is a small corpus by present-day standards. Unfortunately, there are as yet no frequency lists of French words based on larger corpora that can be used for studies such as ours. The Imbs (1971) list is based on a large corpus, but it is somewhat out-of-date, as the corpus consists mainly of 19th- and early 20th-century texts, mostly of a literary nature.

4. The 65 (63) stimulus words represented 1.3% (1.2%) of the Juilland list, and the 390 (378) association words and distractors 7.7% (7.4%) of the list. We thus assessed, albeit in different ways, the knowledge of 9% (8.8%) of the words in the Juilland list.

5. Calculated on the basis of the responses to each association word (correct or incorrect).

6. The p value of a response denotes the percentage of the participants who gave the correct answer; the a value represents the percentage of the participants who gave the incorrect

answer by either ticking the item in cases where there was no relationship or by not ticking it in cases there was a relationship.

7. The frequent words were taken from the list of the *Français fondamental, Premier degré*. The infrequent words were selected from a large French dictionary "by picking only those words which were unlikely to be known by L2 speakers with a limited, *i.e.* non-native knowledge of French" (Bogaards, 2000: 498).

References

Beks, B. 2001. Le degré des connaissances lexicales [The degree of lexical knowledge]. Unpublished MA thesis, Vrije Universiteit Amsterdam.

Bogaards, P. 2000. "Testing L2 vocabulary knowledge at a high level: The case of the Euralex French Tests". *Applied Linguistics* 21: 490–516.

Greidanus, T. and Nienhuis, L. 2001. "Testing the quality of word knowledge in a second language by means of word associations: Types of distractors and types of associations". *Modern Language Journal* 85: 467–477.

Imbs, P. 1971. *Etudes statistiques sur le vocabulaire français. Dictionnaire des fréquences. Vocabulaire littéraire des XIXe et XXe siècles* [Statistical studies on French vocabulary. Dictionary of frequencies. Literary vocabulary of the 19th and 20th centuries]. Nancy: C. N. R. S.-T. L. F.

Juilland, A., Brodin, D. and Davidovitch, C. 1970. *Frequency Dictionary of French Words*. The Hague: Mouton.

Meara, P. 1992. *Euralex French Tests*. Swansea: Centre for Applied Language Studies.

Nienhuis, L., Bogaards, P., Greidanus, T., Van der Linden, E. and De Wolf, T. 2000. "Het toetsen van diepe woordkennis in een vreemde taal [Testing deep word knowledge in a second language]". *Toegepaste Taalwetenschap in Artikelen* 64: 107–115.

Nurweni, A. and Read, J. 1999. "The English vocabulary knowledge of Indonesian university students". *English for specific purposes* 18: 161–175.

Qian, D. D. 1999. "Assessing the roles of depth and breadth of vocabulary knowledge in reading comprehension". *Canadian Modern Language Review* 52: 282–307.

Read, J. 1993. "The development of a new measure of L2 vocabulary knowledge". *Language Testing* 10: 355–371.

Read, J. 1998. "Validating a test to measure depth of vocabulary knowledge". In *Validation in Language Assessment*, A. Kunnan (ed.), 41–57. Mahwah, NJ: Lawrence Erlbaum.

Savard, J.-G. and Richards, J. 1970. *Les indices d'utilité du vocabulaire fondamental français* [The utility indices of French fundamental vocabulary]. Québec: Presses de l'Université Laval.

Schoonen, R. and Verhallen, M. 1998. "Kennis van woorden: De toetsing van diepe woordkennis [Knowledge of words: The testing of deep word knowledge]". *Pedagogische Studiën* 75: 153–168.

Van der Linden, E., Bogaards, P., Greidanus, T., Nienhuis, L. and De Wolf, T. 2001. "Diepe woordkennis als maat voor algemene taalvaardigheid [Deep word knowledge as a measure of general language proficiency]". *Toegepaste Taalwetenschap in Artikelen* 66: 69–77.

Verhallen, M., Özdemir, L., Yüksel, E. and Schoonen, R. 1999. "Woordkennis van Turkse kinderen in de bovenbouw van het basisonderwijs [Lexical knowledge of Turkish children in the upper grades of primary education]". *Toegepaste Taalwetenschap in Artikelen* 61: 21–33.

Vermeer, A. 2001. "Breadth and depth of vocabulary in relation to L1/L2 acquisition and frequency of input". *Applied Psycholinguistics* 22: 217–234.

Wesche, M. and Paribakht, T. S. 1996. "Assessing second language vocabulary knowledge: Depth versus breadth". *Canadian Modern Language* Review 53: 13–40.

CHAPTER 11

Plumbing the depths: How should the construct of vocabulary knowledge be defined?

John Read
Victoria University of Wellington

Abstract

The term depth of knowledge has gained currency in the literature on second language vocabulary assessment, but it has been used by various authors in rather different ways. This chapter outlines three approaches — precision of meaning, comprehensive word knowledge and network knowledge — and discusses the assessment procedures associated with each one. Several studies comparing breadth and depth of knowledge are also considered. It is argued that a single term such as depth is inadequate and should be replaced by more specific definitions of what is being assessed by particular vocabulary instruments.

1. Introduction

The current boom in L2 vocabulary studies has created a need for various measures of lexical knowledge and ability. To a large extent the item types and tasks being used are ones that have long been familiar in work on the vocabulary knowledge of both first and second language learners: the checklist, in which learners simply indicate whether they know each word or not; various types of recognition item which involve the matching of target words with other related words or short definitions; recall-type items which require the learners to supply words deleted from individual sentences or longer segments of text; translation of words from L1 to L2, or vice versa; interviews which are designed to elicit definitions, explanations or other components of the learner's word knowledge; and speaking and writing tasks yielding samples of vocabulary use to which word counts and other lexical statistics can be applied. Perhaps the best-known instrument is the Vocabulary Levels Test, which assesses learners' knowledge of words at various frequency levels by means of a matching (definition — word) format. It has been particularly influential both in its original form (Nation 1983) and in various modified versions (Laufer & Nation 1999, Beglar & Hunt 1999, Schmitt, Schmitt & Clapham 2001).

In order to make choices from among the range of measures available, it is necessary for researchers to have some theoretical basis for classifying them. One distinction that is frequently made in the recent literature on L2 vocabulary testing is that between *breadth* and *depth* of vocabulary knowledge. These terms have been used in the literature on vocabulary in various ways since early in the twentieth century, but an influential definition found in Anderson & Freebody (1981: 92–93) explicitly uses them to distinguish what the authors call two aspects of vocabulary knowledge:

> The first may be called 'breadth' of knowledge, by which we mean the number of words for which the person knows at least some of the significant aspects of meaning. ... [There] is a second dimension of vocabulary knowledge, namely the quality or 'depth' of understanding. We shall assume that, for most purposes, a person has a sufficiently deep understanding of a word if it conveys to him or her all of the distinctions that would be understood by an ordinary adult under normal circumstances.

Anderson & Freebody go on to link the concept of breadth to a large body of work which is concerned with estimating vocabulary size, ie the total number of words known by children of various ages or by adult users of a particular language. Research on the vocabulary size of native speakers of English has a lengthy history (see e.g. Seashore & Eckerson 1940, Dupuy 1974, D'Anna, Zechmeister & Hall 1991) and it has become a significant area of investigation in the case of L2 learners as well (e.g. Meara & Buxton 1987, Hazenberg & Hulstijn 1996, Nurweni & Read 1999). There are several methodological issues involved in estimating vocabulary size which need not concern us here (see Lorge & Chall 1963, Nation 1993, for discussion). The one point which is relevant to the contrast between breadth and depth is that tests of vocabulary size normally need to include a large sample of words and, in order to keep the test to a reasonable length, the learners' task should be a simple one, such as indicating whether words are known or not on a checklist, matching words with synonyms or brief definitions, or supplying L1 equivalents for an L2 word list.

It is this feature of vocabulary size tests which has led to an extension in the use of the term breadth to refer to any vocabulary measure that requires just a single response to each target word and, by implication, gives only a superficial indication of whether the word is known or not. Thus, for example, Wesche & Paribakht (1996: 17–25) include among their examples of 'vocabulary breadth measures' any kind of multiple-choice vocabulary test, a C-test, a dictation, an error recognition task and lexical statistics based on learner compositions or oral production — regardless of whether these assessment methods are being used to make an estimate of overall vocabulary size. In this context, breadth becomes a retronym: it serves as a term to distinguish conventional vocabulary tests from ones that have been designed more recently to assess depth of vocabulary knowledge in particular.

What, then, is meant by depth? If we return to the Anderson & Freebody quote above, we find that it refers to the 'quality ... of understanding' of a word. Other writers (e.g. Read 1993: 357, Nation 2001: 354) have expressed it more succinctly as how well particular words are known. At this level of generality, the distinction between breadth and depth is a commonsense one, since anyone with a cursory understanding of vocabulary will acknowledge that there is a great deal more involved in knowing a word in an L2 than being able to match it with an L2 synonym or provide an L1 translation equivalent.

Nevertheless, for the concept of depth to be useful for research and assessment purposes as a component of the construct of L2 vocabulary knowledge, it needs to be elaborated beyond the level of a simple dichotomy. The problem is that, in their efforts to develop and operationalize the concept during the last decade, scholars have followed somewhat different paths, to the point where the concept has become rather confused and it is questionable whether the term depth can meaningfully encompass the various uses to which it is being put. There are in fact three distinct lines of development in the application of depth to L2 vocabulary acquisition:

(1) The difference between having a limited, vague idea of what a word means and having much more elaborated and specific knowledge of its meaning, which I will refer to as *precision of meaning*.

(2) Knowledge of a word which includes not only its semantic features but also its orthographic, phonological, morphological, syntactic, collocational and pragmatic characteristics: *comprehensive word knowledge*.

(3)   The incorporation of the word into a lexical network in the mental lexicon, together with the ability to link it to — and distinguish it from — related words, which we can call *network knowledge.*

The three approaches overlap to a considerable extent. One can argue that, conceptually, the comprehensive approach subsumes the other two but it is useful to separate them for the purpose of analysis, because each one has been the basis for various authors' accounts of what depth of vocabulary knowledge means and in addition, somewhat different assessment procedures result from adopting one approach rather than the others.

Let us review the three approaches to depth of knowledge, paying attention to the kind of vocabulary tests which have been used in each case. But before proceeding, I should point out some ways in which I have limited the scope of the discussion. The first is that the approaches can be viewed either in terms of the state of the learner's vocabulary knowledge at a particular point or as a process of lexical development. The latter perspective is associated with longitudinal research studies such as those undertaken by Haastrup and Henriksen (Henriksen & Haastrup 1998, Haastrup & Henriksen 2000). However, in practice most depth tests, whether used for research or for learner assessment in a language teaching programme, simply reflect what the learner knows about the target vocabulary at the time they are administered.

The second point is that measures of vocabulary depth have typically been concerned with *declarative* knowledge — which learners can consciously access and report in a vocabulary test — rather than the more implicit *procedural* knowledge that underlies word recognition, proficient listening comprehension or fluent conversational speech. Thirdly, the work being reviewed here generally defines vocabulary knowledge as knowing the meaning of individual word forms. As Bogaards (2001) has noted, this is problematic when it comes to dealing with the polysemous nature of most words as they occur singly or in larger lexical units. In the interests of reducing the scope of the discussion in this chapter, then, I will largely confine it to measurement of declarative knowledge of individual words at a particular point in the learners' acquisition of an L2.

2.   Precision of meaning

Anderson & Freebody's (1981) full definition of depth, as quoted above, states that 'a person has a sufficiently deep understanding of a word if it conveys to him or her all of the distinctions that would be understood by an ordinary adult under normal circumstances'. Implicit in this statement is the problem that words vary in the extent to which they lend themselves to exact definition. Obviously, numerous high-frequency words are inherently vague, particularly when encountered out of context: *thing, make, nice, here, someone.* Other words are polysemous, having various shades of meaning, a range of distinct uses or even quite different meanings: *form, odd, stick, chip, break, draw, proper.* A further distinction is that between everyday uses of a word and more specialized or technical meanings, as illustrated by *fruit, dialect, reaction* and *parameter.* The words which probably lend themselves best to precise definition are purely technical ones such as *phoneme, aneurysm, immunodiffusion* and *tort.*

This variability in the semantic characteristics of words is reflected in the vocabulary knowledge of native speakers of the target language. Thus, for words like *carburettor, mollusc, logarithm* and *haunch* adult native speakers of English may be able to identify the context or field of study in which they are used without being able to attribute a specific meaning to them. Knowledge of specialized, low-frequency vocabulary reflects in the first instance a person's level and field of education but also their social and cultural background, occupation, personal interests and so on. The result is that it becomes quite complicated to define a criterion level of precision that can fit a wide range of different lexical items.

However the 'adult native speaker' criterion is defined, the challenge for L2 vocabulary assessment is to measure whether it has been achieved and, if not, how the learner's knowledge falls short. There are three main ways in which the precision-of-knowledge construct has been operationalized. (See Nagy & Scott 2000 for a five-way classification which covers much the same ground from the perspective of reading research.) Since this is not a well-developed area of L2 vocabulary studies, several of the examples come from work with children acquiring their first language.

2.1   Test items requiring precise knowledge

A first step away from broad knowledge is to design test items which require more specific understanding of the target word in order to be answered correctly. In the multiple-choice format, this can be achieved by writing options which require more than a general understanding of word meaning, as in this example from Dolch & Leeds (1953):

A disaster is ruin which happens

a. suddenly
b. within a year's time
c. to all people
d. gradually

Similarly, in Nagy, Herman & Anderson's (1985) well-known study of incidental vocabulary learning from reading, degrees of understanding of the target words were measured by systematically varying the semantic relatedness of the multiple-choice distracters. The same principle can be applied to other types of test item, such as matching or gap-filling, in which a less frequent meaning or use of a polysemous word is targeted for assessment.

2.2   Self-report of degrees of knowledge

The second method builds on the notion that it is meaningful to identify degrees of vocabulary knowledge in terms of a series of steps or points on a scale. An early example is Dale's four basic stages in knowing a word:

> Stage 1:   'I never saw it before.'
> Stage 2:   'I've heard of it, but I don't know what it means.'
> Stage 3:   'I recognize it in context — it has something to do with ...'
> Stage 4:   'I know it'. (1965: 898).

In a similar vein, Paribakht & Wesche (1993; also Wesche & Paribakht 1996) developed their *Vocabulary Knowledge Scale* (VKS) as an instrument to assess how much knowledge of targeted words was gained by learners as the result of engaging in various reading activities. It follows very much the same sequence as Dale's stages, except that at steps 4 and 5 the learners are required to supply a synonym or translation and to write a sentence containing the word. The sentence-composing task takes the VKS beyond a pure measure of semantic knowledge but up to that point it is a method of eliciting how specifically the learners understand the meaning of each word.

The notion of degrees of word knowledge from vague to precise is a deep-seated one in vocabulary studies. For instance, Melka (1997) suggests that the problematic dichotomy between receptive and productive knowledge should be reinterpreted in terms of a continuum, with an overlapping and shifting transition zone where words that are understood receptively become available for productive use. However, the assumption that acquisition of word meaning can be seen as steady progression along a continuum is challenged by

Meara (1996), who argues that forgetting what a word means is just as much a part of the vocabulary acquisition process as remembering it. Thus, Meara & Rodriguez Sanchez (2001) have developed a matrix model to analyse data from a self-report instrument which uses similar categories to those in the VKS but treats them as discrete states, such that a word could move back and forth from one state of knowledge to another over time. Using longitudinal data from two rating sessions, they were able to make remarkably accurate predictions of the students' ratings of their word knowledge on a later, third occasion. This kind of probability matrix represents a way of avoiding the assumption of a smooth progression from a lower level of knowledge to a higher one, at least in longitudinal studies.

2.3   Elicitation of definitions

The third method of investigating precision of word knowledge is to ask learners to explain the meaning of words and then to evaluate the quality of the explanations they provide for each word. This is a technique that has frequently been used to investigate the developing vocabulary of children in their first or second language. Research has shown that — whether the task be supplying an oral definition (Feifel & Lorge 1950) or selecting options in multiple-choice items (Russell & Saadeh 1962) — explanations of word meaning are predominantly concrete, functional and descriptive for younger children up to around age 10, whereas adolescents tend to opt for more abstract and analytic explanations which resemble formal definitions. Thus, in studies where children's explanations of words are rated according to the level of vocabulary knowledge they represent (e.g. Nagy, Herman & Anderson 1985, Vermeer 2001), more credit is given for a decontextualized response than for one which illustrates a particular use of the word.

   In other research on children's definitions of concrete nouns by Snow and her colleagues (e.g. Snow 1990, Kurland & Snow 1997), the inclusion of a superordinate (e.g. 'a donkey is an *animal* ...'; 'an umbrella is *something* that ...') is taken as a criterial feature of a formal definition. The studies show that both the incidence of formal definitions and the quality of information in the definitions increase significantly from age 4 until around 9 or 10, when a plateau is reached. There is also clear evidence of the effects of schooling on defining ability, with the result that Kurland & Snow (1997) found that 10-year-old children from low-income families in a US city were able to give better definitions (according to the researchers' criteria) than their mothers did. As

Snow (1990: 699) points out, then, giving 'adult-like' definitions of words depends not only on having sufficient semantic information but also having knowledge of — and practice with — the genre of definitions.

Little work has been done on explanations or definitions of words provided by adults in either their first or a second language, but it is questionable whether the ability to supply a decontextualised definition can be taken as a criterion for precise knowledge of a word. For one thing, if learners are being assessed on the basis of a specific set of vocabulary items which they have studied, it is possible that the definition has been simply memorised from a dictionary or textbook rather than being composed as an expression of the learner's current understanding of the word. Another situation is where the learner has a good knowledge of an L2 word but lacks the ability to express that understanding if required to do so through the L2. More generally, Anderson & Nagy (1991) argue strongly for a clear distinction to be made between knowing a meaning of a word and knowing its definition. In their view, functional vocabulary knowledge typically builds up through multiple exposures to a word in different contexts and thus an abstract, general statement of meaning does not adequately represent the knowledge that proficient language users have of most of the words they know, even when we confine our attention to readily accessible declarative knowledge.

This calls into question the whole notion of precision of knowledge, if that implies an underlying core meaning of a word that can be expressed in a general dictionary-type definition. Neither the VKS nor a definition task is designed to elicit learners' knowledge of polysemy or different contexts in which a word can occur. Thus, as Cronbach (1942) pointed out long ago, precision of meaning needs to be complemented with some concept of breadth of meaning — which of course is not be confused with breadth in the sense of vocabulary size, as in the Anderson & Freebody (1981) quote above. Perhaps a term such as elaboration or richness of meaning should be substituted for precision as a way of characterizing this approach to vocabulary depth. Another more far-reaching solution, proposed by Bogaards (2001), is to replace the whole concept of a 'word' with Cruse's (1986) notion of a 'lexical unit', which would allow test designers to target particular meanings and contexts of use for vocabulary items.

3.   Comprehensive word knowledge

A second conception of depth takes a much more comprehensive view of vocabulary knowledge, encompassing not just meaning but various other components as well. Several authors have outlined the scope of the area (Cronbach 1942, Richards 1976, Laufer 1997, Nagy & Scott 2000) but possibly the most influential account in L2 vocabulary studies is Nation's analysis of what is involved in knowing a word (Nation 2001: 27). In summary, Nation's account comprises the following categories:

Form: pronunciation, spelling, word parts
Meaning: form-meaning relationship, concept and referents, associations
Use: grammatical functions, collocations, constraints on use
            (register, frequency ..)

Furthermore, each category covers both receptive and productive word knowledge.

The comprehensive conception of depth greatly complicates test design if we take it to mean that all the various components of word knowledge should be assessed. An indication of what is involved can be found in Schmitt's (1998b) longitudinal case studies of some international students acquiring an advanced knowledge of English vocabulary. It took about two hours to elicit from each student what they knew about five aspects of just eleven words. Perhaps a written version of the task might be more feasible, although my own exploratory study of that possibility was not encouraging (Read 2000: 178–180). An additional constraint is the lack of suitable measures for several word knowledge components, despite Schmitt's recent efforts to develop some (see e.g. Schmitt 1998a).

Apart from the practical concerns of having enough time to carry out an elaborate elicitation procedure and having learners who are willing to cooperate fully in it, there is also the more theoretical question of whether it suits the assessment purpose to have a great deal of data on the learners' knowledge of just a small number of words. Are these target words particularly significant? From this perspective, there is an interesting shift in the Anderson & Freebody (1981) definition quoted above. Whereas their explanation of breadth refers to 'the number of words' known in a collective sense, they define depth in relation to knowledge of an individual word. As Meara (1996) has pointed out, this creates a danger of missing the wood for the trees, if the purpose of a depth measure is to draw some general conclusion about the state of the learners' vocabulary knowledge rather than just reporting on how well the particular target words are known. Focusing on a small set of words can yield important insights in research studies on L2 vocabulary acquisition, but it may not provide useful information for decision-making purposes in language teaching programmes.

What, then, are alternative ways of operationalising the comprehensive framework? One interesting question is whether some kind of implicational scaling of the various components is possible, so that, if learners demonstrate 'more advanced' kinds of knowledge of particular words, we can assume that they have acquired 'basic' knowledge of those same words. One such scaling system was developed by Drum (Drum & Konopak 1987: 79–80) for her research on American children's ability to deploy their vocabulary knowledge effectively in first language reading. Based on the students' attempts to explain the meaning of words presented to them in isolation, she developed a scale consisting of four ranked categories, from lowest to highest:

A. Perceptual – physically similar words
B. Syntactic – internal structure or grammatical function of words
C. Semantic – general meaning dimensions of a word
D. Correct – a specific correct definition

At the upper levels (C and D), this is obviously a meaning scale of the partial-to-precise kind, as discussed above under the precision of meaning approach, leading up to what is judged to be a fully adequate definition of the word. However, Category B brings in grammatical knowledge (the morphological structure and part-of-speech of the word) and the lowest category deals with the students' ability to recognise the word correctly from its spelling and to avoid confusing it with similar-looking words, or 'synforms' as Laufer (1990, 1997) calls them.

This is a useful scale but not a universally applicable one. First, it was developed specifically for *reading*; a scale to account for the vocabulary knowledge required for writing, for example, would need to be defined somewhat differently. Secondly, it was derived from the responses of elementary and secondary students and was designed for use with such students, which means that it could reflect stages of cognitive development in children and adolescents. As such, it may be less relevant to the vocabulary acquisition of older L2 learners.

Very little work has been done by L2 vocabulary researchers to explore empirically the relationships between the various components of word knowledge. The main exception is a study by Schmitt & Meara (1997), who looked at Japanese learners' knowledge of derivational suffixes and word associations, with reference to a set of English verbs. The authors found significant, if somewhat modest correlations (.3 to .5) between the two components. The analysis also showed moderate correlations (.39 to .66) between the association scores and both vocabulary size and general language proficiency (TOEFL), particularly in the case of 'productive' associations (where the learners supplied the associated word through recall rather than selecting it from a list). It was very much an exploratory study and the researchers noted considerable individual variation in results among the participants. Nevertheless, they provided empirical evidence of a relationship between knowledge components and opened up the possibility that certain aspects of word knowledge may be of more value than others as indices of L2 vocabulary development. Obviously more research of this kind is required if the comprehensive approach is to be implemented for assessment purposes, and it would be premature to conclude that there is a developmental sequence in the way that learners acquire the different aspects of word meaning.

In his discussion of testing depth of knowledge from a classroom teacher's perspective, Nation (2001: 346) proposes that his framework summarized at the beginning of this section be used as a kind of checklist to help decide what aspect(s) of word knowledge should be the focus of the test items. He also suggests (2001: 354–355) that some aspects, such as the spelling rule for the doubling of consonants in English or word formation patterns involving productive derivational suffixes, should be assessed as general vocabulary rules rather than as attributes of individual words.

4.   Network knowledge

A third way to conceive of depth of vocabulary knowledge is in terms of the building of a lexical network. The assumption is that, as a learner's vocabulary size increases, newly acquired words need to be accommodated within a network of already known words, and some restructuring of the network may be needed as a result. This means that depth can be understood in terms of learners' developing ability to distinguish semantically related words and, more generally, their knowledge of the various ways in which individual words are linked to each other. This approach has one significant difference from the other two: whereas the others focus on the acquisition of individual words, this one explores the development of links between sets of words in the mental lexicon. Interestingly, in Henriksen's (1999) analysis of the dimensions of vocabulary competence, it is this network approach which she chooses to label as 'depth of knowledge', distinguishing it from partial to precise knowledge as a separate dimension.

The network knowledge approach draws on the fundamental paradigmatic-syntagmatic distinction in structuralist linguistics, as elaborated in semantic theory by Lyons (1995) and Cruse (1986). The work of Miller & Fellbaum (1991) with their WordNet computer simulation of the English lexicon is also significant and in particular their insight that what is important in semantic relations varies according to word class. Thus, for nouns the key relationships are hierarchical superordinate — subordinate ones, as noted above in the discussion of formal definitions, whereas for adjectives antonymy and gradation are basic principles of classification. Although most verbs have hierarchical relationships that are somewhat comparable to those of nouns, they form the most semantically complex word class.

The basic research technique for investigating the lexical network has been the word association task, whereby language users are presented with a set of stimulus words one-by-one and are asked to produce the first word they think of in response. There are well-established findings that adult native speakers produce characteristic patterns of response to this task and that children shift from responses with a syntagmatic relation to the stimulus to the adult pattern of predominantly paradigmatic ones before the age of puberty (Aitchison 1994). In the case of L2 learners, research on word associations was initiated by Meara and his associates in the 1980s (Meara 1984), with subsequent contributions by several other researchers (Söderman 1993, Schmitt 1998a, Singleton 1999, Meara & Fitzpatrick 2000). Debate has centred around the extent to which learners produce phonologically based (or 'clang') responses rather than semantically related ones, and whether their associations can be interpreted in relation to the established native-speaker norms.

In order to assess depth of vocabulary knowledge in a more practical fashion, Read (1993, 1998) used the principle of word association to create the word associates format, which requires learners to select responses to a stimulus rather than supplying them. A word associates item consists of a target word, together with six or eight other words, some of which are related to the stimulus word and some not, as in the following example:

contract

agreement   confident   formal   notice   sign   special

There are three basic relationships between the target word and associates: paradigmatic (superordinates, synonyms), syntagmatic (collocates) and analytic (words representing a key element of the meaning of the target word). Thus, the correct responses in the example above are 'agreement' (paradigmatic), 'sign' (syntagmatic) and 'formal' (analytic). In practice, the selection of words as associates is not based on theory or native-speaker norms, but simply the judgment of the test writers as to which words are suitable for the purpose. Other researchers, notably Greidanus and her colleagues in the Netherlands (Greidanus & Nienhuis 2001, Greidanus *et al.* this volume), have investigated various aspects of the design of such tests and found them to be practical measures to assess the vocabulary knowledge of advanced learners of a foreign language. The word associates format has also had a role in some research on breadth and depth which will be discussed in the following section.

5. The relationship between depth and breadth of knowledge

Having reviewed the three approaches to depth of vocabulary, let us consider the breadth-depth distinction again before drawing an overall conclusion from the discussion. Although the tendency of authors since Anderson & Freebody (1981) has been to contrast the concepts of breadth and depth as if they are — if not polar opposites — at least quite distinct dimensions of vocabulary knowledge, the small amount of evidence that is available so far suggests that they are somewhat closely related. Commonsense would lead us to expect that, as learners expand the absolute number of words that they have some understanding of, they will also be learning more about words that they encounter or use frequently. This parallel development of vocabulary size and depth is particularly pertinent if we adopt a network building perspective on depth, in that vocabulary growth also entails the building of more extensive linkages between items in the mental lexicon.

A strong advocate of this position is Vermeer (2001), who argues that there is essentially no difference between breadth and depth. On a conceptual level, he points out that it is through knowledge of related words that we are able to understand and express the specific meaning of an individual word, as in the differences between *cup*, *mug* and *glass*. Empirically, his evidence comes from his research in the Netherlands on the vocabulary development of five-year-old children, both L1 (DL1) and L2 (DL2) learners of Dutch. He found high correlations between a depth measure, which elicited several meaning aspects of ten familiar concrete nouns, and two breadth measures. The DL1 children had substantially higher scores on all the measures than the DL2 learners and, according to Vermeer, the DL2 children's smaller vocabulary size also meant that they lacked the lexical resources to express verbally the semantic characteristics that were being elicited by the depth test. A follow-up study showed a strong relationship between the vocabulary size of young Dutch children and the frequency with which the words occur in oral and written input in Dutch primary school classrooms. He interprets his finding explicitly from a network knowledge viewpoint:

> The high correlations are a logical consequence of the fact that the lexical elements in the mental lexicon consists [sic] of interrelated nodes in a network, which specify the meaning of an element. The denser the network around a word, the richer the set of connections around that word, the greater the number of words known, and the deeper the knowledge of that word. (2001: 231)

He concludes that a breadth test containing a good sample of words can measure children's vocabulary as well as a depth test.

Another study of Dutch primary school children by Schoonen & Verhallen (1998) compared vocabulary breadth and depth tests with performance on two cloze passages, intended as measures of reading comprehension ability. Like Vermeer, the researchers found that the breadth test (a Dutch version of the Peabody Picture Vocabulary Test) and the depth one (a word associates test) were strongly correlated. Nevertheless, in a regression analysis each vocabulary test made a unique contribution of around 5–10 percent to the prediction of the cloze scores. Thus, Schoonen & Verhallen found that the depth test accounted for some additional variance in the cloze scores beyond what was predicted by the breadth test.

One point to note here is that in young children vocabulary growth has a close relationship to — and may be constrained to some extent — by their cognitive development. This means it is possible that the relationship between breadth and depth may be somewhat different for them than for older learners.

To pursue this possibility, we can look at two studies by Qian (1999, 2000) involving adults learning English as a second language in Canadian universities. He used the reading section of the Test of English as a Foreign Language (TOEFL) as his dependent variable and obtained vocabulary size and depth measures by means of the Vocabulary Levels Test (Nation 1990) and a version of Read's (1998) word associates test respectively. His results were similar to those of Schoonen & Verhallen: the two vocabulary tests were highly correlated (r=.82 in the first study; r=.70 in the second) but, in multiple regression analyses, the depth test added significantly to the variance explained by the breadth measure (11% in the first study; 5% in the second).

One further kind of evidence comes from Nurweni's study of the English vocabulary knowledge of first-year students at a university in Indonesia (Nurweni & Read, 1999). She used a word translation task to assess vocabulary size and a word associates test to measure depth of knowledge. For the whole sample of 350 students, the correlation between the two tests was .62. However, when the students were divided into three groups according to their general level of achievement in English, the strength of the relationship varied considerably. For High level students (just 10% of the whole group), the correlation was much higher, at .81. By contrast, the Middle group (42% of the students) obtained a correlation of .43 and for the remaining half, at the Low level, it was just .18. These figures suggest that, while breadth and depth of vocabulary knowledge may converge when learners are relatively advanced, they are more distinct at lower levels of language proficiency.

It should be noted that the last three studies which found a distinct role for a depth measure all used the word associates format as their test of vocabulary depth. While this type of test has shown some promise as a vocabulary measure, it represents just one way of operationalizing the concept of depth of knowledge, as outlined by the analysis earlier in this chapter. A broader range of measures is needed before we can be more confident about the extent to which depth in some sense makes a contribution to the assessment of the lexical knowledge of L2 learners.

6.   Conclusion

The preceding discussion assumes, of course, that it is useful to continue using the term depth of vocabulary knowledge as if it represents a well-defined construct in the field of L2 vocabulary studies. The analysis presented above makes it clear that, as employed by various scholars, the term refers to at least three distinct ways of conceptualising word knowledge, each of which gives rise to particular forms of assessment. There is a good argument to be made that the breadth vs. depth metaphor has served its rhetorical purpose of encouraging researchers and language teachers to look beyond conventional test items which require learners to indicate their target language words by means of a simple self-report procedure or by matching the words with semantically equivalent expressions in L1 or L2. Once this point is widely accepted, it opens up a whole range of possibilities for other types of test item and alternative ways of measuring aspects of word knowledge.

It may be time, then, to dispense with the term depth and to recognise that any substitute that one might propose — precision, richness, elaboration, quality — is equally problematic as a cover term for the state of a learner's vocabulary knowledge that goes beyond a rough estimate of how many words are known. Whether we focus on individual lexical items or the mental lexicon as a whole, we are setting out to describe something that is inherently ill-defined, multidimensional, variable and thus resistant to neat classification. This does not mean that the quest for new measures of vocabulary knowledge should be abandoned. Rather it suggests that the dimension of knowledge that they are designed to measure should be carefully defined and not simply labelled with a catch-all term like depth. It also remains to be established whether any single measure of what we have been calling depth can make a substantial contribution to assessing the state of a learner's vocabulary knowledge beyond what is measured by a well-designed test of vocabulary size

In addition, it is important to acknowledge the limitations of confining the assessment of vocabulary to declarative knowledge, as we have done for the purposes of this chapter. It is true that the mental lexicon appears to be more available to conscious access than other aspects of language competence and an explicit understanding of specialized vocabulary is necessary in education, the professions and technical fields. Nevertheless, as Nagy & Scott (2000: 273) argue, 'for much nontechnical vocabulary, it may be more useful to conceptualize word knowledge as being primarily procedural'. That is to say, ultimately the question is not what learners know about a word but what they can do with it: being able to pronounce it, recognize it in connected speech and writing, and use it fluently in their own production. Thus, measures of declarative knowledge need to be complemented by tests of vocabulary in use in order to obtain a full picture of the learners' lexical competence.

References

Aitchison, J. 1994. *Words in the Mind: An Introduction to the Mental Lexicon.* Second edition. Oxford: Blackwell.

Anderson, R. C. and Freebody, P. 1981. "Vocabulary knowledge". In *Comprehension and Teaching: Research Reviews*, J. T. Guthrie, (ed), 77–117. Newark, DE: International Reading Association.

Anderson, R. C. and Nagy, W. E. 1991. "Word meanings". In *Handbook of Reading Research*, Volume 2, R. Barr, M. L. Kamil, P. Mosenthal and P. D. Pearson (eds), 690–724. New York: Longman.

Beglar, D. and Hunt, A. 1999. "Revising and validating the 2000 Word Level and University Word Level Vocabulary Tests". *Language Testing* 16: 131–162.

Bogaards, P. 2001. "Lexical units and the learning of foreign language vocabulary". *Studies in Second Language Acquisition* 23: 321–343.

Cronbach, L. J. 1942. "An analysis of techniques for diagnostic vocabulary testing". *Journal of Educational Research* 36: 206–217.

Cruse, D. A. 1986. *Lexical Semantics.* Cambridge: Cambridge University Press.

D'Anna, C. A. Zechmeister, E. B. and Hall, J. W. 1991. "Toward a meaningful definition of vocabulary size". *Journal of Reading Behavior* 23: 109–122.

Dale, E. 1965. "Vocabulary measurement: Techniques and major findings". *Elementary English* 42: 895–901, 948.

Dolch, E. W. and Leeds, D. 1953. "Vocabulary tests and depth of meaning". *Journal of Educational Research* 4: 181–189.

Drum, P. A. and Konopak, B. 1987. "Learning word meanings from written contexts". In *The Nature of Vocabulary Acquisition*, M. G. McKeown and M. E. Curtis (eds), 73–87. Hillsdale, NJ: Lawrence Erlbaum.

Dupuy, H. J. 1974. *The Rationale, Development, and Standardization of a Basic Word Vocabulary Test.* Washington, DC: US Government Printing Office.

Feifel, H. and Lorge, I. 1950. "Qualitative differences in the vocabulary responses of children". *Journal of Educational Psychology* 41: 1–18.

Greidanus, T. and Nienhuis, L. 2001. "Testing the quality of word knowledge in L2 by means of word associations: Types of distractors and types of associations". *Modern Language Journal* 85: 567–577.

Haastrup, K. and Henriksen, B. 2000. "Vocabulary acquisition: Acquiring depth of knowledge through network building". *International Journal of Applied Linguistics* 10: 221–240.

Hazenberg, S. and Hulstijn, J. 1996. "Defining a minimal receptive second-language vocabulary for non-native university students: An empirical investigation". *Applied Linguistics* 17: 145–163.

Henriksen, B. 1999. "Three dimensions of vocabulary development". *Studies in Second Language Acquisition* 21: 303–317.

Henriksen, B. and Haastrup, K. 1998. "Describing learners' lexical competence across tasks and over time: A focus on research design". In *Perspectives on Lexical Acquisition in a Second Language*, K. Haastrup and Å. Viberg (eds), 61–95. Lund: Lund University Press.

Kurland, B. F. and Snow, C. E. 1997. "Longitudinal measurement of growth in definitional skill". *Journal of Child Language* 24: 603–625.

Laufer, B. 1990. "'Sequence' and 'order' in the development of L2 lexis: Some evidence from lexical confusions". *Applied Linguistics* 11: 281–296.

Laufer, B. 1997. "What's in a word that makes it hard or easy? Some intralexical factors that affect the learning of words". In *Vocabulary: Description, Acquisition and Pedagogy*, N. Schmitt and M. McCarthy (eds), 140–155. Cambridge: Cambridge University Press.

Laufer, B. and Nation, P. 1999. "A vocabulary-size test of controlled productive ability". *Language Testing* 16: 33–51.

Lorge, I. and Chall, J. 1963. "Estimating the size of vocabularies of children and adults: An analysis of methodological issues". *Journal of Experimental Psychology* 32: 147–157.

Lyons, J. 1995. *Linguistic Semantics: An Introduction.* Cambridge: Cambridge University Press.

Meara, P. 1984. "The study of lexis in interlanguage". In *Interlanguage*, A. Davies, C. Criper and A. P. R. Howatt (eds), 225–235. Edinburgh: Edinburgh University Press.

Meara, P. 1996. "The vocabulary knowledge framework". Unpublished paper. Available online at www.swan.ac.uk/cals/vlibrary/pm96d.htm

Meara, P. and Buxton, B. 1987. "An alternative to multiple choice vocabulary tests". *Language Testing* 4: 142–154.

Meara, P. and Fitzpatrick, T. 2000. "Lex-30: An improved method of assessing productive vocabulary in an L2". *System* 28: 19–30.

Meara, P. and Rodriguez Sanchez, I. 2001. "A methodology for evaluating the effectiveness of vocabulary treatments". In *Reflections on Language and Language Learning*, M. Bax and J-W. Zwart (eds), 267–278. Amsterdam: John Benjamins.

Melka, F. 1997. "Receptive vs. productive aspects of vocabulary". In *Vocabulary: Description, Acquisition and Pedagogy*, N. Schmitt and M. McCarthy (eds), 84–102. Cambridge: Cambridge University Press.

Miller, G. A. and Fellbaum, C. 1991. "Semantic networks of English". *Cognition* 41: 197–229.

Nagy, W., Herman, P. and Anderson, R. C. 1985. "Learning words from context". *Reading Research Quarterly* 20: 233–253.

Nagy, W. and Scott, 2000. "Vocabulary processes". In *Handbook of Reading Research*, Volume 3, M. L. Kamil, P. B. Mosenthal, P. D. Pearson and R. Barr (eds), 269–284. Mahwah, NJ: Lawrence Erlbaum.

Nation, I. S. P. 1983. "Testing and teaching vocabulary". *Guidelines* 5: 12–25.

Nation, I. S. P. 1990. T*eaching and Learning Vocabulary.* New York: Heinle and Heinle.

Nation, I. S. P. 1993. "Using dictionaries to estimate vocabulary size: Essential but rarely followed procedures". *Language Testing* 10: 27–40.

Nation, I. S. P. 2001. *Learning Vocabulary in Another Language.* Cambridge: Cambridge University Press.

Nurweni, A. and Read, J. 1999. "The English vocabulary knowledge of Indonesian university students". *English for Specific Purposes* 18: 161–175.

Paribakht, S. and Wesche, M. 1993. "Reading comprehension and second language development in a comprehension-based ESL program". *TESL Canada Journal* 11: 9–29.

Qian, D. D. 1999. "Assessing the roles of depth and breadth of vocabulary knowledge in reading comprehension". *Canadian Modern Language Review* 56: 282–307.

Qian, D. D. 2000. *Validating the Role of Depth of Vocabulary Knowledge in Assessing Reading for Basic Comprehension* [TOEFL 2000 Research Report]. Princeton, NJ: Educational Testing Service.

Read, J. 1993. "The development of a new measure of L2 vocabulary knowledge". *Language Testing* 10: 355–371.

Read, J. 1998. "Validating a test to measure depth of vocabulary knowledge". In *Validation in Language Assessment*, A. Kunnan (ed), 41–60. Mahwah, NJ: Lawrence Erlbaum.

Read, J. 2000. *Assessing Vocabulary*. Cambridge: Cambridge University Press.

Richards, J. C. 1976. "The role of vocabulary teaching". *TESOL Quarterly* 10: 77–89.

Russell, D. H. and Saadeh, I. Q. 1962. "Qualitative levels in children's vocabularies". *Journal of Educational Psychology* 53: 170–174.

Schmitt, N. 1998a. "Quantifying word association responses: What is native-like?". *System* 26: 389–401.

Schmitt, N. 1998b. "Tracking the incremental acquisition of second language vocabulary: A longitudinal study". *Language Learning* 48: 281–317.

Schmitt, N. and Meara, P. 1997. "Researching vocabulary through a word knowledge framework: Word associations and verbal suffixes". *Studies in Second Language Acquisition* 19: 17–36.

Schmitt, N., Schmitt, D. and Clapham, C. 2001. "Developing and exploring the behaviour of two new versions of the Vocabulary Levels Test". *Language Testing* 18: 55–89.

Schoonen, R. and Verhallen, M. 1998. "Aspects of vocabulary knowledge and reading performance". Paper presented at the Annual Meeting of the American Educational Research Association, San Diego, April.

Seashore, R. H. and Eckerson, L. D. 1940. "The measurement of individual differences in general English vocabularies". *Journal of Educational Psychology* 31: 14–38.

Snow, C. E. 1990. "The development of definitional skill". *Journal of Child Language* 17: 697–710.

Singleton, D. 1999. *Exploring the Second Language Mental Lexicon*. Cambridge: Cambridge University Press.

Söderman, T. 1993. "Word associations of foreign language learners and native speakers: The phenomenon of a shift in response type and its relevance for lexical development". In *Near-native Proficiency in English*, H. Ringbom (ed), 91–182. Åbo: Åbo Akademi, English Department Publications.

Vermeer, A. 2001. "Breadth and depth of vocabulary in relation to L1/L2 acquisition and frequency of input". *Applied Psycholinguistics* 22: 217–234.

Wesche, M. and Paribakht, S. 1996. "Assessing second language vocabulary knowledge: Breadth vs. depth". *Canadian Modern Language Review* 53: 13–39.

List of contributors

Adolphs, Svenja
School of English Studies
The University of Nottingham
Nottingham NG7 2RD, UK
svenja.adolphs@nottingham.ac.uk

Boers, Frank
University of Antwerp
Faculty of Education and Information
    Sciences
Universiteitsplein 1
2610 Antwerp, Belgium
frank.boers@docent.ehb.be

Bogaards, Paul
Leiden University, French Department
P.O. Box 9515
2300 RA Leiden, The Netherlands
p.bogaards@let.leidenuniv.nl

Cobb, Tom
Département de linguistique
    et de didactique des langues
Université du Québec à Montréal
Montréal, Québec, Canada
cobb.tom@uqam.ca

Demecheleer, Murielle
Université Libre de Bruxelles
Institut des Langues Vivantes et de
    Phonétique
Avenue F. D. Roosevelt 50
1050 Brussels, Belgium
murielle.demecheleer@ulb.ac.be

Dewaele, Jean-Marc
Birkbeck College
University of London
jmdewaele@aol.com

Eyckmans, June
Erasmuscollege Brussels
Trierstraat 84
1040 Brussels, Belgium
june.eyckmans@docent.ehb.be

Greidanus, Tine
Free University Amsterdam
French Department
De Boelelaan 1105
1081 HV Amsterdam, The Netherands
dt.greidanus@let.vu.nl

Horst, Marlise
Department of Education
TESL Centre
Concordia University
Montreal, Quebec, H3G 1M8 Canada
marlise@education.concordia.ca

Jiang, Nan
Department of Applied Linguistics & ESL
Georgia State University
P.O. BOX 4099
Atlanta, GA 30302–4099
U. S. A.
njiang@gsu.edu

Laufer, Batia
Department of English Language and
    Literature, University of Haifa
Haifa 31905, Israel
batialau@research.haifa.ac.il

Linden, Elisabeth van der
ACLC/University of Amsterdam
Department of Second Language Acquisition
Spuistraat 134
1012 VB Amsterdam, The Netherlands
e.linden@uva.nl

Mondria, Jan-Arjen
Dept. of Language and Communication
University of Groningen
P.O. Box 716
9700 AS Groningen, The Netherlands
j.a.mondria@ub.rug.nl

Nation, Paul
School of Linguistics and Applied Language
    Studies
Victoria University of Wellington
P.O. Box 600
Wellington, New Zealand
paul.nation@vuw.ac.nz

Nienhuis, Lydius
University of Utrecht
Department of Roman Languages
Kromme Nieuwe Gracht 29
3512 HD Utrecht, The Netherlands
lydius.nienhuis@wanadoo.nl

Qian, David D.
Department of English
The Hong Kong Polytechnic University
Hung Hom, Kowloon, Hong Kong
david.qian@polyu.edu.hk

Read, John
School of Linguistics and Applied Language
    Studies
Victoria University of Wellington
P.O. Box 600, Wellington, New Zealand
john.read@vuw.ac.nz

Schmitt, Norbert
School of English Studies University of
    Nottingham
Nottingham NG7 2RD, UK
norbert.schmitt@nottingham.ac.uk

Vermeer, Anne
Linguistics Department,
Tilburg University
P.O. Box 90153
5000LE Tilburg, The Netherlands
anne.vermeer@uvt.nl

Wiersma, Boukje
Contact Jan-Arjen Mondria

Wolf, Tom de
University of Amsterdam
Department of Second Language Acquisition
Spuistraat 134
1012 VB Amsterdam, The Netherlands
t.dewolf@uva.nl

Index

Index

In the *Language Learning & Language Teaching* the following titles have been published thus far or are scheduled for publication:

DATE DUE

7/30 6pm			

Demco, Inc. 38-293